CAVEMAN TO PRIEST

A Journey of Healing,
Becoming Poppa God's Favorite Best Friend

By Mike Collins,
through the Power of HOLY SPIRIT

Caveman to Priest: A Journey of Healing, Becoming Poppa God's Favorite Best Friend

Trilogy Christian Publishers

A Wholly Owned Subsidary of Trinity Broadcasting Network

2442 Michelle Drive, Tustin, CA 92780

For information, address Trilogy Christian Publishing

Rights Department, 2442 Michelle Drive, Tustin, Ca 92780.

Trilogy Christian Publishing/ TBN and colophon are trademarks of Trinity Broadcasting Network.

For information about special discounts for bulk purchases, please contact Trilogy Christian Publishing.

10 9 8 7 6 5 4 3 2 1

Library of Congress Cataloging-in-Publication Data is available.

ISBN 979-8-89333-135-6
ISBN 979-8-89333-136-3 (ebook)

Acknowledgments

Corey Russell—thank you for your book *Gift of Tears*; it helped me significantly during the most difficult season of my life. "HE" gave me the gift of tears and taught me how valuable my tears are to "HIM." Also, thank you for all your teachings and your passion for JESUS CHRIST.

Andrew Bucksot—thank you for your friendship and all the advice on this book. I truly appreciate you.

Jeff and Amy Lyle—thank you both for your teachings and love for me and especially for JESUS CHRIST.

David Dusek—thank you for your book *Rough Cut Men*, speaking at New Bridge Church's Men's Group in 2018, and your posts on social media. You gave me the courage to walk through the most difficult season of my life.

James Lawrence, the Iron Cowboy, thank you for your inspiration and for firing me up to hit the trails running. You got me running my first triathlon, and that was a major catalyst for a lot of my Healing. You spoke at the SFPE conference (Society of Fire Protection Engineers) in Duluth, Georgia, in 2020. Bless you.

Fifty Ironman triathlons in fifty states in fifty days. Fifty. Fifty. Fifty.

Kim Zember—thank you for the excellent advice on the covers of this book. I greatly appreciate it.

DEDICATIONS

Michelle McKirahan—I Love You and will Love You ForEver.

Alexandra Collins (Ali)—to my oldest little girl. Thank you for being the woman *JESUS* made you to be and loving me well. I love you, Ali. I'm so proud of you. Some of my fondest memories are teaching you to roller skate with Megan's Barbie skates, all the sled riding on the hills I built in the yard, and playing in the piles of leaves at the Rhinebeck house and you learning to ride a bike in the driveway.

Catherine Collins (Cate Mike)—to my youngest little girl. Wow, what an incredible and beautiful woman you have become. Thank you for also loving me well. I so look forward to what *JESUS* has for you. Some of my most fond memories are all the sled riding on the hills I built in the yard, as well as when I would tie a rope around a guardrail and your tube so I could pull you up. Remember the first time when I didn't make the rope long enough? Sorry! You playing in the piles of leaves at the Rhinebeck house, one of your first bicycle rides, doing the entire north and south Millerton rail trail, and then driving in the snow at Tech City! I love you so, C. Mike Collins. Your dad, P. Mike Collins.

My ministry financial partners—to each of you, I love you, and I'm so grateful for your friendship, Prayers, and financial partnership. This project wouldn't have come about without you all. Thank you for believing in me:

Mark Penk, Chris and Carol Rosenbusch, John Michael Hightower Jr., Tom Guzzardo, Matt and Nicoleta Gardier, Bobby and Nan Bullard, Richard Dalton, Lonnie and Cathy Funk, Steve Pennington, Ben and Melissa Melancon, Stephen and Bev Carlson, Scott and Rhonda Stevens, Michael Green, JD and Jasmin Russell, Bob Herrmann, Gary and Trish Clem, Aaron Blodgett, Nathan and Lisa Camp, Bryan and Laura Bactel, Bart and Michelle Jones, Tony and Whitney Ramos, Will, Etta and Family Shehee, Mark Aslam, Tim and Gayle Frost, Trey and Holly Lewis.

My entire family—I love and appreciate each and every one of you. Thank you for how you've loved me and contributed to my life. I love you all. Eileen and Al Bernard, Larry and Joyce Collins, Kathy and Michael Pietroforte, Patty Cohen, Kerry and Patty Collins, Timmy and Angel Collins, Sean Collins, Terrance and Sally Collins, and all of their families and all the cousins.

Barbra—this book would have never happened without you, and more importantly, I don't think I would have gotten my HEaling in *JESUS* without you. Your counseling skills are incredible, but your love for *JESUS CHRIST* and your Spirit are what changed my life through HEaling.

Dustin Pennington—I don't know if I would still be here in Atlanta and GateCity without you. You loved on me, mentored me, and became a dear friend. I love you, man.

Billy Humphrey—thank you for being my Spiritual leader for eight years. You, your teaching, and your covering were instrumental in my HEaling and still are.

Ben Melancon—boy, were you there for me and us…I love you, Ben. Grace and peace…

Will Shehee (Pastor Will)—you were there for me on one of the darkest days of my life. You pastored and loved on me in the GCHOP parking lot. I'll never forget you, Pastor Will.

Rolando and Olivia Gonzalez—thank you both for allowing me to serve with you at 212 High School Youth Ministry.

The Stern family (Jim's hymns)—thank you all for allowing me to Prayer Lead for you and accepting me into your family in such a loving way. Each of you has a special place in my heart. From Jim, Jess, Kennah, Eva, Jadyn, Shaya, Maximus, and you also, Phil.

Jamie Boy Pridgen (the white Hulk)—your teaching style and knowledge have opened my heart to the Word like no other.

Don and Iris Valley—thank you for your ministry and the amazing HEaling I got through Restoring the Foundations Ministry. Bless you.

Kathy and Michael Pietroforte—thank you for always believing in me and all you've done for me!

Some of the young men in my life:

Aaron Blodgett, Aaron Brumer, Adam Wells, Akeem Robinson, Andrew Bullard, Andrew Faletti, Andrew Potter, Andrew Smith, Andres Franky, Angel Alicea, Angel Colon, Anthony Mwangi, Anthony Peduri, Arnold Oh, Ash Bolden, Bailey Ewing, Ben Malancon, Beto Amorim, Billy Fonfrel, Brandon Berry, Brett Mclaine, Brett Milner, Bryan Wigton, Bruce Wham, Caleb Andrews, Caleb Bachtel, Caleb Compton, Chan Pridgen, Casey Ryon, Chris Peterson, Chris Vollo, Clinton James, Coby Humphrey, Dakota Merriman, Daniel Korgua, Daniel Oehrke, Danny Cressey, David Bryant, David Middleton, David Bridges, David Ricca, David Williams, Dean Mikolyski, Emanuel Roro, Eran Barnes, Evan Humphrey, Felipe Saldana, Eric Hunter, Femi Enigbokan, Emmanuel Kiganda, Forrest Garrett, Frank Tirado, Gamaliel Tosado, Gabe Palmer, Gee Liebenberg, Grant Garner, Greg Hunsinger, Gregory Peck, Greg Yost, Greg Owen, Gus Ruballo, Hazen Stevens, Henri Liebenburg, Isaiah Murray, Isaiah Ram, Jacob Solomon, James Hanes, Jamie Pridgen, JD Russell, Jeremy Bruce, Jeremy Campbell, Jerimiah Jones, Jesse Digges, Jim (Slim Jim) Nahlik, Jim Stern, Joel Gonzalez, Joel Konacou, John Pritchett, John Michael Hightower Jr, Jon Padilla, Jonathon Bucksot, Jonathyn Carter, Josh MacDonald, Joshua Fry, Joshua Olson, Joshua Perez-Rijos, Joshua Ransom, Justice Jeffries, Justin Thomas, Kevin Carter, Larry Salay, Landon Camp, London Vaughan, Mark Aslam, Mathieu Gillet, Matthew Gardier, Matthew Pennington, Michael Boal, Michael Green, Michael Shivers, Miles DiBona, Nathan Camp, Nick Koebert, Patrick Bing, Peter Keller, Preston Bing, Randy Ducasse, Robby Randall, Ryan Sharky, Rolando Gonzalez, Ryan Lambert, Shaun Campbell, Siah Humphrey, Son Byrd, Stephen Hataway, Tony Ramos, Trey Lewis, Troy Cooper, Wesley Anderson, Weston Kephart, Will Shehee, Zach Stilwell, Zach Riddle, Zech Gettig, Tim Wood.

Men in my Men's over Fifty Bible Study:

Lonnie Funk, Mark Penk, Cedric Williams (Shadrach), Bob Boal, Chris Rosenbusch, Tom Guzzardo, Scott Stevens, Irville Smith, Ozzie Giles, Bart Jones, Rene Glover, Mike Redden, John Duffey, Joseph Scott, Daymon Southerland, Chris Bridges, Bill Durham, Andy Neely, Wesley Silva, and Rich Jones.

Other men in my life:

Dustin Pennington, Bobby Bullard, Steve Pennington, Stephen Carlson, Bob Herrmann, Gary Clem, Bryan Bactel, Tim Frost, Richard Dalton, Bruce Williams, Chris Mauro, Quincy Bulla, Bobby Campbell, Anthony Laniewicz, Daniel Flagg, Pete Ramirez, Scott Keller, Brad Michael, Craig

Jackson, Jeff Lyle, Bobby Humphrey, Rodney Miller, Mike Price, Marcus Robinson, Andrew Bucksot, Rick Wheeler, Rob Compton, Denise Mitchell, Sam Whatley, Alain Fabius, Jeff Tullis, Chance Wrigley, Bishop John Bosco, Michael Collins, Tommy Johnson, Phil Wint, Marlow Dunham, Terry Dunham, Mark Huffman, Tom Lawton, Gary McGowan, Phil Stern, John Byer, Billy Humphrey, Jeff Tarbutton, Robert Shepitka, Curtis Simpson, Pete Gitto.

All my IHOP-ATL, GCHOP, and GC brothers and sisters.

Richard Dalton—I'll always remember five feet, and don't tell me about Mike...

Andrew Bucksot—thank you for taking time out of your busy schedule to read my manuscript and advise.

Quincy Bulla—quincybullaart.com—thank you for the outstanding job of painting JESUS' face for the back cover.

Gus Ruballo—Create Together, LLC—thank you for your love and for creating, building, and maintaining mikecollinsministry.com and cavemantopriest.com. I couldn't have done it without you and your team.

Landon Camp—StartCHURCH—thank you for your love and encouragement and for filing and creating Mike Collins Ministry, Inc., the 501.c.3. I couldn't have done it without you and your team.

ENDORSEMENTS

I first got to know Mike in 2018, right before the events of this book took place. I went back to the mission field and didn't see him again until 2021. When I returned to our church, I saw a stranger with a beaming face and a childlike innocence, always dancing and worshipping wholeheartedly by the Altar. When I introduced myself, I was shocked to discover it was my friend Mike Collins! I literally didn't recognize him as the same person. Until reading this book, I did not know the depth of the journey God took him on during those years I was away. But what has always been evident to me is the fruit—a life transformed literally beyond recognition. Mike's transformed life is itself the strongest letter of recommendation that anyone could give to read this book.

William Shehee

Cofounder and Vice President of Send56 Ministry, Inc.

I've been incredibly privileged to witness Mike's extraordinary journey of transformation from a front-row seat. Rarely have I encountered someone who partners with the work of the Holy Spirit as diligently as Mike does. Within these diary-like pages, he extends a heartfelt invitation for you to join him in exploring the remarkable story of how his transformation unfolded.

Dustin Pennington

Lead Pastor, GateCity Church

Mike Collins has the heart of an encourager! He has traversed many life situations that require a person to stand strong in the grace of the Lord and refuse to be disheartened. The revelation he has gained in God through trials he longs to give away. Mike's story is the tale of a man refusing to give up in the face of setbacks, and along the way he has discovered the power of true God-given identity as a priest and son.

Hazen Stevens

Executive Pastor, GateCity Church

As a member of the Promise Keepers Movement and pastor of men's ministry groups over a period of thirty years, I can say that this book is a masterpiece of the process men go through, despite the failures and struggles we have, of how the grace of God and the Holy Spirit never gives up on us as we develop into the priestly image or image of Christ that God has ordained since the foundation of the world. A must-read.

Pastor Richard C. Dalton

"Joshua Transformation Project"

"Recipient of the 284th Point of Light from the White House" for a Drug Prevention Initiative;

SCLC Wings of Hope.

Table of Contents

INTRODUCTION

I want to thank you for purchasing my book. I am honored you did and Pray you get as much HEaling from it as I did and even more.

This book was written to bring Glory to POPPA GOD, *JESUS CHRIST*, and HOLY SPIRIT!

Here is a breakdown of some of the unique ways I write:

» POPPA GOD, "HE," "HIM," "HIS," The FATHER

» *JESUS CHRIST, HE, HIM, HIS, The CHRIST, The SON*

» HOLY SPIRIT, HE, HIM, HIS, The SPIRIT, BOB

» Michael The Archangel, He, Him, His, Mike A., Bear

» Ali, Cate, and Quinn, she, her, Michelle, Her, She, Marriage, Wife

» Heaven, HEaven

» HEaling

» Prayer, Pray

» CHRISTian, CHRISTmas

Welcome to a glimpse into my life. This book is in a journal entry style; it chronicles the last four years of my life of HEaling through trauma counseling and inner Healing/deliverance. Some of the notes are from my journal; others are presession notes, session notes, and post-session notes of trauma counseling. All of this describes how I became POPPA GOD's favorite best friend! I've been a degreed electrical engineer for over thirty-five years. For the last twelve years, I've been a code enforcement officer/fire protection engineer. In this arena of work, there are codes that builders must follow when building. If the design professional (architect) prefers, they can use what is called a prescriptive method, which is a step-by-step method of design. I believe POPPA told me that this book is a prescriptive method of becoming "HIS" favorite best friend. That doesn't mean it's the only way, but it's mine. "HE" had me start writing *Caveman to Priest* Thanksgiving week in a cabin up in the North Georgia Mountains in 2022. I finished it and filed for the copyright on Friday evening, February 17, 2023. I wanted to go to the revival at Ashbury University in Kentucky but needed to complete the work. "HE" said Friday night, "You're done; go to the revival." I was in the auditorium for the last Sunday before they had to shut it down. What an amazing act of GOD. I feel it was a revival of the Peace of GOD. The real miracle came after I received my copyright on March 22, 2023, and could now send the manuscript out to publishers. Saturday, April 8th, I clicked a link on Instagram to publish *Cavemen to Priest* at about 07:00. I had an email to forward my manuscript at 07:45 and a contract on April 14th. This contract includes a ninety-second commercial on national/international television with TBN, the largest CHRISTian TV network in the world, reaching 1.6 billion households in 178 countries! (Come on!)

You will be walking through my day-by-day life for the last four years. This includes traumatic events, dreams, visions, Spiritual conversations with POPPA, *JESUS*, HOLY SPIRIT, Mike A. (Michael The Archangel), Michelle, other angelic beings, demonic beings, three of my daughters (two are here on earth, Alex and Cate, and one sadly wasn't born, Quinn Michael) and other people in my life...

My trauma counseling came in the forms of EMDR and (*CHRIST*-based) IFS. We would start every session in Prayer, and then I would close my eyes and take a few deep breaths and an inventory of my body. Shortly, I would have pressure or light pain in an area of my body. This often occurred in my core, and I tried to write down where it was each time. I would speak to the pressure/pain and start a conversation. Eye movement desensitization and reprocessing (EMDR) has been a helpful tool in my healing. Through this technique, I was able to explore the painful trauma in my life without being exposed to the hypersensitive feelings that originally came with them. The way I describe it, you're more in a dream state and don't feel the emotions as intensely. The technique of *CHRIST*-based internal family systems (IFS) was helpful when we hit the ceiling in EMDR. I would speak with my feelings/emotions, which we called my parts and other times with my mes. My parts consisted of protectors, messengers, and other hurt emotions... kind of like the Pixar movie *Inside Out*. My mes are my younger and older self. It was absolutely wild to meet my parts, both male and female and my mes.

My inner HEaling was done through a ministry called Restoring the Foundations. I was first introduced to the ministry some twenty years ago in New York. It's a very powerful and anointed ministry. I highly recommend them.

Enjoy the book, and please send me any comments to testimonies@mikecollinsministry.com.

Some of the characters from my trauma counseling—these are my parts and messengers:

Quinn Michael Collins: A messenger, my unborn, sweet, beautiful second daughter. She's a messenger and is protecting and watching out for me.

Tim (True Mike): My true me with I in the middle. Basically, my Spiritman.

False Mike: The me that I operated in most of my adult life that caused a lot of the trouble and pain.

Bobby: My part/feeling who was mostly rejected and pushed down by my false me most of my adult life.

Popp'n: My part/feeling who is protecting and watching out for me.

Mary: My part/feeling who spoke obsessively, won't listen, and be a scatterbrain my entire adult life. As she says, the dizzy or bobblehead blonde.

Francis (Frank): My part/feeling who was the firefighter or extreme protector, often overreacting to protect me.

Gary: My part/feeling who was a rageful, extreme protector, often overreacting and arrogant in his protection of me.

Sal: My part/feeling, another arrogant guy.

Jim: My part/feeling with a pot belly who enjoys sweets.

Pam: A messenger trying to warn and defend me.

Harry: My part/feeling who was very insecure.

Joel: My part/feeling who is the creative one.

Jane: My part/feeling who missed having Michelle around to talk with.

Peter: My part/feeling who had a very strong, aggressive, religious spirit.

Paul: My part/feeling who had the religious spirit but wasn't as aggressive as Peter.

Bob: My part/feeling who also had the religious spirit and was very hurt by Michelle. After being healed he became Robert.

Helen: A messenger, and she's a big fan of Michelle.

Patty: A messenger to encourage me to stand up for women.

Joe: A messenger who came as darkness warning against women who have and may hurt us.

PREFACE

Moses was eighty years in the desert. Forty years on the back side and forty with the Hebrews.

David was forty years hiding out from Saul in the desert. Saul was forty years chasing David in the desert.

Joseph waited twenty-one years before his dream came true. He was thrown in a pit, sold as a slave, thrown in a dungeon, in a ruler's house, back in a dungeon, and then second in command of Egypt. I originally thought I was going to have to wait forty years for my HEaling after I was saved at thirty-nine. I thought, *Well, at least seventy-nine is going to be awesome.* Then a friend said, "Did you ever think of Joseph, twenty-one years in the desert..." Sure enough, here I am at sixty! I don't have my Michelle, but other than that, wow, is The Triune GOD all over me in Love!

Cate, Ali, and me kayaking in the Hudson Valley of New York

Cate, Ali, and me apple picking in Red Hook, New York

Chapter 1

"HE" Whispers in My Ear Insight, Discernment, Wisdom, and Understanding

Notes from Barbara

07.27.20: I just didn't have the drive, the push, the fuel, or the fire on the circuit. And I believe HE; you don't have the rage, anger, hurt, pain, or sorrow. "Now it's just your big beautiful Heart that 'I' gave you that will push you, which will be fine, but let's walk together in the cool of the day in this beautiful garden." This was POPPA, and "HE" really spoke to me right at that spot from Tues. Then I got to the car, and I lost my key. So I turned around, and POPPA and I continued walking and talking. When we got a hundred feet in, I said, "It's probably the other way," and we decided to keep walking. Of course, the key was sitting right on the path in almost the exact place I started running in the opposite direction, just as I thought, and "HE" just smiled. Thank "YOU," POPPA, for being so absolutely deliciously wonderful and kind and loving to me.

07.29.20: My Aunt died, so, of course, I had to call the girls. I physically spoke with Ali. Oh, it was so needed. When I told her that Loretta died, she understood—she was old. I reminded her that I have a fifty-one-year-old nephew who came close to drinking himself to death two years ago and is knocking on death's door again. It really hit her hard. We've lost three nephews and nieces in four years in their thirties. I told her, "You don't have to be a *JESUS* freak like me, but you have to know *HIM*. If you don't know if you're going to give *HIM* a big hug and kiss, you probably don't know *HIM*." She got it. Let's see what happens.

She just kept talking. When I told her I was going to be fifty-seven, she called me an old fart, and we both laughed. When I told her I run around five miles a day, lost fifteen pounds, and I'm the same weight I was in high school, she was impressed. She told me she loves her house most because of the privacy of twelve and a half acres, and it adjoins state land all around it.

06:58: This is how I know I'm "HIS" best friend. "HE" gives me such hope by whispering truths and secrets of "HIS" great plan in my ear. Things that I would never have or be able to know. Insight, discernment, wisdom, understanding… Why? Why me, LORD? Why have "YOU" chosen me to be "YOUR" best friend? Who am I that "YOU" would choose me?

08.04.20: Barbara's Presession Notes

"HE" is just all over me. It is so different. I don't know; I should be crying my eye out, and I'm not. It seems like so much peace, confidence, stillness…yes, now is the time. Thank "YOU," LORD… I don't see my brokenness anymore… I'm seated at The Table of The LORD… "YOU" carried me, my LORD…Leeland's song, "Carried to the Table." It's so different, and "HE" said, "It has all been for 'such a time as this,'" and I just heard the lion roar his battle cry.

> *"For if you remain completely silent at this time, relief and deliverance will arise for the Jews from another place, but you and your father's house will perish. Yet who knows whether you have come to the kingdom for such a time as this?"*

> Esther 4:14 (NKJV)

07:32: "HE" said the reason it's different is I'm on the other side of the season of sorrow, brokenness, heartbreak, and pain, and now I'm in the season of conquer, claiming ground back and much new ground. I will be leading the captive home. Leeland, "Tears of the Saints." FATHER, We will lead them Home! There is no more brokenness, and it is far from me. Thank "YOU," LORD.

07:47: "HE" is inundating me with so much.

» In the old season, I was running out of a broken spirit, heart, and soul.

08.08.20: Barbara's Presession Notes

Triozathon! Today was the official day that I trained for it.
Run: 10.28.19. Swim: 08.06.20. Bike: 08.04.20.

Okay, last swim practice before game day. Five hundred meters, twenty-three minutes. Now I know why they put the swim first in the triathlon. This way I don't drown from exhaustion in the end.

08.26.20: Barbara's Presession Notes

Caveman to Priest: A Journey to Full Healing in JESUS CHRIST!

By The LORD *JESUS CHRIST* through "HIS" best friend Mike Collins (not imperfect but constantly getting back up in the Spirit)

"What's better than that? Sitting at 'MY' feet, gazing into 'MY' heart, through 'MY' eyes, knowing you, Mike, are ravishing 'MY' heart. 'I' *love* you, Mike, always have and always will. Believe 'ME,' trust 'ME'!"

07:40: *HE* brought me such peace with thoughts of my week with Michelle from Saturday, March 7, to Monday, March 16th, 2015. But as soon as I got back to New York, JFK, from visiting Michelle for the first time, I called Terry, one of my pastors, and we were chatting. I got to the Throgs Neck Bridge toll booth like I've done, seriously, a thousand times. I have E-ZPass, so I don't expect to stop. A toll guy was there outside, almost in the lane, so I stopped. He started screaming at me, "This lane is closed. Didn't you see the red light, you idiot?" I said, "I'm sorry, sir; the light wasn't red, or else I wouldn't have come through." He was mad and said, "You could have killed me." I once again said, "I'm sorry," and he said, "Oh yeah, what if I take my gun out and stick it in your face? What about that?" At this point I was really mad but knew this could be very dangerous, so I said, "Please don't do that..." And then he said, "Go on" or something. I called the Port Authority the next day and filed a complaint. They did call Terry and said there were a lot of complaints against this guy, but I never heard a thing.

12:40: We were just talking, and "HE" said, "When you really get Song of Solomon 6, Mike, when it gets down deep and entirely in your entire heart, mind, soul, strength, and being, then the pettiness just doesn't matter. Why waste your time and effort on it? Just sit with 'ME' and know how much your attention and gaze melt and affect 'MY' Heart. What else matters? Just be with 'ME'! Mike! Like you yearn in your heart for Michelle to come back, love you, hold you, and give you Her heart. I'm GOD; 'MY' heart and desires are infinite, and it's all for you, Mike, 'MY' best friend! Just be with 'ME' always in everything you do—always! That's what 'I' want more than anything. Believe

'ME,' trust 'ME.'" I asked "HIM," "Why me, LORD? Why me?" "HE" said, "'I' have given you a heart so much like mine. 'I' *LOVE* everyone on earth who has ever been or will ever be, but you, Mike, you truly have a heart like and for 'ME.' There aren't many that, first, 'I've' given a heart like that but even fewer who have sold out so for 'ME.' You're not perfect, Mike, but 'I' am. You've fallen so much and many times, but you just keep getting up, praising 'ME,' and loving 'ME' through it all. Keep it up!"

19:47: There was such peace in the counseling today. I felt like Stephen, the first CHRISTian martyr...we didn't even do counseling because by the time I shared my heart about how much *love* I was feeling from *JESUS*, it was 6:15, and that was all right...*HE* has me in such a place of having my head on *HIS* chest and hearing *HIS* heartbeat...nothing else matters...nothing...no matter what it is...

08.27.20: BARBARA'S PRESESSION NOTES

Strawman contest (triozathon): 06:06–09:43. Zero-point-three-mile swim, fourteen-mile bicycle, three-point-three-mile run. Actual contest time: three hours and fifteen minutes.
Full duration: three hours thirty-seven minutes.

06:16: I count ten, think I'm done, jump out of the pool, say goodbye to Todd, and think, *Wait, ten minutes, no way. I just cut my time in half. That's only ten lengths, not ten laps, so I have to jump back in and continue. Thank YOU, JESUS, for catching that. It really would have stunk if I did everything else and it didn't count.*

07:45: At mile nine of the bike ride, I hit a huge wall big time. I'm crying and working so hard coming down off of the Collins Hill side, just past the path home. I'm really having a tough time, and this older black woman (around sixty-five) says, "You can do it." It is a word from GOD. Everyone is fairly quiet, actually silent, until the run. I guess they all knew I had the first two disciplines (swim and bike). Boy, I didn't know I had anything.

09:01: Of course, Mike A. is on his stump just inside the west side of the north power lines (the absolute killer part of the circuit). It was so good to see Him.

09:05: I'm approaching Big Red (the huge uproot with all the red clay in the roots), and Michelle comes running up to me. I say, "Sweetheart, I'm only a mile in." She doesn't even listen to me and gives me a huge hug and kiss. She says, "I'm proud of you. I love you. You can do this. Go get 'em, tiger." Oh, how I needed that.

09:07: I come out of the wood on the west side of the south power lines, and there is everyone! Right at the spot where all the HEaling has been taking place. I mean all of Mike A.'s boys, all of mes, and my parts...I turn and head down the hill, and there are Mom and Dad on the bench. I get a super big hug, and the rest of the family is behind them. Now I see Norman, Mor Mor, and Pop Pop...I saw Jessie, Alaura, and Jace, and they were all so excited!

09:12: I get to CJ Lane, and the boys are jumping up and down and screaming, "Go, Dad!"

09:43: I'm done. We did it! A heavenly group hug from POPPA, *JESUS*, and BOB (HOLY SPIRIT, Big Old Buddy)! THEY said THEY watched it from up there to give everyone else the view and the ability to support me but weren't going to let anyone get the first hugs, not even Michelle or the boys, but of course right immediately after THEM. There was my beautiful, amazing Wife again for a heart-crushing, ginormous, loving hug and kiss, and then the boys right behind and with Her. It was more than I could have ever imagined or wanted. I got my certificate out of the van, and Michelle, the boys, and I sat at the lower bench on the south end of CJ Lane and just hugged and kissed, and they all loved me well. I was in the middle of Michelle and the boys, which was so powerful and healing, but then I asked the boys to sit between us. I took a couple of pictures. I just really missed the girls, but *JESUS* let me know they didn't know their Spirits yet.
I texted.

10:09: "Michelle, I just completed my first triathlon. Boy, were You there Spiritually. I don't know if I would have made it without You and *JESUS*..."

10:19: "Hey, Ali. This old man just finished his first triathlon at fifty-six! I love you."

10:41, Ali: "Oh wow, that's awesome!"

10:21: "Hey, Cate. I just finished my first triathlon at fifty-six! I love you."

10:22: "Rodney, I did it! Only with *JESUS*! Thank YOU, LORD."

10:35: "That's fantastic!"

10:28: "Dustin and Ben, I just finished my first triathlon at fifty-six! It was all *JESUS*, the whole way! Michelle was there Spiritually, and boy, did that help! I love you guys! Thanks for helping me through this so far. 'HE' keeps telling me, 'Soon, believe 'ME,' trust 'ME'...'"

10:31, Dustin: "Well done."

The men's group: "Hey, guys. I just finished my first triathlon at fifty-six! It was all *JESUS*, the whole way! I love you guys! Thanks for helping me through this so far. HE keeps telling me, 'Soon, believe ME, trust ME...'"

Kathy and Mike: "Hey, guys. I just finished my first triathlon at fifty-six! It was all *JESUS*, the whole way! I love you guys!"

10:34, Mike: "Hey, Mike. Well done! Congrats."

14:22, Kathy: "Very impressive at any age! Congrats."

08.28.20: Barbara's Presession Notes

19:45: I was walking into the garage admiring my bike and said, "That's a machine." *JESUS* said, "You are a machine."

HE just told me that *HE* was so excited that I was not hurt, angry, offended, or feeling rejected. *HE* said, "Good—since that is the case, now WE can work on Her heart since you're not trying to influence things physically, Spiritually, or emotionally!" This is amazing. I'm not letting this affect me in any way, and, therefore, I have no influence on it and am not interfering with the Spiritual realm. They now have 100 percent full access to Her heart. Thank *YOU*, LORD *JESUS*. Have *YOUR* way!

08.31.20, 08:45: Barbara's Presession Notes

10:44: I need this every day, all day!

11:03: My new place is such a Blessing. I went from a 160-square-feet to a 415-square-feet suite. Not including shared space (a full shared kitchen, unlimited attic space for storage, and around 50 square feet in the garage). Of course, while typing this that IHOP-ATL dude is singing "I Want to Build You a Garden."

11:52: "HE" gave me sixteen purple calla lilies; they are so beautiful. Thanks, POPPA.

Billy Humphrey and Jamie Boy Pridgin's Song of Solomon class. Fifteen Prayers (I added two and comments on his).

JESUS:

1. Kiss me with the kisses of *YOUR* Word! A whole new understanding! 03.18.22!

2. Always remind me that *YOUR Love* is better than anything. Anything! (It's better than being with Michelle or having Her in my life. Please help me process this Grace and truth fully and receive it in the depths of my heart and soul.)

3. *JESUS, YOUR* name and *YOUR* nature are pleasure.

4. Draw me away.

5. Let's run together.

6. I'm dark but lovely (poor but beautiful) (and *YOU love* me so [08.30.21]).

7. I'm *YOUR* favorite one.

8. *YOU* say I am beautiful. (Often I don't feel beautiful [08.30.21], but it seems to be less now. Thank *YOU*, LORD *JESUS* [12.30.21]!

9. *YOU* love my emotions. (Used to so often be a huge box of a mess [04.18.21]—sometimes still are [07.31.21]. They haven't been for some time now [01.06.22].)

10. *YOU* love my desire to do *YOUR* will. (Please help me do *YOUR* will no matter the cost.)

11. *YOU* are life to me. (*YOU* are Everything I want and all I need. Please help me to really believe that in my heart and emotions [10.07.21].)

12. *YOU* are beautiful to me. (*YOU* are the most beautiful! *YOU* are beauty [11.22.21].)

13. *YOU* say I am beautiful.

14. *YOU* say I am faithful. (I just love this one [around 08.15.21]!) *YOU* have given me the Spirit of Faith.

15. I'm safe with *YOU*.

16. *YOU* tell me, and *YOU* tell me, and *YOU* tell me that *YOU love* me and say, "Have *I* told you how much *I love* you, Mike?"

17. "I'm driving to do my TJ (Trader Joe's) ministry on 01.20.21, and "HE" starts saying, "Have 'I' told you how much 'I' love you, Mike?" "HE" keeps telling me and telling me and telling me that "HE" loves me and tells me, "Have 'I' told you, Mike, that you're 'MY' favorite best friend?" "HE" doesn't stop. I can't breathe, and "HE" keeps on saying it and saying it and saying it... I guess this is the beginning of the title...

08.30.20, 06:00: Barbara's Presession Notes

07:11: I looked out the dining room window to see a doe; she jumped into the woods, and a beautiful small six-to-eight-point buck jumped out and then back in.

11:11: Today was the first day I serviced at New Bridge Church. I was on camera one! Thank *YOU*, LORD *JESUS*; it really was awesome to be part of things. A guy came up to me after church and asked how it was going, I was honest, "Okay, good, horrible." But *JESUS* just reminded me of the book *A Tale of Two Cities* by Charles Dickens; it's the best of times and the worst of times. But it's all good in *HIM*!

08.30.20, 06:00: My Notes

I told him (the enemy) that *JESUS* has me and I have nothing to worry about. I told him what *JESUS* said to me yesterday. "I'm so excited that you are not hurt, angry, offended, or feeling rejected." *HE* said, "Good—since that is the case, now WE can work on Her heart since you're not trying to influence things physically, Spiritually, or emotionally!" This is amazing. I'm not letting this affect me in anyway, and, therefore, I have no influence on it and am not interfering with the Spiritual realm. THEY now have 100 percent full access to Her heart. "Thank *YOU*, LORD *JESUS*. Have *YOUR* way!"

I couldn't believe it and was amazed. Now *JESUS* is at the table, and *HE* hasn't said anything, but *HE* smiled a huge *JESUS* smile to reassure me. The little guy just looked at us and said, "*HE* is GOD, and *HE* talks with you like that?" I said, "Yes, *HE* loves me so much, but also, *HE* likes me. *HE* really likes me. That's why I have nothing to worry about at all! Do you understand that? Why would I waste any time, effect, or thought in worrying?"

He looked at *JESUS* and me, then looked at Mary, and asked, "Is this really true?" And Mary said, "Yes, I didn't know this a few weeks ago, but yes, it's true." He looked right at *JESUS* and said, "I want to have this relationship with *YOU*—may I?" *JESUS* just hugged him and Mary, and they all disappeared. I felt such a wave of peace. Thank *YOU*, LORD *JESUS*, my best friend. I just cried and cried.

09.01.20, 05:15

07:17: I'm driving by the house, and I hear pretty clearly, "Put in an offer." I said, "Are 'YOU' serious? How do I do that?"

07:27: I feel it's definitely "HIM," so I have to move on it. I called Bryan, my realtor, and Sam, my mortgage guy, and left messages.

07:38: Leave a message for Bryan and Sam.

07:47: "HE" just told me, "It's 'ME.' Move forward; 'I' know what 'I' am doing." Of course, "YOU" do. I'm moving. It's not me! I just realized I was walking out of my room and that girl from IHOP-ATL was singing "You Make Me Brave." It was 7:43, and I think to myself, *It's almost 7:47!*

09:58: I call Sam and tell him that *JESUS* wants me to put an offer in on this house. My credit stinks. I owe $100k…

17:51: Sam (my mortgage guy) calls and says he doesn't know what I'm talking about. I am in the top tier for a mortgage; Michelle can't have a better mortgage rate than me because it doesn't exist. He says this over and over because POPPA knew I needed to hear it four to five times. No problem! Thank "YOU," POPPA! It's all "YOU."

19:05: "HE" said, "Don't touch the numbers, budget—trust 'ME'..."

19:41: I said, "Who am I that 'YOU' love me like this? "HE" said, "Oh, most favored of men..."

23:30: Done with all the paperwork—it's all in *YOUR* hands, *JESUS*.

09.07.20: My Notes

05:24: I had a dream last night about Michelle; part of it was in a store, and I clearly saw Her walk by in an aisle intersection not even seeing me. She looked stunning, and it was clearly my baby. Then, I think it was Ali saying, "Mom and Michelle are both in the store, and we should leave." The next screen was at home, but what's home? Once again, I don't think She saw me when I was on the other side of the room and behind Her. This time She was very large and had gained at least 150 to 200 pounds; it was clearly Her, and She looked even better than stunning, and She was doing some kind of dance. She looked great!

Once again, I believe this was *JESUS* showing me that I love Her no matter what. I've always told Her that I would still be "crazy about Her, even if She put on 150 pounds or anything happened to Her," and this proved it to me. Thank *YOU, JESUS*.

12:39:

And HE said to them, "Go into all the world and preach the gospel to every creature. He who believes and is baptized will be saved; but he who does not believe will be condemned. And these signs will follow those who believe: In MY name they will cast out demons; they will speak with new tongues; they will take up serpents; and if they drink anything deadly, it will by no means hurt them; they will lay hands on the sick, and they will recover."

Mark 16:15–18 (NKJV)

13:17: Andrew, the director of the Prayer Room, texted me: "Thank you for all of your hard work. Can't keep the fire burning twenty-four seven without Gatekeepers like you." I texted him back: "Thanks, man. I really appreciate and receive that." Of course I was ready to encourage him, and I could feel *JESUS* waiting, waiting. Are you going to just receive the Blessing? And thank *YOU, JESUS*. I did. Actually, it's funny—yesterday, before the nine o'clock service, I was talking with Dean, the assistant director, and *JESUS* was doing that same thing while I was listening to him talk...

15:00: Gary (my landlord) came and took all of his stuff out of my new room and crammed it in my old room. He said, "I feel like I lost a bet to you and had to move out, trade places with you." I said, "I hope not, but I do appreciate it so much. I can't stop crying. This place is huge for just me...*JESUS, YOU* are amazing and so very kind to me."

09.08.20: Barbara's Presession Notes

05:07: LORD, please help me tame my tongue, *JESUS*.

05:11: When I asked *HIM* what I could do for *HIM*, *HE* said to tame my tongue; it's going to be so powerful when you can just listen. Thank *YOU, JESUS*. I will—with *YOUR* Grace.

06:03: "HE" said, "'I' *love* you, Mike; you are going to be so powerful and affective when you learn to listen more intently than wanting to share. You are beginning to, and 'I' know soon you are going to listen well, with a yearning to understand and receive much wisdom from everyone you open your ears and heart to. And more importantly, you are going to help 'ME' heal and empower many! Keep doing what you're doing, letting 'ME' heal and work in and on your heart, mind, and soul. 'I' am building much strength, humility, wisdom, meekness, gentleness, understanding, and *love* in you. 'I' am proud of you; trust 'ME,' believe."

06:20: "HE" said, "'I' know you only want to share what 'I' am doing in your life because you're so excited to share with them, but they will listen and receive better if you listen with understanding and receive their heart, then sow into fertile, rich, loving soil."

07:02: Pastor Dustin. Text—"Thank you for my red hat." "Proud of the work of the Spirit you have yielded yourself to. It is such a powerful testimony and so rare..."

10:47: I feel like we're on vacation, a gorgeous beach island. We get in the room, and it's tiny, nice but tiny. The phone rings, and it's the front desk; they say, "We made a mistake. Drop everything where you are and go to the beach; all drinks and food are on us. We will move you to the correct room, and this is the number. Please give us an hour, and your room will be ready." We go to the most beautiful beach, have ice-cold yummy drinks, and eat shrimp, streak...of course, heavenly cheesecake, brownies...you know...come back to our room, and it's the presidential suite—I mean presidents stay here. We don't deserve it, but that is what "HE" wants us to have. That's how I feel with this room, POPPA. "YOU" are so kind; I don't deserve it. Who am I?

05:45: I drop my contact, and in the past, I would get anxious and nervous. Now I just say, "LORD, I know 'YOU' want me to find it. Please help me," and sure enough, I turn the overhead light on, I look down, and it's on the floor at my feet. In the past, my anxiety and nervousness would frighten Michelle.

06:00: The anxiety is gone!

6:30: I have a vision; a wave comes over my goggles, and I would normally freak. It's going to hit my nose, "man the decks," but I don't. I just don't breathe! Wow! What a concept—no anxiety. I'm going to need a lot less energy to run life like that. Then I hear POPPA say, "That's 'MY' boy! 'I'm' proud of you, Mike. Believe and trust 'ME'!"

08:00: Haven't had my first cup of tea until now! I go out to the kitchen to make breakfast; the refrigerator is so unorganized, and it is frustrating. Then I notice the pork loin that is in a baggie dripped all over; that would normally really uptight me. The cleaner is in my room. It's okay. I start taking stuff out and find it is a sticky mess! I take most of it all out, walk down to my room, and get the cleaner and find that I have to use the sponge because it's bad. I take it all out, wipe down the entire shelf and the bottom of all the contents, and put it back neatly. It is so refreshing to not get anxious, and look at what time it is—I've got to say...

Thank *YOU, JESUS*. Now I did grunt once slightly, and I shouldn't have, but that little bit, I believe would have frightened Michelle. Please, LORD, heal us, give us much Grace, and help us.

08:10: I'm outside stretching, and I hear a dog I don't recognize bark once. I cannot get a sense of the size since it only barked once. I immediately say to myself, *It's okay—no matter how big it is, I'm only three feet from the door.*

08:30: I want to get back to work! This breakfast break is taking a lot of time. I could clearly hear the enemy say, "So you think you have patience and gentleness—we'll see about that." I just said, "*JESUS*, please give me Grace..."

09.09.20: Barbara's Presession Notes

07:20: POPPA had a real heart-to-heart with me this morning on the trail. It was the first time I've run since the triathlon.

"HE" said, "Michelle has never felt safe with you, unfortunately. She does now because you are nowhere near Her and don't know where She lives. She also felt safe with Her phone because you weren't supposed to text Her personally. She doesn't get email or anything else directly from you on it. For Her to wake up and see a text and a picture of you when She doesn't even like you right now— it was unnerving."

09.15.20: BARBARA'S PRESESSION NOTES

00:15:

"Let me hear YOUR promise of Blessing over my life, breaking me free from the proud oppressors."

Psalm 119:122 (TPT)

07:07: I drove past the house I'm bidding on, and there was a nice bookshelf in the garbage. I just asked *JESUS* for a bookshelf when I went to sleep last night, and here is it from possibly my new home! How cool is that? Thank *YOU, JESUS.*

08:03: No, I was not a good husband. I thought I was. I was so deceived. I didn't love Michelle, let alone love Her well. I was so selfish, self-centered, so very wounded! I trust the promises that *JESUS* gave to me face to face, especially when I keep all the promises I made to *HIM* about the man I will be for the rest of my life with *HIS* Grace.

09.11.20 BARBARA'S SESSION NOTES

07:03: I think I clearly heard *JESUS* say, "Make the offer."

We spoke about some of the above, but not all. I'm trying to limit how much I share. Barbara said to do the IFS (Internal Family System), and immediately my gut just tightened up so tight. I guess I'm now beginning to feel how tight my gut is getting with all the running, swimming, biking, and no starch. It really hurt, but it's been so long since we've gone here, I wanted to take it in. Sure enough, this guy came out, and he looked like Genie from the Disney movie *Aladdin.* He took us to one of the Hudson River mansions near Rhinebeck, New York. At first, he didn't want to with Barbara there; he shared how so many ladies had hurt me. They've told me they know how much I can love and that it is amazing, but my junk isn't worth it. Then I asked him to show me these times, and he did until we got back to my first girlfriend at about fifteen or sixteen.

Then I met Mike; he is the one after the one who got hit by the car (ninth grade) and before the one who I guess must have been right up to graduating from SUNY (State University of New York) Farmingdale; he is with *JESUS* and Michelle now. He said that he was really hurt since he had to move away and knew it wasn't working with Sue, but, really, when she found someone else, he wished that he had worked something out. She never threw it in his face or even spoke about him getting drunk and walking into the car driving at least fifty miles/hour on a parkway or made a big deal about all the acne on his back, shoulders, chest, or face. He said she really did love him. Then I remembered this is the one that I have been ashamed of. The one that got hit by the car shamed me, but this one I am ashamed of because of all the stupid mistakes, all the stupid drinking...he is the one I was just thinking and speaking badly about last night. I got my Farmingdale transcript and had four Ds. One in precalc that I forgot about and the three from Professor Zipper, which I thought I had even more than that. (This is the professor who hated me and gave me Ds every semester I had him except my final one. He had to give me a C because I had the highest grade on the midterm. Boy, did that annoy him. He also fought to keep me out of the bachelor's program at SUNY Farmingdale. Thank GOD Drs. Petrella and Fiorillo fought for me.) I really looked down on him, getting in trouble in HS, like what he wrote in the yearbook about traveling to France and finding Jim Morrison...he kept on trying to tell all his good things, and I just kept trashing him; it was the exact opposite for little Mike in the grade school yard; when he told me that I only remember the good things and he had it tough...I felt so bad. He reminded me that he worked at Bryant's Supermarket almost every single Saturday from 6:00 a.m. to 6:00 p.m. and worked so hard through engineering. (It reminded me that I hope I wasn't too hard on Ali.) Boy, did we hate Zipper for how much he hated us. I forgot he tried to keep us out of the engineering program. I was so glad the other week when I heard that he may have died. I felt so bad; that was not right of me.

Suddenly an older Mike appeared, and he said or signaled this was his time. He said that I worked with each of the other Mikes (*JESUS* and Michelle), and now it was his time to be with me. He just looked at me and cried. I said, "I am so sorry. I'm not ashamed of you; I was ashamed of myself, but, of course, that is me telling you I am ashamed of you." I saw him at each of these stages: early high school on Long Island, twelfth grade upstate, Columbia-Greene, and Farmingdale colleges. He (I) used to wear the old cowboy hat and an orange suede jacket and drive that hand-painted-with-a-brush, allied-green 1950 GMC pickup truck with the push button started on the floor. I gave him such a big hug and kiss. We just cried, and I asked him if he would please forgive me, and he said, "Of course." I told him that I loved him and that I was so proud of him. Boy, did that make us both feel so good. Then he looked me straight in the eye and told me how much he loved me, and then he asked, "Could I meet *JESUS*?" And there *HE* was, the Man in the White Robe hugging on him. Mike and *JESUS* wanted to make sure I had my time with him, but then they both took off. They had so much time to make up for. We all just waved and loved on each other while they walked away. They were walking down the beach. When I was sharing with Barbara, suddenly I could see him turn around while walking with *JESUS* and wave, like "Thanks, I'm really well, and I love you…"

13:05: I just told Barbara that I haven't been deep crying lately. I got off the phone with Bryan, and he said, "Let's put the offer in." I couldn't stop deep crying.

Me, my hand-painted, allied-green 1950 GMC pickup,
and my dad (my girls called him Pop Pop)

09.17.20: BARBARA'S PRESESSION NOTES

"Let me feel YOUR tender love, for I am YOURS. Give me more understanding of YOUR wonderful ways."

Psalm 119:124 (TPT)

"So with deep love, I Pray for MY disciples. I'm not asking on behalf of the unbelieving world, but for those who belong to YOU, those you have given ME."

John 17:9 (TPT)

Oh, LORD, what about my girls? Hear my Prayers for them. Have mercy on them.

08:00: Someone at IHOP was looking for a tent and a Bible for a homeless couple, and I was able to give them my eight-man one. Three-room tent and a Bible. It was such a Blessing. Thank *YOU, JESUS.*

"As a lovesick lover, I yearn for more of YOUR salvation and for YOUR virtuous promises" (Psalm 119:123, TPT).

It annoys me beyond a lot! When they don't even cap the first letter of HIM, I'm ready to stop using their translation!

The session: At first, there was nothing! It was like, "Wow, that's never happened." Then it hit me; at first, I said to myself, *That has never happened.* Then I remembered that last time, it hit my gut unbelievably, but then it did hit there. I waited, and it was clear. I asked it to come out, and it wouldn't—then it started but hung there...it was a woman with blonde hair, and I couldn't see anything else, and she didn't want me to. Okay, then she was back where the guy was the other day: at a mansion in Hyde Park/Rhinebeck, New York. And she was afraid of something big in the water. We stayed there for a bit. I addressed her fear and said, "Yes, I know what you are feeling..." I asked, "When did you first feel this?" And she took me to Dean's Creek in East Durham, New York (Upstate), at about seven years old. I asked, "Was there anything earlier?" Then Grand Ave Elementary School, a little glimpse of the lake next to the Southern State Parkway, me getting my foot stuck in the spokes (which just jolted me in my seat with pain), barefooted on the handlebars of the bike at about ten years old on Long Island. When Barbara said, "Ask if she will address the location of the area on my body to a muscle memory," then she went right to that area that was used to do the act with Wilber. Michael was healed by being taken to Glory, but I'm (me) not. Then she said, "That was vile, but then you"—me—"also you were with a lot of women in a sinful way..." She said she represented all of those girls and women Spiritually and there is a lot of pain. I needed to repent and ask for forgiveness from her for hurting so many women and *JESUS* for what happened with Wilber—she knew I didn't know but still needed to. Also, I needed to repent to Barbara and ask for forgiveness because she represented all the women physically. When I told Barbara this, I repented and asked for forgiveness. Please, I have to forgive myself also. Barbara was very kind and forgave me and said I had been forgiven myself. That was so Healing; as soon as I started, I saw myself forgiving me in every stage of my life for inappropriate behavior, being...I forgave each one of them up to now—wow, was that freeing. Then I repented to the blonde, and we both cried, and she forgave me and just wept... then suddenly, she turned into Michelle...and I repented with such sorrow and asked Her to forgive me, and we just cried and held each other...then of course here came *JESUS...HE* held us...then *HE* put *HIS* hand on each of our hearts and healed and healed and healed. Suddenly it was just me, and I repented of the heinous act with Wilber. *HE* cried, forgave me, and really laid *HIS* hand on my heart, and then *HE* poured *HIS* oil of intimacy in a vile of my heart, which *HE* couldn't before because it was so impure. Now it was pure; *HE* gave me:

Isaiah Called to Be a Prophet

> *In the year that King Uzziah died, I saw The LORD sitting on a throne, high and lifted up, and the train of HIS robe filled the temple. Above it stood seraphim; each one had six wings: with two he covered his face, with two he covered his feet, and with two he flew. And one cried to another and said:*

> *"Holy, holy, holy is The LORD of hosts. The whole earth is full of HIS Glory!"*

> *And the posts of the door were shaken by the voice of him who cried out, and the house was filled with smoke.*

> *So I said:*

> *"Woe is me, for I am undone! Because I am a man of unclean lips,*
> *And I dwell in the midst of a people of unclean lips. For my eyes have seen the King,*
> *The LORD of hosts."*

> *Then one of the seraphim flew to me, having in his hand a live coal which he had taken with the tongs from the Altar. And he touched my mouth with it, and said:*

> *"Behold, this has touched your lips. Your iniquity is taken away,*
> *And your sin purged."*

Isaiah 6:1–7 (NKJV)

I couldn't believe this happened, and I was telling Barbara this, and there was still so much heaviness, which usually wasn't the case when this happened. *JESUS* began speaking with me, and I told her that she represented all the women and I shouldn't have done any of this, and there was still heaviness until I confessed, and I said I never did this without their consent, but it was still wrong and I was sorry. *HE* told me *HE* was healing each of these women of guilt and shame in their hearts for fornicating with me, like the shame and condemnation women who have abortions have for what they've done. *HE* showed me, not the woman but that *HE* was doing it; the heaviness lifted, and then Michelle came and told me She forgave me (I didn't get forgiven by Michelle because *HE* came in and ministered to us) and that *JESUS* healed Her heart even more than from before. Oh, did we cry!

I felt such peace, no guilt...no shame...*JESUS* had purified my heart before, but it was different, like Michelle just said.

HE purified our hearts, but we still needed forgiveness to free us! Then Barbara said:

"When you speak with anyone, be sure to tell them that I have a tendency of running on when I speak, so I'm learning to watch and weigh my words to not overtalk and to become succinct."

I may want to start thinking about how I may begin sharing some of this with Michelle when She calls. I must remember She has no grid for Her being such a big part of all of this Healing; She didn't handle the text well—perhaps because of the way I shared how much She was involved in the triathlon.

08:15: I had a great two-hour meeting with my boss in the fire marshal's office; then I went to planning and met my newest brother, Pastor Femi, who is building a church. He is the one whom I had tea with the other day, and he opened me up, truly, like the book I tell you I am. It was, once again, another divine appointment, and he shared this time!

09.22.20: Barbara's Presession Notes

My home sold. I texted my realtor Sunday night after, I believe, POPPA said, "Did 'I' tell you to make an offer!"

07:20: Running is different now; it's like I've experienced something different. I saw Mike A. It's been a long time. Then the boys, and they were so excited. Then at 07:53 I saw Michelle in the Spirit again. I didn't expect to. I came up to Her and gave Her a hug and told Her I missed Her. Then I said nothing. She, after a moment, knowing I wasn't going to talk, said She missed me and appreciated and needed this time! When I looked down in the natural on the stump, there were these beautiful white morning glories.

My NPD (narcissist personality disorder), my pride, would get upset when I cooked the steaks perfectly, and Michelle would dillydally or just want to talk...because She would just microwave it, which was unacceptable to the pompous and prideful fool I was. I now purposely stall after the steak is perfect because I want to honor Her. I now even eat like Her, purposely only eating half of the steak to leave it for tomorrow. I would always eat it like a lion, making sure the hyenas get none! What a "fool." Thank *YOU*, *JESUS*, for saving me. Please show Michelle it's real, and if it isn't, please make it real!

09:03: I've always known the *love* of GOD and that I've been "HIS" favorite, since a very young age. I'm now seeing that, like everything else in my life, it was a fraction of a micron in depth. Therefore, when someone didn't respond well or got mad, so did I. I believe my shallowness, pride, apathy, wounds, rejections, selfishness, and self-centeredness held me back from going deeper into really meeting *JESUS*. It kept me from knowing *HIS* pain and suffering and experiencing *HIS* manly, powerful bridal *love*. Also, my very shallow, high-percentage-of-milk-teaching, seeker-friendly church experience and very immature life kept me goofing off and thinking it was funny with *JESUS*. As Billy Humphrey said yesterday, he was for thirteen years a youth pastor—he went to IHOP-KC and was blown away! He hears the bridal paradigm, the depth of cross-sectional references in the Bible, from the minor prophets to major to Revelation to John and then Genesis...to seeing that it is one book.

From start to finish, it's all *JESUS*. The wrath of GOD was against those who were against POPPA's Son's (*JESUS'*) bride—me! It's like sitting at the depths of the ocean and taking HIS Word, *HIM*, and all the above in at the extreme pressure of 30,000 feet. You drink deep the knowledge, *love*, wisdom, and awe of *JESUS*. What's cool about that is it's not like a fire hydrant that just blows you away—it's a deep, soaking, penetrating pressure from every side and goes to the depth of your being.

11:46: Also, I believed that I had no sorrows to speak of my entire life; during counseling one of the Michaels even said to me directly, "You are like Mom; you only remember the good stuff. I"—he—"had some real pain and sorrow. I've hurt and never received anything from you"—me—"I believe those rose-colored glasses also prevented me from going deep with *JESUS*; all I saw were the mountaintops, and now I see how *HE* really meets us in the deep, deep valleys of sorrow, but only when we allow this sorrow to take root in our being and deal with it, knowing we can only do it in *HIM*, is that *HE* meets us there and we can then share in *HIS* time of sorrow and become a man of joy in deep, painful sorrow.

09.29.20: Barbara's Presession Notes

09.25.20

04:30: 154 days into my fast of all starch, Billy calls for a forty-day fast up to election. I will now fast my favorite at this time and have no candy, gummies. Help me, LORD—it's only by YOUR Grace that I can do this and that YOU can heal this land, as well as have the closing on IHOP go smoothly. In the Name of *JESUS*. Amen.

I had a dream that Cate and I were in a river. I wasn't swimming, but she was. She was having so much fun, and there were a lot of ships that were just rusting. She was like a dolphin, swimming and going in and out of the water. Suddenly, she stopped coming out of the water and was gone. I slightly panicked. HE had me breathe, find her underwater, breathe in her mouth, and free her foot that got stuck in something, and she was fine. There wasn't a monster or scary fish. Her foot got stuck—that's all. Nothing to be scared about or panic.

07:33: It is so incredible to have this new heart. I'm working and listening to voicemail after voicemail from foreign-speaking people whom I can't really understand. In the past I would have had such an attitude toward them. Now I enjoy their dialect. Wow! Not only that, but when they call and ask about their job, I'm not getting anxious. *Oh no, did I not do my job? Is there a problem with what I did…?* I just calmly pull up their job, look for a status, and call them back. What an awesome way to live, not being anxious and haphazard. Thank *YOU*, LORD *JESUS*!

07:47: I spoke with my oldest brother, Larry, yesterday and explained some of how *JESUS* has healed me through trauma therapy. He was so excited to hear this; he has been so sick and messed up from Vietnam, agent orange, working in LILCO's furnaces with asbestos, being mugged and divorced. He knew only too well about the anxiety and drive…

09.24.20: Fifty-Seven!

21:30: Just before I closed my eyes, I heard from the last of my siblings. Thank *YOU*, *JESUS*; it was such a sweet day. I really felt loved. I heard from two important men in my life, both the girls, most of my brothers and sisters, and a bunch of folks on FB. I spoke with three brothers for a long time. It had been years since I'd done that. I really didn't expect to. Thank YOU, LORD. I had a great big rack of pork ribs for dinner with coleslaw I made!

09.29.20, 07:00: Down twenty pounds. I think another five, and I'm going to have to do something to stop the loss.

Work is going really well until an applicant completely disrespected and belittled me…he just kept going on, and I didn't even hang up on him…

Well, it got worse. The president of an architectural firm tried scaring me into allowing him to not install a sprinkler system. My boss emailed and said maybe we all should meet. I spent three hours on an email response to my boss, and he called me the next day. He said, "I want to make sure you know I have your back." I thanked him and said something like, "This needs an immediate response." He said, "Send it!" I didn't get nervous, scared, or mad. The dude's email said something like, "I've sent you everything you need; it would be prudent for you to accept and approve it. I calmly emailed him and said, "We reviewed your additional documents and are standing by our original decision. Send the new plans in, and we will expedite the review." I had already spoken to the owner of the business, a believer who commented on my email signature of "Be Blessed in the Name of *JESUS CHRIST*." I said, "It will go a lot easier if you sprinkle the places," and he seemed to agree. The architect probably convinced him that it was going to cost $250,000 and he should push back. Now they may still try and push it; if they do, they will be tied up for at least months and lose a lot of money in lost construction time.

I'm only saying all this to describe the peace I have dealing with these situations. I'm so different than I've ever been my entire life. Thank *YOU, JESUS.*

09.28.20, 07:00

09:19: Major cold-cranking amp battery needed to start this brain this morning.

16:40: Major tugging on my heart when Billy Humphrey was sharing during the all staff about being full time. I believe I'm to pursue both full-time ministry and work equally and see what *JESUS* decides!

19:23: Missing my gummies major; they were a big food group in my diet.

09.27.20

11:15: I came home from church, and there was Mow Mow (a stray outdoor cat I feed) in the middle of the kitchen; he was not supposed to be in the house! Normally I would flip, but I didn't; he saw that and wasn't upset. He knew he was wrong and calmly walked unafraid out the door. That had never happened; it was so peaceful and kind of *JESUS* to show me that.

Post-Session Notes

We tried a new part of IFS; she asked me to tune into my heart to see if there were any feelings or sensations, and immediately I felt not pain but pressure on about a third of my heart on the right side toward the bottom. At first I didn't know if someone was holding it or leaning on it. It didn't hurt, but I wasn't sure if someone was holding my heart lovingly or restricting it...as we continued, I could see that it was a metal plate riveted and welded to my heart. There were two men there watching the patch, like people used to do hundreds of years ago, watching a dike for a breach. The rest of the heart was huge, bright, and pumping or pulsating. This was when Barbara asked what my heart was feeling; the rest of the heart was alive, loving, kind, and sweet. The part with the patch wasn't very deep, alive, or bright; it was dark. Then she asked, "Is the patch to protect your heart or to keep things in?" I saw that it was to keep the contents in because I could see that it would all pour out if the patch gave way.

She asked, "What can we do to help this patch?" I tried to ask the two guys, but they were workers, like dike workers...then their boss came, and it was POPPA. Yay! "HE" popped "HIS" beautiful face into the scene. "HE" was tremendously large with beautiful big eyes and a heavenly smile, and "HIS" countenance was brighter than the sun. "HE" said, "That patch is to hold back the poison of your heart that is still hurt and rejected, prideful and arrogant...all you have to do is continue going deeper in the knowledge of 'MY' *love*, get it deeper into that heart, and pour it back out. Realize the testing 'I'm' doing, enjoy it, love it, and keep growing in 'MY' *love* and pouring it out lovingly. This will heal your heart completely." (IHOP-KC, 01.03.20, 9:00 a.m. Aaron V. is singing "I Will Pour out All My Love to You" [1:40.10].) It's now 19:45 that I'm writing all this down. When I explained this to Barbara, the patch exploded, and it shrank to around a third of its size. "HE" said it was because I understood what "HE" had told me. I explained it well to Barbara, showing that I was going to do it.

What happened was my entire heart, except the little piece that still has the patch is what exploded. It is now gigantic, brilliant in color, and pulsating with such new energy. It made the patch look tiny and barely able to hold on. "HE" knew I wanted the full Healing today, and she said, "What else can we do?" It was so funny because I was watching "HIM" and knew we couldn't do anything right now. "HE" said, "'I' could Heal you completely today, but 'I' am not going to; it's not like the permanent limp that 'I' gave Jacob for wrestling with 'ME.' 'I' am going to Heal you and your heart 100 percent, but for now, 'I' am going to leave this patch in place. You will see and feel as you grow in depth of 'MY' *love* and pour it out freely on all; you will see and feel this patch pop, and you're even going to hear it. It is going to explode off soon." When I read this to type it, I said to myself, *That's just repeating it; maybe I will rewrite it.* I believe "HE" said, "Yes, 'I' often do that in the Bible. I repeat the same thing over in the same paragraph—originally there were no paragraphs—it's to bring emphasis to it! When you grow more in the depth of the knowledge of 'MY' *love* and show it continually. It's soon—trust 'ME,' believe 'ME'..."

"HE" also told me my heart, which exploded tonight, was the new heart that "HE" gave me a few weeks ago. I was only operating in the huge, beautiful new heart at the capacity of my old heart. Tonight, it exploded into the full size of the new heart; that very little patch part is actually my old heart. I'm telling you this new heart is glorious; it shines with the secret colors an illumination of Heaven. We don't know these colors or Glory, but "HE" has them richly in this new heart of mine. "HE" just said, "Wait until you see it when it's 100 percent healed and operating in 'MY' *Glory*!" The pop was going to be heard Spiritually around the world, all the universe, and heavens. "'I' am well pleased with you, Mike! You're doing great—keep going. You've earned this new heart. It will serve you well, and 'I' know you will continue serving 'ME' well." "HE" gave me an eternal hug and kiss. 20:15.

06:04: The other day I passed another test at the lap pool. Some dude was in my lane, lane number three! The lifeguard said, "I know…" And I was okay with it; I said, "No worries, The LORD is working on me." Well, today I failed. I saw a man getting ready to get into the pool. I looked down and thought, *Sure enough*. He was getting into the lane next to lane four; now Todd was in the second from the end, and I thought that would mean he was in lane three, which was mine. Had I analyzed things first, I would have known/seen lane two on this side of four or remembered that the numbers start in the other side. Well, I didn't, and I approached him and asked him, "Before you jump in, I believe that is lane three." He is a nice man and has been there a few times. He calmly said, "This is lane five," and pointed to lane four next to it. I apologized, and, thankfully, it was over. I was embarrassed, but not humiliated like I would have been in the past.

My dream with Michelle—She and I were at an event, conference, or something, maybe even a Marriage conference. We were walking together—Her in front and winding through (zigzag) row after row from the back to the front. We got to the front, and there was only one seat, and Her friends were all there, just ladies, so I looked at Her and said, "I'll go into the back," and I had purity in my heart. Normally, I would immediately think, *What about me? I'm the one who likes the front row, not for attention, but there's less distraction.* None of that went through my head or heart. I just smiled lovingly to acknowledge it and waited to see if that was okay, if She wanted to stay there, and I would go back. I also wanted to clearly give Her a chance to acknowledge me; that is what She wanted. The old me would make the decision and just leave, and maybe that would be taken as my being upset. I looked Her in the eye and waited with kind, loving eyes to make sure She understood it would be okay if She sat without me. I wanted to give Her a chance to weigh in… Thank *YOU*, LORD *JESUS*. Then I walked away and sat all the way in the back, and that was more than okay. I honored my wife with purity in my heart. *HE* kept me in this moment for a while, even when I woke up. In the past I would be so insecure and needy. I would want or need to be with Her. I was always so smothering and suffocating to Michelle. Thank *YOU, JESUS*, for healing me.

14:00: I read a letter from a PE (professional engineer) yesterday that sounded like his client built a building without a permit—second one in a week! So I spoke with him today, and sure enough, they did!

Twenty lengths, 500 meters. I pushed myself like when I was running before the triathlon, and I couldn't see well, even after around six hours, three cups of tea, one DC (Diet Coke), and the shock of finding another app built without a BP (building permit).

06:10: There was a contractor who waited fifty-five days for us to help him. The day it came to me I called him at 06:10. "You are a breath of fresh air." I cried inside and thanked him for his kind words.

10:06: I believe "HE" is teaching me to be like *JESUS*, a man of great joy in the middle of such excruciating sorrow. "HE" has me in the secret place. "HE" is holding me, hugging me, loving me, kissing me, smothering me—sometimes I can't breathe. "HE" has me eating, sleeping, and drinking the FATHER's heart all day and all night long, so it's all I know...so all I can do is try and love others well.

16:29: My heart grieves with immense pain for all the poison I've spewed on Michelle for five years. I had such rejection and woundedness in my heart. I had no idea it was there and didn't believe it or that it was so bad that I was a monster to Michelle. I've said it to Her, but this season is making me taste it in such a profound way. I can't stop crying about it. My most important focus right now is to really soak in POPPA's *love* and deepen my understanding of it so that no matter what I face, I can only love...it's all about that.

POST-SESSION NOTE

This session was so tender and kind. Barbara said, "Let's just see what 'HE' wants to do." I felt something strong. It was so strong and immediate that it came out of me, and I believe it was a female. I couldn't see her at all, but that was what I thought. I addressed her and asked her who she was. At first it was clear, but I still couldn't see her, and then it looked like there was a man on the bench in the place where the angles are on my run circuit. He was leaning over her, and I didn't know what was going on. She said that I still had impurities that I didn't repent of or get cleaned of. These are all the thoughts that I have had my whole life, even the thoughts of Michelle, which I shouldn't be having. *You think it's pure because it's Michelle, but it's not because you're separated from Her*. She said, "That has hurt you"—me—"my whole life. You"—I—"need to address it, repent, and ask for forgiveness." I said, "Yes, I want to." I asked her if she could wait one moment so that I could update Barbara. She said something like, "Thank you for asking me if I would wait. I appreciate that, and yes, please do." When I explained this to Barbara, she spoke more about how I need to address this because I've gotten such Healing and freedom from all the junk that has gone through physically, but not the thoughts. I said, "Please help me; I want to repent for all of this." She started walking away; there were such beautiful, bright but soft colors, and I asked her, "Please don't go." I was now deeply crying, feeling lonely and rejected. I was not ready; there was still so much we needed to work on. I didn't want her to go, and she said, "I was just here to let you know this," and HOLY SPIRIT was the man talking to me on the bench, making sure I knew the plan. She said, "You're going to do fine," and she walked away. Then HOLY SPIRIT (BOB) came. HE is so beautiful, kind, and sweet…I'm just crying and crying about how sweet and kind HE is to me! HE said, "It's time to sweep that house clean entirely and make room for US to have you completely." I repented of all the impure thoughts I've had my entire life. HE started pulling so much junk out of me. I started writing these down and not telling Barbara because HOLY SPIRIT was lovingly working on getting all of this out of my heart:

- » impurity

- » anger

- » greed

- » rejection

- » insecurity

- » pride

- » idolatry (love of money)

- » vanity

- » haughtiness

- » superiority

- » anxiety

- » dumbness

- » tiredness (need for sleep)

- » need for caffeine

- » need for attention (from others other than HIM)

- » affection (from others other than HIM)

- » need to be right (to have to prove it)

- » drive (striving)

He then put in me:

- » humility

- » love

- » gentleness

- » patience in waiting

- » meekness

- » tenderness

- » sensitivity

- » clarity

- » focus

- » purity (HE highlighted that)

When I started explaining this to Barbara, I could see it all like sediment floating down in water. *HE* was telling me that I was so immature, and this sediment was all of these characteristics floating down into this new heart of mine.

Then the water was gone. I was watching all this. All the sediment started taking root. I was watching this happening...

Then they started growing...

First, low growth, beautiful big green leaves—immature but good growth.

Second, now trees—big, beautiful, big, big trees. Mighty "oaks of righteousness" (Isaiah 61:3), 200 feet tall with strong roots and majestic branches and leaves. Maples and beautiful dogwoods...

Third, birds resting and raising families.

Fourth, all the living creatures.

Fifth, rich, lush, gorgeous gardens with fruits and veggies.

The three of THEM are the biggest lions playing with me, wrestling with me, loving on me!

My heart is Healing, no patch, and THEY are 100 percent in 100 percent of me as mighty lions.

Then the lions said THEY needed me to settle, get comfortable, peaceful, and strong in my new heart and garden. "Trust 'ME,' believe 'ME.'"

At the end Barbara said, "There's more resistance"; she could see it in my face. Immediately *HE* let me know that there was still unbelief. I was still missing Michelle and holding onto Her too much...I didn't believe in my heart that *HE* was enough. I said, "I'm sorry, *JESUS*. Please help me with my unbelief."

Me in Israel 2005 net fishing on the Sea of Galilee

A pic I took of HOLY SPIRIT in a window on Mount Tibor (Mount of Transfiguration)

10.06.20 Barbara's Post-Session Notes

We started talking about how she saw something in my face, and *JESUS* said it was unbelief. We didn't do the normal—this time hit it head-on. She said rejection, and boy, that opened the floodgates. Immediately I felt the rejection of when that lady walked away. I cried that she didn't want to continue talking and felt so rejected...then we were back to kindergarten...then the womb. Wow! We hadn't heard or felt something from pre-birth in a while but still couldn't get there. We got there today...pre-birth Michael was in the womb, and there I was...I couldn't believe I was actually in my mother's womb. It all felt like:

> *JESUS replied, "Very truly I tell you, no one can see the kingdom of GOD unless they are born again." "How can someone be born when they are old?" Nicodemus asked. "Surely they cannot enter a second time into their mother's womb to be born!" JESUS answered, "Very truly I tell you, no one can enter the kingdom of GOD unless they are born of water and the Spirit. Flesh gives birth to flesh, but the Spirit gives birth to spirit. You should not be surprised at my saying, 'You must be born again.' The wind blows wherever it pleases. You hear its sound, but you cannot tell where it comes from or where it is going. so it is with everyone born of the Spirit."*

John 3:3–8 (NIV)

I'm telling you; I was there. I felt the warmth of the fluid. I was there…I was with preborn Michael, and I was preborn Michael. Then I felt someone there. Barbara asked, "Is it a boy or a girl?" I thought it was a girl, so I thought for a moment, *Twins?* No, it's Mara. Mara Collins the fourth girl, eighth child? But it wasn't! It was Mom wishing I was a girl, Mara…I saw such darkness, rejection—big time—tormenting me… It was so sad. Mom didn't want me…I was so hurt. Mom didn't want me; she wanted Mara, and she told me many times. She didn't know I was a boy, but she sure wanted Mara. Maybe that's why they called me Michael instead of Patrick. Supposedly my Aunt Loretta lost a son, and she was going to call him Patrick, but maybe Michael reminded Mom of Mara, and that was really what Mom wanted. My full name is Patrick Michael. By the time Terrance, number nine, came in, the joke was Dad said, "No more"…I never met or heard of a Mara before an instructor the other week at work, and that's why the name meant so much to my heart.

It was so bad; there was so much torment rolling around and surrounding me (us); it was part of the fluid. Barbara said, "Talk to him—let him know how much he is, was, and always will be loved." I started speaking to and into him (me), and the darkness disappeared. I kept telling him how much everyone loved him. He was a chubby (just like my girls), sweet, lovable boy, always smiling… How when he got a little older, Larry would bring his friends over to see me (us), always smiling, and the name Chopper (Chopper was a bulldog we had) wasn't a mean thing. He loved you (us) so much, but boy, did the girls (our older sisters) say you had the smelliest big poops, and you always had such knots in your shoes. Much, much later. Mom would forget everyone's name, but not yours… she always remembered her Michael…in high school, she would say, "You're not fat; you're husky," and we would just laugh and laugh and laugh…I believe the last thing Dad said before he died was, "Michael…" He had the biggest smile on his face when he saw you. I don't think he said another word, and then while watching Monday night football, the Bears against the Lions, he passed away while we were holding his hand at 12:02. I had to kiss him to tell if he was breathing; he went so peacefully…

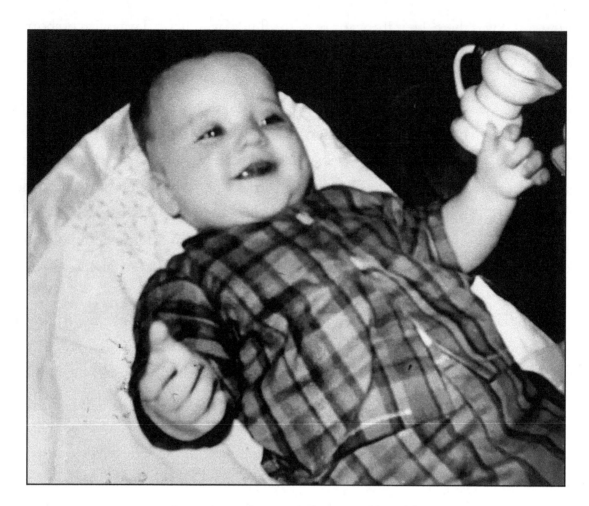

A picture of me at a few months old.

Then suddenly, it was time for us to be born, and it was the weirdest thing. I was him being born. I was watching as me now, and Barbara said, "Don't tell anyone this, but, buddy, I gave birth to you"—me—"so please don't share it with anyone." I mean it—it was strange but so cool. I was part of my own birth in third person. It was such a wonderful experience. I was there with him (me) and everything... Then we didn't want to come out. I believe we were scared...I told him (me), "It's okay. Ali was a forceps delivery; she didn't want to come out either." Then we crowned and just stayed there for a moment...then we came out, and they swooshed us up and put us on Mom's belly; she was so excited to see us (me)...boy, she loved us. It was so peaceful, but then darkness came, and Barbara believed that was when they took us from Mom.

Then *JESUS* came...the loving, beautiful Man in White with the most incredible smile... We were so scared, but not anymore. *HE* was playing with newborn Michael, and I wasn't able to approach—like middle school Michael, who went to Glory. I just watched lovingly as HE held him and bounced and cuddled him. *HE* was like the proud FATHER *HE* is...I couldn't get close, but it was me, so I was the one being cuddled and loved on...once again it was so strange...then *HE* invited me in, and newborn Michael was on *HIS* right lap, and I was on *HIS* left...and *HE* just loved on us and made us feel so secure...*HE* just kept loving on us...Then suddenly, little baby Michael was there. He sat on the outside of *HIS* right leg, and once again, *HE* just kept loving on us all. *HE* said *HE* was Healing me (us) from pre-birth to baby Michael. This was every Michael, except the one who is still with HIM from Joan to Michelle...Then *HE* wanted the three of them alone, and baby Michael took my place. It was so satisfying to see *JESUS* loving on the two of them (us), and *HE* was talking to them, hugging on them, kissing on them...and playing with them...

Then baby Michael left, and Dad came in. I watched Dad love on him (me), and he was so happy to see and hold him (me). *JESUS* was right there 'cause Dad and Mom sure loved *JESUS*. Dad was kissing us and just holding us (me) so tight. Then Dad brought him (me) over to Mom, and the three of them loved on him. This was when *JESUS* said *HE* wanted me to leave and give them time together. Just alone time, like each one of the Michaels.

Billy Humphrey started saying during the 16:00 Prayer meeting that JESUS was breaking the chains around people's hearts of performance to earn HIS love. Think you have to work to gain HIS love? "It's not who I am!" It's not who HE is. It's not what I have to do to be loved by others. There is no striving in love. HE is seeing the chains breaking over our hearts. HIS love for me has nothing to do with what I can do; it's not my works. It's JESUS on the cross only! "'I' have loved you with everlasting kindness."

10.07.20

06:27: *HE* let me know that last evening I was emotionally born again, healed, and freed in the Name of *JESUS CHRIST*! Thank *YOU*, LORD *JESUS*.

08:47: Okay, so yesterday The LORD allowed me to experience in three persons. I was pre-birth Michael, feeling the pain of the rejection of thinking Mom didn't want a boy and wanted Mara (HE also let me know that Mom didn't have any girls named Marie; Dad had three boys with the middle name George). I was also Michael, the adult, watching my birth, which was incredible. The LORD allowed me to experience my own birth as Mom, Michael (me) being birthed, and me, adult Mike watching. HE gave me this so I could actually feel how happy mom was to have me (something like what I felt about my own girls but different since obviously I'm a man). So that when I spoke to Michael and told him Mom was so excited to have me, I was actually speaking the truth because I experienced it as Mom.

"As in water face reflects face, so a man's heart reveals the man" (Proverbs 27:19, NKJV). I would look in the mirror and be lied to, to my face, by me. I was very ugly, mean, rotten, and deceived. *JESUS* has Healed my rejected and wounded heart to see this and all the pain I have caused.

I'm talking to Michelle in the Spirit. I believe I understand now what You told me weeks before this last separation. You said something like, "I put You on a roller coaster of emotions. I tell You that I love You, then in seconds get mad at You for…" There is so much to unpack with You about what this season is teaching me and healing me from. I look forward to one day soon doing that… "HE" has told me that I have such a wide understanding and experience of "HIS" *love*, but it has been a fraction of a micron (one millionth of a meter or 1/26,000 of an inch) deep, and as soon as "you" scratched it ever so slightly, the rejection would pour out…

Post-Session Notes: Written Saturday, 10.10.20, 16:00

We chatted shortly and jumped right into EMDR (which we hadn't done in weeks). Barbara wanted to set all the incredible things that POPPA did in Tuesday's session with the pre-birth Michael's Healing and the filling of this awesome new heart of mine with a new heavenly garden. It was so peaceful; we had a very slow frequency tapping, and I could feel all of the GODly traits being firmly set in my heart and soul.

- » Humility
- » *Love*
- » Gentleness
- » Patience (in waiting)
- » Meekness
- » Tenderness
- » Sensitivity
- » Clarity
- » Focus

There are nine of them!

It was so powerful. Then we went right back into Tuesday, and there we were. I could see *JESUS*, PB (preborn/post-born) Michael, Mom, and Dad. *JESUS* made it clear to me to leave them alone, to give PB Michael max time with *HIM*, Mom, and Dad. I immediately felt something, and it came right out. It was a man, but no details to his shape. He sat next to me and stared at Michael and *JESUS* in amazement. Then he would look at me with the same look, but he had no detail, so I couldn't tell, but I could tell…he was clearly part of Michael, but that was me, so there is/was a connection to me. He was there Tuesday, and I had no idea. He was just so bewildered in awe and love but didn't know love; he was apart, not a human, and on top of that, he was a part of Michael, who experienced such torment and never really got away from it because they were never birthed—at least that is what I'm being told. That's why I experienced such a strong third-person experience, which was a fourth-person experience. It was with Michael in his torment in the womb—I was me witnessing his/my birth; I was Mom giving birth (so, so weird and only *JESUS*), but now I'm hearing post-birth Michael. I don't know how to explain it. I just try and write it down as I hear it; if I'm wrong, "HE" will usually correct me later. What I'm hearing now and may have been told Tuesday—pre-birth Michael never birthed because he was trapped in torment that never ended until Tuesday, so very sad, and this guy was with him the entire time. Remember I was there; the torment was so evil, mean, powerful, and intense. We thought it was a twin because Mom wanted Mara so badly, it had Michael trapped there, so it was a fight. They never believed in *JESUS*. Mom knew and loved *JESUS*, read Scripture, Prayed, and spoke with *HIM*, but they felt hatred because she wanted Mara so badly that they only felt hatred and hypocrisy. When I came in there Tuesday, it was a stark difference. I'm not better than Mom or saying anything like that; they are saying they were stuck inside the womb for around fifty-eight years (fifty-seven years plus nine months). The enemy was so mean, strong, and ferocious—then I came into the womb with *JESUS* in my heart and full of *HIS* love, and it changed everything. He couldn't feel it or comprehend because he isn't human, but Michael did. This guy was so confused and was separated from Michael shortly after I came in and during the birth.

Then Michael was with *JESUS*, and this guy couldn't approach him—like I couldn't. It was just like when *JESUS* took middle school Michael to Glory. He so wanted *JESUS*, and this was when Michael (who was still with *JESUS*, Mom, and Dad, just to the left, the entire time) turned around and smiled at us as well as *JESUS*, acknowledging that "it was good." Then suddenly POPPA came out of nowhere and started hugging me, clothing me in my armor like "HE" did a few weeks ago. "HE" was laying hands on me, then the robe and crown. "HE" turned into a gigantic lion again, but this time even bigger. "HE" stood up on "HIS" hind feet with "HIS" front feet and hands on my chest and started roaring. "HE" was letting the enemy know I'm "HIS" and "don't mess with 'ME.'" It was absolutely wild! Then HOLY SPIRIT came over for a huge hug fest. One of the newest heavenly saints, Derek Duncan, came over to join this hug fest since *JESUS* was with Michael. It was so good to see Derek, and the four of us hugged and kissed.

Here was this guy. I didn't even know his name—if he had a name—and he so wanted in. Then who do you think came running over? Mary, one of my parts, of course. She came running over and hugged this guy and immediately loved on him. Both *JESUS* and Michael turned around, and *JESUS* said, "*I* have anointed her with *MY* oil of intimacy, like Mary Magdalene, and *I* am becoming very fond of her." This guy just melted. Then I got it; he was poisoned by Mom's thoughts of Mara. Here was Mary, the root name of Marie and Mara…loving on him with the oil of intimacy that *JESUS* has anointed her with… He then told us his name was Mark.

10.13.20: Barbara's Presession Notes

10.10.20, 08:47: I grabbed a Bartlett pear, and "HE" took me back to fond memories of two Bartlett pear trees growing up. One on the north and south end of the village of South Hempstead, New York. I would sit in those trees for hours eating fresh pears as a very small kid.

10.12.20, 05:30: My Notes

12:58: I was washing dishes, and someone walked in the side door. I would normally turn around and say hi. I didn't this time, and I wasn't trying not to…but what *JESUS* said was that I was healed of the people pleasing, insecurity, and the need for attention. It happened to be Jose, and I was so glad that I didn't, but it's not about being mad of hurt by him. He also said that this proved my *indistractionability* and *focusability*.

Chapter 2

SO YOU THINK YOU'RE UNFLAPPABLE?

10.15.20: BARBARA'S PRESESSION NOTES

06:32: "HE" said, "Have you seen 'MY' girl, Amy Barrett? That's how 'I' am working you—'unflappable,' like Neil Armstrong, first man, 'solid, unchangeable in conviction.' That's you, Mike, and 'I'm' setting it in you like stone." It's the second time I heard, "Thus saith The LORD." I'm not saying that. "HE" did!

10:03: So I hear this voice, "Unflappable? It looks to me like you're getting flapped around a lot!" I said, "I'm in training—speak to my teacher!" I didn't hear anything after that. Thank *YOU, JESUS*!

10.14.20, 07:24: When I was making my second breakfast. PB (post-birth) Michael said he was talking to *JESUS* about that surgery that came right after birth. He wants to know why I didn't warn him.

08:35: I was chatting with Mark and Mary. Mark was still a little scared of that dude from yesterday, and I said, "You have *JESUS*," but then I thought, *Maybe he doesn't.* Then I thought, *The rest of my parts do—why wouldn't he?* I told him, "I believe you can have *JESUS* in you, and, therefore, you have nothing to fear." "There is no fear in love; but perfect love casts out fear" (1 John 4:18a NKJV)

18:32: "HE" let me know that "HE" is allowing me to stretch my wings. (I'm not an angel, but you know what I mean.) But WE are never far. Thank "YOU," POPPA. I know that.

POST-SESSION NOTES

Barbara said, "Let's go to your peaceful place." I felt peace for a moment, but immediately I felt something in my chest. It'd never been in my chest, and there was so much pressure that I couldn't breathe. I mean I seriously couldn't breathe. I knew it was the big guy from Thursday, and I got mad! I couldn't breathe. Then she reminded me to ask for space. I did, and it subsided almost completely. But I couldn't see anything; I was in my Adirondack chair, but there was nothing. She said, "Invite *JESUS*." *HE* is so kind and sat right next to me. We sat there, and an image of a heavy fellow was sitting opposite us in a rocking chair. He reminded me of a friend of mine named Bill Durham.

He was kind-looking and seemed gentle like Bill but serious. He said, "This is serious. I started seeing and feeling pagan worship." He let me know that "they," not him, were using it against me. He was really serious and expressed again how serious it was. I looked at *JESUS*, and *HE* was so at peace. Barbara said, "Be curious!" *HE* didn't say much after that. Suddenly, this big guy came, big dude, and he was mad but quiet. I asked him to sit, and they were on the opposite side of the firepit, and he was mad! Raging but wouldn't say anything.

After some time, I looked at *JESUS*, and *HE* said, "Don't take your eyes off him—this is serious." The big guy finally, after a lot of silence, was trying to play me. He said he was mad that I took Michael and that guy away. When I told Barbara he meant Michael and Mark, he said something derogatory about me like I'm a little turd...and that thing has a name! That was when I raised up a bit and noticed a lot of his troops coming around. I told Barbara and said, "I don't know if he sees all our troops coming around behind me." It was amazing, and I could feel how serious this was getting. *JESUS* was just sitting there and giving me such peace and courage. The big guy said, "Something like I had you from the beginning, and I had you good. I have the last you also." He was reminding me that they haven't come completely to *JESUS* yet; speaking of pre- and post-birth Michael, I realized that Joan and Michelle Michaels still aren't healed yet. Then Barbara reminded me that I needed my armor of GOD on, and I started speaking each piece into place; it was so cool. There I am in full battle gear, and this guy was getting even madder. I stood up, and he was huge! I took my sword out and jammed it into the ground. I said, "In the authority of the Name of *JESUS CHRIST*, I command you to leave me, all my mes and my parts, and this place now. You go back to hell and never return—in the Name of *JESUS CHRIST*!" I turned into a mammoth lion and started roaring louder than I ever have! They all left except for the heavy guy. I meant to say while things were heating up, he gave me a genuine smile and nob. I didn't want to smile back because I didn't want him to get in trouble.

I looked at *JESUS*, and *HE* was well pleased with me. Then POPPA came and said, "No more lovey-dovey; this is real." "HE" said I have done a great job, but there is more to be done, and to pick up my Sword. "HE" was so proud of me, but "HE" was very serious. I don't remember "HIM" like this, except this morning. Then "HE" hugged me big time and was huge. I was like David up against that dude, but I'm not a child, but POPPA made him look tiny. Then BOB, HOLY SPIRIT, came over and hugged and kissed me big time. I really didn't know how serious it was until THEY hugged me and just poured into me, and, of course, *JESUS* then jumped up to give me a big squeeze. Each of THEM separately and purposely had alone time with me to impart some of each of THEM into my heart, Spirit, and being. It was very clear, especially how POPPA was stern (like this morning), serious, and focused...letting me know that the next season is upon me. Then "HE" poured "HIS" *love* all over, around, and in me! The three of THEM hugged me and hugged me and hugged me and poured even more into me...once THEY were done loving on me, Mike A. came up, hugged, and encouraged me. He told me that He and all His boys were there, which were a lot, were there for me in support. He also said He knew something was up, and that was why He came to see me yesterday.

Then suddenly we were all at a table. It was POPPA, *JESUS*, HOLY SPIRIT, Mike A., and me. It was a huge table with incredible food (Heavenly food like Billy Humphrey talks about). I was eating the largest chicken leg, bigger than any turkey leg, and then there was this huge bowl of the most delicious-looking roasted potatoes I had ever seen. POPPA was right next to me and said, "Go ahead." I said, "No, I'm going to keep my fast," and "HE" gave me such a big smile. Then the roast of beast and a huge bowl of green beans and almonds. At the table POPPA was on my right and then BOB (HOLY SPIRIT) on "HIS" right—*JESUS* on my left, and Mike A. on *HIS* left. I didn't notice for a while, but POPPA let me know that I was at the head of the table, and it was not because I was a guest. I said, "No, that can't be." I started crying. "'YOU' must be at the head, at least one of YOU three, and then even Mike A. over me."

THEY refused and said, "No, it's you." Then I was in my crown, robe, and slippers, no more battle armor. I looked at each of THEM smiling at me with such *love*, even Mike A., and then THEY showed THEIR *Glory*, and it lit up the room; it was amazing. As the Bible says, "The city had no need of the sun or of the moon to shine in it, for the glory of God illuminated it. The Lamb is its light" (Revelation 21:23 NKJV)

Then I was in The Throne Room. POPPA, *JESUS*, and HOLY SPIRIT were on THEIR Thrones, and I was seated just below THEM and on their left. It was me, then Mike A. to my left. POPPA came up to me and said, "Grab your sword next to you." It was a brilliant, beautiful sword with the biggest ruby on the end. "HE" reminded me of the energy and power in a ruby and said that was why "HE" gave me that one. Then "HE" took the crown off my head, placed it in front of me, and placed a new, more elegant, and royal one on my head. "HE" said that other one was for battle, along with that sword. "This one is for peace, and I am to interchange them for the specific duty." I just cried and cried. I could see the "emerald-colored Sea of Glass." I've only seen that from farther away, like all the times for the last two years. I'd be sitting on the ground next to POPPA, holding onto "HIS" ginormous leg like a small child with Dad at work. "HE" said, "Now you are up here and in your place. You have much to learn, much to grow, and much to do." Mike A. was looking at me like

Mark was looking at *JESUS*, pre- and post-birth Michael, and then me in astonishment. I realized He was an angel and didn't or wasn't capable of feeling this *love*… It blew me away. Here was Mike A., Michael the Archangel, looking at me like that, and then He said how He was assigned to me around January of this year and how He hung around me even more because He likes me so. This was Mike A., the most powerful angel, and He was telling me He liked me so much and enjoyed hanging with me. He loves being assigned to me because He likes me so much. I'm bawling my eyes out. Who am I? What have I done? THEY said, "There is nothing you can do," that *JESUS* had already done it all. Then I thought and said out loud, "Are YOU taking me *Home* to Glory?" I was genuinely scared THEY were taking me, right now, right in our session…I cried. I hate to admit it—I was so scared and didn't want to go. It was so beautiful and amazing, but I wasn't ready, and I really thought, with everything that was going on, that THEY were taking me. *I'm sorry, POPPA. I really want some time with Michelle before YOU take me—please allow me to have a great Marriage before YOU bring me Home.*

THEY knew how serious I was, and POPPA started telling me how proud "HE" was of me and how I was allowing "HIM" to HEal me. I said, "Barbara has so much to do with it." "HE" agreed and told her how special she was to "HIM" and she has done her job very well.

10.20.20 Barbara's Presession Notes

EMDR flash technique. EMDR has disassociation, so we did IFS and some EMDR.

10.17.20: I think "HE" said, "Don't be too certain that you won't have to cut the head off that dude if and when he comes back. You're ready—be ready!"

Before we started the session, while we were talking, Barbara told me the reason she was spending so much time with me was that she was seeing so much of what *JESUS* was doing in me right in front of her eyes…she is learning so much from *JESUS* during these sessions…every single session *HE* blows it up! Who am I, LORD! Why me? Why are YOU so good to me? Who am I?

10.19.20: I'm beginning to respect others' privacy, not striving to communicate or be with others, and it's so peaceful!

Session Notes

We went into the session, and it was that lady from a few times ago. The one who was only there to bring something to my attention, and then HOLY SPIRIT took over. *I don't know what she looks like. I don't think she's part of me.* I was Upstate New York at the little house in the '60s, maybe early '70s. We were hanging in the tall grass, shooting BB guns in the sun, and I believe "HE" reminded me this scene is a big part of what my peaceful place is. She didn't want to come out; she said, "That dude or someone is around." She was not afraid but said he or they have more authority, dominion...than she. Barbara said, "Ask her if she would come out and go behind you." I didn't even have to ask. I was in my armor, and she came behind me.

Then Barbara said, "Have her put her hand on your shoulder," and she did. As soon as this happened, things changed; there was something out in the grass. It was the enemy. I could see them, and they were coming from the woods, up from the ravine. Before this, I was seeing the time when Terrance was in the driver's seat of the Oldsmobile; we were pushing it to get it out of the way so we could play. It got away from us, and we were young. Terrance could barely even see through the steering wheel.

Dad came running, jumped in the window, and put it in gear and stopped it. If he didn't, it could have gone over the ravine. That was where they were coming from. Suddenly, they started charging, and I was on a horse. I drew my sword, and they turned into a huge fire storm raging toward us. I immediately said out loud, "This battle belongs to The LORD!" And they all retreated. While I was putting my sword back, I shouted, "*JESUS*... Hallelujah..." That was my battle cry...

I asked her if I could update Barbara, and she just so appreciated that I asked and said yes, but she went back inside... After I told Barbara, she said, "Let's go back," and I did. She came out, and there was POPPA in the clouds; they were dark storm clouds, and "HE" was so proud of me. "HE" said, "Well done," and let me know that this was number two—I did very well this time. And "HE" said I had more authority this time than Thursday. "HE" reminded me that I was looking more to *JESUS* Thursday for guidance but still won the battle with my authority in *CHRIST*. This time THEY made sure I was by myself. I'm never alone with THEM (not alone but by myself), sure and steady in my authority and ready for the battle. When I firmly proclaimed the battle belonged to THEM, it was over! In the beginning, the enemy was a strong adversary in the fire storm but nothing! Because of THEM. I stood strong and confident in THEM and won. "HE" told me "HE" loved me and was very proud of me and left in the cloud. It looked like:

> *And above the firmament over their heads was the likeness of a throne, in appearance like a sapphire stone; on the likeness of the throne was a likeness with the appearance of a man high above it. Also from the appearance of His waist and upward I saw, as it were, the color of amber with the appearance of fire all around within it; and from the appearance of His waist and downward I saw, as it were, the appearance of fire with brightness all around. Like the appearance of a rainbow in a cloud on a rainy day, so was the appearance of the*

brightness all around it. This was the appearance of the likeness of the glory of the Lord. So when I saw it, I fell on my face, and I heard a voice of One speaking.

Ezekiel 1:26 KJV

Mike A. was right behind "HIM" and acknowledged that I did very well, nodding, smiling, and cheering me on.

Mike A. and I are beginning to have a very close relationship. When He first came into my life, I think it was much earlier than January of 2020, but He really started hanging with me then. I was always so concerned—why was Michael the Archangel here with me? LORD, what is He protecting me from? Sure enough, He was there a lot, day after day...I remember seeing Him take things out around me so many times. He was there protecting me...then I would see Him while running or walking...Wednesday while I was looking for the bench in Peachtree City, Georgia...then there was Thursday, and it changed everything. He was there with all His boys for the battle; He was so proud of me. He was there in the war room at the table and next to me in The Throne Room. He was next to me on my left, with THEM on my right. He and I were one level below THEM but at the same level, and He was looking at me and THEM and at me, like Mark was... It was at the table when POPPA had me at the head and then at The Throne. There I was looking down onto the Sea of Glass... It's so different now with Him and THEM. I'm beginning to have a personal relationship and friendship with POPPA, *JESUS*, HOLY SPIRIT, and Mike A.... Why me? Why me? It's so different...I'm beginning to have an individual, intimate friendship with each of the GODhead, knowing their voice and heart, and Mike A. It is just so amazing... How could this be?

Then I told Barbara this; she said, "Let's go back and make sure there are no loose ends." When I went back, there were Mike A. and the lady. POPPA said, "There are plenty of loose ends because there is plenty going on." It's okay; it's more than okay! This is not done; it's actually just the beginning of this new season in The LORD...I'm beginning to walk, talk, and battle in the new authority POPPA and *JESUS* Prayed into me on Thursday. The full armor, the robe, the slipper, the sword, and the crown.

When I told Barbara this, she asked if there was an object that could wrap up today and the last few sessions that we could tap in. Immediately I saw my crown, clear as day. I wanted to wait and make sure, unlike I used to do... Then she said, "Picture it and then take three very deep breaths. As soon as I started doing this, distraction and condemnation came; it was the enemy trying to steal it from me. So I grabbed it and held on to it; he wasn't going to get it from me, and I took three giant breaths and set it deeply in me...

She wanted me to draw it or picture it and have it with me always.

CAVEMAN TO PRIEST

10:28: "HE" gave me something so powerful and so confirming…that I'm becoming a thermostat instead of a barometer. It was so deeply encouraging to me that "HE" is seeing in my heart, that I'm not being changed by my surroundings as much as I'm changing my surrounding or environment.

12:45: Dustin told me again that I am his hero! Who am I?

10.25.20, 14:45: "HE" once again showed me my crown! It's big; it's solid, solid gold and thick rubies and some emeralds, diamonds…

10.21.20, 05:00

08:58: I was such a fool. There was a huge fire (lava) just slightly under the surface of my skin. I was so kind until you scratched it ever so slightly—then, boy, would it come up.
"I rejoice at YOUR word As one who finds great treasure" (Psalm 119:162, NKJV).

Post-Session Notes

We started the session, and immediately it hit me hard, but I didn't say anything because Barbara was describing the peaceful place, what I see, what I feel, and what I smell, and it was good because I went right there. It was clearly the little house, not the other beautiful cabin up in the mountain. Once she said something like, "What part of you wants to come out?" We were sitting in the Adirondack chair; it hit me harder, and I said something to her, and it immediately came out of me but was so different. It shot out of me, disappeared, and went right down the ravine. I thought right away, *Oh, no!* Then nothing else—she once again asked, "Does someone want to come out…?" And we waited. Mark wanted to come out but was afraid, and Mary wasn't comfortable because of what ran into the wood. Then suddenly I felt it once again strongly, but it was that lady. I didn't know her name or anything about her. She came out and said something like, "This is big and serious…" She sat right next to me to my left in the chair. I got a look at her for the first time. I could see, but I couldn't see…it was strange…I think she had blonde hair, but I couldn't see any other details. She was just so absolutely loving and kind and reached out for my hand. I melted when I held her hand. They told me SHE was the loving feminine heart of GOD, not a woman… Instantly *JESUS* was in the seat to my right, and I held *HIS* hand. They were polar opposites. *HIS*, so strong, powerful but gentle. HERS (notice the case) was loving, soft, gentle but equally powerful but in a polar opposite way. Immediately they started uploading *love*; it was like Spiritual intravenous. SHE was HOLY SPIRIT (no, HOLY SPIRIT isn't a woman, like GOD isn't a woman), and *JESUS* on my right; it was amazing. Blue *love* was coming from *JESUS*, and pink *love* was coming from HOLY SPIRIT; it was charging or flowing into and filling my heart like you wouldn't believe. Like oceans being drained from the bottom, such pressure but no pressure because it's the *love* of GOD. They are filling me up and filling me up.

One side of my new, big, giant heart is filling with blue on the right and pink on the left. I looked, and POPPA was in front of me in the fire, and "HE" was huge. "HE" was an all-consuming fire and was burning it or baking it into my heart. "HE" was like the burning bush, immense heat, power, and fire, but not burning me. "HE" said, "You can keep your sandals on because your feet are on the chair, not on holy ground."

> *And the Angel of the Lord appeared to him in a flame of fire from the midst of a bush. So he looked, and behold, the bush was burning with fire, but the bush was not consumed. Then Moses said, "I will now turn aside and see this great sight, why the bush does not burn." So when the Lord saw that he turned aside to look, God called to him from the midst of the bush and said, "Moses, Moses!" And he said, "Here I am." Then He said, "Do not draw near this place. Take your sandals off your feet, for the place where you stand is holy ground."*
>
> Exo 3:2-5 NKJV

THEY kept pouring it in and burning it in and filling me up more and more and more...

THEY let me know that I had an idea of the *love* of the FATHER, *JESUS'* love, and the *love* of the Man *JESUS*, but I have such a vast, empty canvas, void of feminine *love* of the FATHER or the love of a woman...and I just cried, and cried, and cried and cried...this was filling and filling every part of every part of my heart, all the Michaels and the parts. I was getting such healing from it. "HE" showed me everyone looking on in awe and being HEaled.

Then after the session I called Kathy, my sister, back, but *JESUS* told me, "Brien is gone." I believe *HE* told me that Brien, my nephew, came around before *HE* took him. I cried and cried. I'm going to miss him. I really loved him so very much—what a sweet, lovable guy...

Post-Session Notes

It started very strangely. Barbara had us at the peaceful place, and we were at the little house. It went from happy little people, maybe Ali in the field dancing, to a white horse and a man with no shirt, bare back a distance out toward the new house—he was between me and Ali...I don't know if he was the big dude—nothing else. She said, "Go approach him," and I did. I smiled and said hi. He dismounted, and there may have been another man, and they backed off. The horse seemed to come to me. I love horses. I think they are one of the most beautiful creatures with those big eyes. It was strange—get used to the phrase. I felt myself talking to and caressing the horse, but visually it was different. I felt her, the horse, be affectionate or at least letting me pet her, but visually she wanted nothing to do with me, walking away and eating grass...Barbara said, "Ask the horse if it is part of you"; she said, "This may sound strange." I said, "No, it doesn't sound strange," and the horse wanted nothing to do with me...so Barbara said, "Ask her if she would take you to where you need to go," and I felt that was fine, and she started leading me toward Big Rock, which is a beautiful stream not far from the house in Upstate New York. She led me, and she started to take off, but I didn't feel that at all. Barbara said, "Ask her to show you where or how you're being disconnected." It was nice because I could feel like she wanted me on her back, and then there I was on her back in the water, and it was so relaxing and exhilarating. I love the idea of riding a horse in water—never did it, but...I felt something down in the water, and there were snakes or something black in the water, but the horse either didn't see it or care, which I thought was very strange. We continued, and suddenly I could see a beach but didn't feel like we were there. Then a train on the left, beach on the right, and Big Rock to the right but more like behind me. I remembered hearing that 100–200 years ago an old passage train used to ride through here. I could see a few people in it, and then so was I, but they had nothing to do with me...then there was a beautiful timber wolf, a male, but he had nothing to do with me—then a beautiful black female wolf that approached me. It seemed to acknowledge me kindly and then stopped! Barbara asked again about the disconnecting. Then I saw lions, stopped, a giraffe, then nothing...then some lady in black way off, and then a few white wolves circled her and gone...strange! I asked *JESUS*, "What is going on? Pease help me."

I told Barbara she asked about the lady way off, and I saw her again, and she started coming toward me. Then she had a red hat, then black, and then lighter hair. Then red, and she didn't seem to notice me. Barbara said to speak to her, and, of course, when I did, she disappeared... It didn't faze me but was so strange... Then the entire area didn't go blank but was plain...some patterns but almost nothing...Barbara did or said something. I still wasn't upset, hurt, or mad about being disrespected.

Then, after Barbara said or did something, I was back on the trail at Collins Hill Park in Atlanta, Georgia, where I live. It'd been a while, but it was so strange...I thought no one would talk to me. I spoke with them and nothing. So I said, "I'm going to sit here against this tree." I think The LORD said shhhh, and I started getting upset or hurt at this point with being ignored by everyone.

I felt something but not strong, so I asked, and it turned strong; it went right up to my upper gut and ripped me big time. I hadn't had that in a long time, and I didn't know if ever at this location. Not wrenched but tight—it felt good. My gut hadn't been that tight for a while... When I spoke to it, it came right out and was a big brown bear, real big. I felt like there was a religious spirit or something. Once I understood, sure enough, I could see it clearly. I could see me, then my Spirit, and another spirit. Then something ugly came out of the side of it and was disrespecting me. Barbara asked if he was part of me; when I asked, he said, "I'm not a part of you, you piece of crap" or something...I didn't get phased, but the bear said something like I was about to take him out. I felt like Elisha sending the bear to eat the kids that called him baldie.

Then he went up from there to Bethel; and as he was going up the road, some youths came from the city and mocked him, and said to him, "Go up, you baldhead! Go up, you baldhead!" So he turned around and looked at them, and pronounced a curse on them in the name of the Lord. And two female bears came out of the woods and mauled forty-two of the youths.

2 Kings 2: 23-24 (NKJV)

It was funny 'cause the bear was really mad...but, of course, Barbara said no and had me invite the three of them back to the peaceful place. *JESUS* already had the fire ready and was waiting. So we all sat down. *JESUS* on my right, the spirit on my left, the rude dude next to him, and the bear opposite me. The dude was mad... Bear (the bear, I believe, is Mike A.) once again asked, "Should I take him out?" But Barbara said no, so I asked him, "What can I do?" He didn't speak to me and was still mad, but not as bad. Now I think he feared Bear at this point. Barbara said something like, "The bear is my protector." I told Him, "It's okay; He is my protector and won't do anything unless I ask him to. I'm not going to hurt you because I want to get to know you." I asked the spirit if he had anything to say. I would gladly talk with him. I think he was also scared of Bear...Barbara had to go, so she said, "Let's have this dude and Bear either take a walk in the woods or clean up the mess at the beautiful place where we were." The dude said, "How do I know I'll survive a trip in the woods with him...?" So we said, "Then why not clean the mess?" And he got mad or maybe hurt because he knew we knew—it was his mess... Bear said, "No problems," but the dude wasn't going for it;

suddenly Mary popped in and said, "I'll go." I could see *JESUS* smile, but I was wondering about Mark not having Mary...Barbara loved the idea, and then Mark wanted to also come. Barbara said something like, "I've been looking for Mark." So we ended here until next time.

11.03.20: Barbara's Presession Notes

10.31.20, 15:00: THEY put all of them in my heart. I asked Bear, "You didn't eat him yet, did you?" He said no. I asked, "You didn't nibble on them, did you?" And He said no. I asked Mary and Mark, and that dude got upset...I said kindly that I was saving the best for last, and he genuinely appreciated it. He said it was going well...even the spirit dude said so.

We jumped right in, and it was peaceful with nothing going on in my body. I was at the little house in front of the fire; Mary and Bear came and sat down. They started telling me that this dude was tough.

He was wired and wound tight. They said he hadn't and was probably not going to clean up. He knew it was his junk, knew it was affecting me, and either didn't care or wouldn't because he knew it affected me. Bear asked if I wanted Him to eat him. Barbara and I agreed—no. She wanted to invite him, the spirit dude, and Mark to get together. He was pretty upset and said he didn't appreciate being told to clean up his stuff. I said, "We didn't intend this time to make you clean up; we wanted you to get to know the others and spend time together." He understood and was okay with it. *JESUS* came and was sitting next to me.

HE was on my right, Bear next to *HIM*, Mark, the spirit dude, the dude, and Mary next to me. Mark suggested that the four of them would go with Bear.

HOLY SPIRIT took them and walked right down the raven because of the dark spirits down there, and they were gone. At once *JESUS* brought post-b Michael, and he was just so cute and chubby...*JESUS* was just hugging him and loving on him. *HE* handed him to me, and I just melted. This was me as a newborn, and he was healed and whole. Hallelujah! He knew *JESUS*! Mary was loving on him, me, and then I gave him back to *JESUS*, and he was either talking with or sitting on Bear's lap. I got scared for a second because Bear was mad! He was roaring and very mad! He shot off into the ravine. Bear was my protector, and I didn't know, but I didn't think He knew about what happened to pre- and post-birth Michael, and He was going to tear that big dude apart for what he did to pre-birth Michael, me, and also for Mark...I didn't know, but I was sure we'd find out... Stay tuned—like the show in the '70s, "same bat time and same bat channel"...

Then *JESUS*, post-birth Michael, and I were at the peaceful place, and it was like Heaven. It was the real peaceful place; I hadn't been there for a while. Suddenly, I was back at the little house, the peaceful place, but not the real peaceful place. I could see Kerry's junk car...Mary and I were sitting in front of the fire; it was nice for a moment, and right away there was something small like, you guessed it, the Tasmanian devil from Bugs Bunny. A small powerhouse of evil, darkness, ugliness...it scared Mary, and she moved to my right side. It was strange; it wasn't like anything before (you know, like always...). It didn't seem to be a part of me, and, boy, was it evil and demonic. I asked *JESUS* for help, and *HE* said, "You got this." Maybe I shouldn't have, but I told it if it didn't cool out, I was going to cut it in half (Barbara likes me to be curious)! It did cool down, but warfare broke out all around big time. I wasn't scared at all and told it there were lions and knights with their swords drawn, all around them, real dark...evil...and it seemed genuinely scared. I asked it, "Are you trying to warn me, scare me?" Then it seemed like something like when the guy that reminded me of Bill Durham was there with that big dude whom Bear is probably eating or tearing limb from limb right now. It definitely was scared, and Barbara said, "Stay curious and talk to it" (like I said above). It seemed to want to get close, and at first, I said no! After Praying, I decided to let it close, and I held its hand. If it had a hand to hold—and I let it sit in my lap. It obviously saw post-b Michael there and couldn't believe how kind I was being toward it. It suddenly turned into more of a sphere with such evil in it, strange. I think this was when Mary took off. It started *skitzing* out, jerking, abnormal, spacing out, and it was strong...it reminded me how I would scare Michelle with my jerkiness and sudden fast movements. It seemed to be telling or showing me what it was like for Michelle or how She felt when I used to do that. I felt something like it was part of me but a curse or generational sin or something. I was getting ready to rebuke it, and Barbara said to hold off! I did, and it was like the way we begin our sessions. I felt something, not extreme but strong; it went into my gut hard and got very strong. It even went into my legs like never before. This was strange! It felt wrong, maybe even demonic... maybe something like succubus? It was so big and strong and strange...then it came out of me...and it was huge—this was when Barbara got disconnected, and I was stretching my neck looking up at this thing; maybe a better word would be tall instead of huge. I mean gigantic, tall, like a giraffe.

Super tall in the way of a giraffe... At first it was really scared, jerking or flailing round as if lions were around, kind of kicking or preparing to start kicking. *JESUS* came, and it calmed right down. I asked *HIM* to help again, and *HE* said that I have this. *HE* said *HE* was proud of the way I was handling it. It was still hurting my neck to look up at this very tall giraffe. I asked it if it could reach down, so it did, and its beautiful face was right in mine...it was so cute, but then I think it said it couldn't stay there long. We were on the trail, and I think that was why it was okay with leaning down. We went out to the powerlines so it could stand up straight. It stood up and was so very tall. Wow, even taller than before! It said it could see way off in the distance, and she didn't like it...she said the generational sin, curses...are strong and bad—if I don't get them eradicated, it's going to be bad! I asked, "Could you help me?" And it said no.

It was done here, and he started walking away. I said, "Please help me," and it said, "I'm just to point things out to you," and walked away. She was so much like that lady, and then I noticed it was goldish, and so was she...I believe this was the lady that I liked so much, and she was gone. I got a strong feeling, and Barbara said it was probably talking about all the death in the family. It clearly skipped our generation, but all of Mom and Dad's siblings are gone—three nephews and nieces and one great-niece, all in four years.

My dad's sister Dot drank herself to death; Jimmy, her son, drank himself to death, and her daughter Darleen was beaten to death in her bed. Dad's sweet brother Normal died of cancer; after taking care of his mother and father (my Mor Mor and Pop Pop) until he was around fifty, he then took care of his wife's parents, then married his wife, Jean, and died in a few short years.

Mom and Dad were both Prayer warriors and lived past ninety-two—now gone—but I know they're both in Heaven. I handed Dad off to *JESUS*...

Eileen: None of her kids died, but Alaura, her granddaughter, died.

Larry's son Brien died.

Kathy: Many miscarriages, then had Magen at around forty.

Patty's daughter Jessie died with an aneurism from prescription migraine meds.

Kerry's son Jace died.

Timmy.

Sean raised his grandson and granddaughter.

I got drunk out of my mind at around fourteen and walked into a high-speed parkway looking the other way and got hit by one of my sisters' or brothers' friend.

Terrance.

**Mom's funeral. Sean #7, Kerry #5, Kathy #3, Patty #4,
Eileen #1, Terrance #9, Timmy #6, Larry #2, and me #8.**

11.02.20, 06:13: THEY gave me a pic of Mary feeding Bear honey on a spoon, and she's an older lady, which makes sense. It's *JESUS* that has changed her so quickly. Bear is huge. He said He's receiving needed understanding of the dude, and no matter what, he won't eat him.

11:30: Today is my nephew Brien's (he was fifty-one—he sadly drank himself to death) funeral. I cried until "HE" said, "He's with 'ME.'" At the funeral Kevin said they would make fun of him because he was supposed to be a girl. This really hit me hard after the experience with pre-birth Michael. But also to lose such a sweet, loveable guy like Bri and to think of my aunt Dot (my dad's sister) and her son Jimmy losing both of them to drinking and her daughter Darleen being beaten to death in her bed decades ago... Now lately Jessie (around forty-two, niece), Alaura (around twenty-eight, great-niece), Jace (around thirty-five, nephew)—all within four years.

11.05.20: Barbara's Presession Notes

I've been sleeping so well since Tuesday, like a rock, almost no dreams. Maybe because I gave Barbara my word not to let things happen or something?

We didn't talk except to discuss how it seems that since pre-b Michael has come around, it seems more scattered, unclear, more demonic...more animals...

So just as we started, I believe I clearly heard from Michael and that lady, and I also had a whisper on Tuesday that maybe Bear was Mike A. I believe I'm being told that the lady was the giraffe.

We went from there...it hit me in my right chest, not extreme but clearly there...then the gut and then the legs, the first time all of this...it was a lady. I said, "It looks like you, Barbara," and she said immediately, "It can't be me." I said, "She looks like you in a white down vest"; turns out it was the lady, and she looked like Barbara. She said it was because I respected Barbara and could trust her. She made it clear this was serious. I thought she was scared. I asked her if she wanted to get behind me, and she did right away. I could clearly feel her hand on my right shoulder. I asked whatever this was to come out; it was big, and it took almost all of me—from my right chest and gut and down my right leg. It appeared to be a man with a round shield, then two men with round shields, and a wolf...the one was a clean-cut Captain America or Superman type; the other a brawly guy with a wolf. They were all tough in their own way. When I locked eyes with the wolf, he got big, and I could see Bear around him. He most certainly must be Mike A.... It was cool, but I didn't tell Barbara because she was asking me something else and we went that way. It turned out that they were part of me but more a part of my Spirit man (True Mike). They wouldn't tell me their names, but the clean-cut guy is my protector from believers in the church and the world. Clearly believers, but probably mostly hurt believers. The other guy is my protector from nonbelievers, demonic, and worldly people. They said that the clean-cut guy works more closely with HOLY SPIRIT and the other guy with Mike A. The rough-cut guy was more like a Scottish or Irish warrior like in *Braveheart*... She asked, "When you mess up, what happens?" Rough-cut said he overprotects and hurts others, and Clean-cut said he operates in *love*, and when he messes up, it usually allows darts to hit my heart. They got along well; she asked me to speak to them about when they helped me. I was okay with that but had to Pray. So, after getting clarity, I said to the rough-cut guy that I needed him to not come out so heavy each time and to check with me first. I told the clean-cut guy the same about checking with me; suddenly the giraffe stuck her pretty head in and reminded me that these guys see ahead of me, like her. They will warn me first, and we'll all get on the same page unless it's really bad, and then, they may have to jump right in, but they will make sure that's not the norm.

Then Barbara asked, "Do they know the lady? They all know each other well; it seems that they operate under her, and she's under HOLY SPIRIT and Mike A." She asked how long they had been in my life. "Rough-cut" said my whole life, but "Clean-cut" made it sound like only for a year or two since

I'd really become a mature or fruitful believer in that time frame. They reminded me that Rough-cut has been dealing with Michelle and that was another reason why it didn't go well as well as my whole life... The lady has been there as well; they made it clear this was post-birth, that pre-b Michael was completely different, and she made it clear—like before now, she had a clear job, and that was why she walked away when her job was done the last few weeks as the giraffe. But now it seemed to be different...I didn't know if it was because we now had a relationship. Barbara asked, "What else needs to be done today?" I checked in and now noticed that the entire time the lady (giraffe) was behind me to my right, that entire side was goldish and sunny. I noticed it was very dark from 180 to 360 degrees, and I could see lions, wolves, and ugliness...Clean-cut left; the lady and Rough-cut let me know that it was going to get bad. The huge dude was nothing compared to this. Bear (once again, I believe he is Mike A.) showed up and let me know that He took that huge dude out. He said I could have done it myself, no problem, but He wanted to do it for pre-b Michael, and we won't be seeing that dude anymore. *I must be ready, and I'm ready for this next season THEY are preparing me for...* This was when we wrapped up...

11.10.20: Barbara's Presession Notes

11.08.20, around 11:00: Worship was awesome. A different song, "How I Fight My Battles." Everything that's been lost "*love*" is returning. Then Pastor Hazen got up and Prayed with a word of discernment about men and women who lost a baby through miscarriage (I did in approximately 1995). It rocked me and has since he mentioned it. I don't know for certain, but I think that young lady may be my baby girl, middle girl. Multiplying and compounding the loss of Michelle and Cate. I'm just thinking now how hard it was for us to get pregnant during the first marriage; the doctors said it was me. There was a lot of shame, especially when my brothers found out and, of course, said they could help...

11.10.20, 05:25: Seeking intimacy with *JESUS* with every ounce of my being has profoundly changed my life like nothing else. I think even more life-altering than salvation, not more important but life-altering! Of course, it wouldn't have come about without salvation. Trauma counseling has significantly helped with that and has made me more whole, and I'm not even there yet! Thank YOU, POPPA, *JESUS*, and HOLY SPIRIT, and thank you, Barbara.

Post-Session Notes

We started out at the peaceful place; I saw the little house. But wanted to wait and see, make sure that was where we were. She asked to invite my parts and then for *JESUS* to come; immediately *HE* came and sat down on my right. I felt something down in the ravine and thought something dark or bad. Then Mary came out and immediately sat to my left. We waited. I felt like that lady was around and checked my heart and realized that it was me wanting her there, so I quickly removed that thought. Barbara said in the beginning to focus on the true me, not parts or desires...it's so cool how "HE" does that. Barbara was amazed because that was what she meant. Then from the ravine came HOLY SPIRIT, the religious guy, and Mark—then I thought another part was going to come out, and it turned out to be the spirit guy that went with HOLY SPIRIT and them. I couldn't see him but knew Mark was there.

The religious guy (RG) was different; he was smiling ear to ear, and so was Mark. The RG jumped right next to *JESUS*, and I could see that Mark wanted to also; it was just amazing. Then *JESUS* started speaking directly to him, not quietly or in secret, but I couldn't hear. Mark was looking at *JESUS* and RG like he was looking at *JESUS* and PB Michael and then me weeks ago. This time was like he knew, like he knew HOLY SPIRIT and, therefore, knew *JESUS* and was connected, nodding his head in agreement. Then the RG was clearly a guy, and I could see him in a dark green long-sleeve oxford, felt, or flannel shirt, and everything was clear, and that was good. It was different. I could see the religious spirit come right out of him. It reminded me of when *JESUS* called the spirits out of the crazy naked dude and sent them into the pigs.

And when He had come out of the boat, immediately there met Him out of the tombs a man with an unclean spirit, who had his dwelling among the tombs; and no one could bind him, not even with chains, because he had often been bound with shackles and chains. And the chains had been pulled apart by him, and the shackles broken in pieces; neither could anyone tame him. And always, night and day, he was in the mountains and in the tombs, crying out and cutting himself with stones. When he saw Jesus from afar, he ran and worshiped Him. And he cried out with a loud voice and said, "What have I to do with You, Jesus, Son of the Most High God? I implore You by God that You do not torment me." For He said to him, "Come out of the man, unclean spirit!" Then He asked him, "What is your name?" And he answered, saying, "My name is Legion; for we are many." Also he begged Him earnestly that He would not send them out of the country. Now a large herd of swine was feeding there near the mountains. So all the demons begged Him, saying, "Send us to the swine, that we may enter them." And at once Jesus gave them permission. Then the unclean spirits went out and entered the swine (there were about two thousand); and the herd ran violently down the steep place into the sea, and drowned in the sea. So those who fed the swine fled, and they told it in the city and in the country. And they went out to see what it was that had happened. Then they came to Jesus, and saw the one who had been demon-possessed and had the legion, sitting and clothed and in his right mind. And they were afraid.

Mark 5:1–15 (NKJV)

The guy was different again, like healed, and then he and Mark were holding hands; HOLY SPIRIT grabbed Mark's hand, and it was awesome; it was all so clear...they seemed to become spirits and left. I started telling Barbara. I said, "I'm not certain," and I stopped and looked at *JESUS*, and *HE* said you're certain. Yes, they disappeared, and *JESUS* acknowledged that they weren't parts of me or pre-b Michael; they were spirits. Mark was tormented with pre-b Michael, and RG was a religious spirit; they were both away from *JESUS* and didn't know THEM. After spending time with HOLY SPIRIT, HE softened or healed or transformed them, and I believe they left as spirits of GOD. I don't know if that's biblical, but Mike A., as he said to me, explained that they weren't parts of me and pre-birth Michael but were tormented spirits around us. They were separated from that big dude that Bear shredded, He said, made minced meat out of him, and, therefore, he didn't have control or dominion over them. HOLY SPIRIT loved on them. HE and *JESUS* transformed them, and then all three of them (Mark, the spirit guy, and the religious spirit are spirits) disappeared... *JESUS*, HOLY SPIRIT, and Mike A. said that pre-b Michael and I have received HEaling over the big dude and that was why everything was so clear today. Mike A. (Bear) took out a very high-level demon that tormented pre-b Michael and me this entire time—since the other week (and essentially my entire life since conception). Remember THEY said to not be surprised if I had to cut the head off that dude (who was an officer or someone high up in the demonic ranks). I didn't have to because Bear got so mad after playing with post-b Michael and took off to tear him to pieces (minced meat...). He was so mad that I didn't even recognize Him. It was so peaceful and clear now.

Barbara said for me to ask *JESUS* if everything was good or done. I didn't have to ask, and *HE* said no! I immediately felt something strong. Then between Barbara, *JESUS*, and I, I got the feeling *HE* was telling me, "Oh no, there's so much more," and then I remembered it was Tuesday and Barbara needed to end early, but then I checked myself and knew I wasn't supposed to speak for her or allow the fear of man...and I looked at *JESUS*; it was just so cool. *HE* was nodding *HIS* head and telling me, "Good, you just pay attention to *ME*, not your heart, your mind, thoughts, cares for Barbara...*ME*!" Then *HE* told me that *HE* was proud of me for not letting my heart get in the way and pull the lady in. *HE* said *HE* knew how much I loved her but didn't acknowledge who she was but acknowledged how proud of me *HE* was that I was allowing THEM to orchestrate these sessions. Then I could see (Aaron at IHOP-KC [11.09.20], fifty-four-minute set, is speaking *so* loudly to me. "'I' am Praying for you, and you don't even know it. 'I' am fighting for you, and you don't even know it. I'm returning all that has been taken and lost..." It was so powerful! *JESUS* is Praying for me...wow! Thank *YOU*, *JESUS*...) when I lifted my eyes the real beautiful, peaceful place was there. There was no clutter or junk, and the sun was booming, and everything was so crystal clear. I could see the little house down, way down, but wouldn't look because I was fixed on the beautiful, peaceful place. THEY reminded me that the clutter was the RG, and he's not around, and it's all clean. The beautiful, peaceful place is so sunny, crisp, clear, and not hot but nice warm...the little house was clear but different and then different again. The lady, she, and her atmosphere in goldenness, misty, beautiful but different, such a contrast...THEY said, "This is a good place to leave off." *JESUS* and HOLY SPIRIT each nodded and smiled, and there was so much peace...

I then gave her an update on Dr. Schiff, my neurologist, and said that I think seeing him has also brought clarity to this session as well...

11.12.20: Barbara's Presession Notes

11:11: IHOP-KC, Aaron Valdiviez, 11.09.20, 13:00, at 51:20–58:20. "I hear The Father saying, 'I'm coming for *you*! Son! With all "MY" strength, "I" am drawing *you* up out of many, many waters... "I" am coming to *your* rescue. "I" have seen *you* holding on...getting beaten down...just keep holding on...all *you* have lost, "I" will redeem. All that's been taken away "I" will give it back...'I" am fighting for *you*. "MY" name is "Mighty Man of War." "I" am coming for *you*. "I" have seen *you* Praying; *you* never stooped; *you* never stopped lifting *your* arms; *you* never stopped lifting *your* eyes up..."I" saw it, and "I" am coming for *you* with all of "MY" strength...' *HE* said, '*I* am Praying for *you* with all of *MY* strength; *you* don't even know it. *I* am fighting for *you*, and *you* don't even know it... Praise GOD— *JESUS* is Praying for *me*...'"

11.11.20: I'm experiencing remorse at such depth; it seems to sink deeper and deeper into my heart and soul now. The only way I can explain it is I've felt remorseful before (especially with and for Michelle). I would always hear someone inside me, a part of me, say, "What about...?" In trauma counseling, I'm learning that parts of me thought they were protecting me. I'm meeting them and finding that they are or were hurt badly and overprotecting me in their woundedness. I'm not hearing or feeling them anymore. I'm experiencing the pain I've caused not allowing myself to excuse it away or diminish it because of...I'm not allowing myself to block it anymore. I don't think I've ever allowed myself to sit long (long-suffering...what a concept...) and patiently in sorrow, feel it, learn from it, abide in it with *JESUS*, and get through it. I would have to be the encourager! I would say, "That's my job; that's my Spiritual gift..." I now say, "No, shut up. Leave me alone. Let me experience it." I'm not afraid of sorrow anymore...I'm not the man of joy through it yet, but I'm beginning to understand a little more about it. Have you seen the movie *Inside Out*? This is basically the parts I'm talking about. The introvert told the extravert, "Let the guy who's feeling sorrowful be sorrowful..." The extravert had no grid for it...I can now feel deeply how much I've hurt so many people and not allowed myself to experience the depth of the feelings I've blocked my whole life. I believe this has been the enemy blocking me from intimacy. You can't be intimate if you're only there for the good times. It's the really hard, painful times that you make it through that build intimacy. Michelle said something years ago like, "You can only go as high as you allow yourself to go low." I believe that's in humility but also emotionally.

Yesterday, before we began the session, Barbara said something like I needed to be aware of being in my True self (True Mike, TM). In IFS (Internal Family System), the powerful tools we've been using, I've watched and listened to what was going on in me like I wasn't me. Instead of hearing, "Yeah, yeah, I've got it. I know; I know! I don't have to worry about that; no worries, I don't do that...blah, blah, blah..." I was listening, hearing what she was saying, not thinking about what I was going to say, how important what I wanted to say was, or defending myself, talking to, or encouraging myself...it was so foreign. I watched and heard myself doing it "right." It was so strange! What THEY are doing in me and how THEY are showing me, sitting with me...like I'm a different person. I am different, a completely different person, watching and listening to me. I can't explain it. I can only enjoy it and cry...why fifty-seven years...so much pain, such destruction... It reminds me of the endorsement from my dear friend and Ministry partner Will Shehee: *I first got to know Mike in 2018, right before the events of this book took place. I went back to the mission field and didn't see him again until 2021. When I returned to our church, I saw a stranger with a beaming face and a childlike innocence, always dancing and worshipping wholeheartedly by the Altar. When I introduced myself, I was shocked to discover it was my friend Mike Collins! I literally didn't recognize him as the same person. Until reading this book, I did not know the depth of the journey God took him on during those years I was away. But what has always been evident to me is the fruit—a life transformed literally beyond recognition. Mike's transformed life is itself the strongest letter of recommendation that anyone could give to read this book.*

I have such deep pain in my heart...I'm so sorry for all the hurt I've caused by not allowing myself (or maybe not being able) to feel or experience and express all the pain in me or others.

I told Barbara, "One day you're not going to find me...I'm going to explode; it's going to be a beautiful mess—the place is going to be covered with 'HIS' Love and Word. Like people would say, it would be like if Disney exploded, there'd be color all over the place...like when they went from black and white to Technicolor."

POST-SESSION NOTES

We spent a lot of time on the above...I cried and cried and cried...Why me, LORD! Barbara wanted to check in on PB Michael. I closed my eyes, and I was in Upstate New York; there was Cairo-Durham HS, the high school I spent my senior year at. Michael was on the back deck of the house; it was sunny and beautiful. I thought, *Let's give it a moment...* But he wasn't going anywhere. He wasn't like scared or trying to get my attention, so I kept looking around being curious like Barbara likes. He was on the right side, and then the right side started opening like the woods, but not like the woods on the side of the house. I was open and let it develop, and sure enough, it got dark, and there was a bear, not a bear but Bear! My buddy (Mike A., Michael the Archangel!)—boy, was it good to see Him, and He was huge! He gave me such a big hug. We were talking about Him before—how I really believe He is Michael A. I told her that I feel this connection to and with Mike A. I know He loves me, but He doesn't know love. I guess He likes me because He's an angel...but there's something...He loves me, and when Bear was next to *JESUS* with post-b Michael on *JESUS'* lap, playing with him (me), and then he got really, really mad! But He wasn't just mad... His mouth opened almost 180 degrees, and He told me He tore that high-level demon to shreds... it was so good to see Him! Like I said, He's huge! There was post-b Michael on Mom's lap right in between Bear and high-school Michael. He was just sitting there so happy, and you should have seen Bear with a huge smile, seeing and showing me Michael...I was looking at post-birth Michael and noticed he looked bigger than I thought—just as I was going to say something, here came Mom with infant post-birth Michael. They are just so awesome...and then HOLY SPIRIT comes and brings with HIM HIS fresh, warm breeze of peace...here I am watching this, seeing HS Michael on my left, Mom and infant post-birth Michael next to him (me), short months to my left—then *JESUS* was next to me on my right and Bear on *HIS* right. HS Michael was looking with such love, knowing post-b Michael was HEaled on Mom's lap; it obviously brought HEaling to him. Then I saw kindergarten Michael in between HS Michael and post-b Michael, and I had such a strong word of knowledge and revelation that this poor guy, when Mom left him that first day of kindergarten, he thought, *Now she's getting what she's wanted; she didn't want me, and now she's leaving...and I'll never see her again.* The enemy never allowed me to know that she cried the whole way home, not having me... It wasn't that it was a word of knowledge and revelation because he was HEaled months ago by *JESUS* bringing him (me) into class and just loving on me and showing me such fun and *love*, but it was the knowledge of the deep pain and understanding how and why it was sooo gut-wrenching on us...but it wasn't sad or painful any more...because we had already been HEaled of it.

**A picture of me at about three years old in front of my house
in South Hempstead, Long Island, New York.**

This was even so much more...deeper, and you could see it on every one of my faces. This was when Barbara said, "Let's tap this in," and we did...oh my, was this such HEaling? Deep, deep HEaling and sweet HEaling from post-b Michael and HS Michael and me now! Fifty-seven years later!

Then Barbara asked who was closest to me, and I said, "HS Michael," and she wanted us to check in with him. When I did, he was on the back deck with Dad, and they reminded me that Dad was about my age then...it sunk in. Wow, Dad, my age...then I was taken inside, and there I was at about thirty with infant baby Ali; she was a beautiful newborn...then there was POPPA...oh my, did POPPA come with all "HIS" majesty. That word is so beneath what it was; this is YHWH... not just POPPA; this is YHWH, the ANCIENT of DAYS (ATIK YOMIN), GOD of Israel...I Am (*Ehyeh*)...I can't stress enough how high and lofty..."HE" spoke of HEaling and showed me Mom, me, Ali & my grandbaby...four generations that were just HEaled...*JESUS* and HOLY SPIRIT are GOD, but even *JESUS* said in red letters how *HE* doesn't compare to YHWH, the

FATHER..."HE" is the One that does this HEaling. "You have heard Me say to you, 'I am going away and coming back to you.' If you loved Me, you would rejoice because I said, 'I am going to the Father,' for My Father is greater than I" (John 14:28, NKJV). "HE" reminded me of how dark and ugly the sin we saw last week was, and "HE" is here now! Bear took out that dude, and I saw Bear, and He was smiling, not like "yeah, I did that." No, it was a "so grateful to have been chosen to help..." YHWH said, "Watch this!" "HE" took over...I could feel that it was the masonic spirit (I could feel and remember it from a lot of the HEaling from Restoring the Foundations Ministry). "HE" showed me Mom and then Dad and started counting the generations. Granny, Mor Mor, and Pop Pop, then people I didn't know...and "HE" (YHWH) is counting back generations. Loud, boldly...and I could see the numbers—it was unreal! "HE" was calling back the generations one after another; they weren't just numbers—this was generations of my heritage, my line, and "HE" was the One doing it. I wasn't trying to get more; "HE" just kept going back and back after Mom and Dad...one, two, three, and "HE" stopped there and made a big deal about it. I think this was the part about March of 2015; when another ministry was Praying, I was manifesting extremely from one part of the masonic spirits to a certain level, and then he said he didn't see or feel anything else or something, and I could remember clearly the junk that came out of me. It was around my feet, and I was getting so tired because the demons were so strong. I think "HE" said something like "HE" wasn't letting anything get away, not one little drop of evil. This was YHWH...then "HE" went back to counting four, five, six, seven, eight, nine, ten, eleven, twelve, thirteen—and I was jolting around, but this was POPPA, and "HE" kept on going: fourteen, fifteen, sixteen, seventeen, eighteen, nineteen, twenty, twenty-one, twenty-two, twenty-three, twenty-four, twenty-five generations back. "HE" started pulling this root all the way back twenty-five generations, that was 560–1,120 years (at twenty to forty years per generation). "HE" was pulling the root...then I could feel it in my chest, and "HE" was now pulling it out of my future generations...I was crying and being jolted around even more...and "HE" was showing me Ali, my grandbabies, and more and started counting again...one, two, three, four, five...that's five generations forward...that's a total of 5 + 3 + 2 + 25 = 35 generations; now that's 700–1,400 years...how, oh, how, POPPA? Why me...? Why are "YOU" so good to me? "How Great Is Our GOD" is on Aaron V's set from above at around 154:00 in...that's what I'm saying...1,400 years' worth of HEaling through and in me. How, LORD...?

My great-grandfather on my dad's mother's side.

**My great-grandfather on Dad's side (top right)
and my grandfather (Pop Pop), third from left.**

Then Barbara said, "Let's call all of the Michaels together," and there all of my *mes* were. It was every me, from pre-birth Michael all the way to me, and they were all there. I was wondering if the last me was going to be here because last me was with Michelle and *JESUS*, and we haven't heard much from him…and there he was right next to me…I looked at each of me. Barbara started saying something, and I said, "I'm looking into the eyes of each of me…" I cried! I saw pre-b Michael, molested Michael (we believe he's in Glory, and he looked different, like he's from Glory…I don't know—I'm just telling you what I'm seeing and feeling…), then ninth-grade Michael (the one who got hit by the car)…then Michael who got mugged, and I thought these guys really went through a lot, and each of them did, and they reminded me that each of me went through a lot. Like the one of the mes said on the Grand Ave Grade School playground, "You're just like Mom; you don't remember the bad," so I apologized and agreed—this way, you'll be reading about it. We've all been through so much…I looked at all my mes, and there were so many mes; it was so THEM showing me and having me look into the eyes of each of me after each of us (me) got so much HEaling…all of my mes were on my left; when I looked to my right, there were all future mes. I couldn't see them clearly but told her some of them are really old…they were future me…right there were all my future mes…there were a lot of them, but I couldn't see them clearly, and I can't say exactly how many. I'm believing THEY don't want me to think that so many of past mes had problems, issues, needed HEaling...THEY didn't want me to think of it like that but wanted me to know that I have a very long life ahead of me. Thank YOU, LORD!

I looked around again, and suddenly to the left...I could see all of mes and twenty-seven generations of my family all the way to the beginning. I think it was the generations HEaled and then all the way to Adam. (I just looked it up, and, of course, there are around 127 generations since Adam! So I saw the generations here plus a hundred!) Then I looked to the right and saw all the future mes and seven generations, then to eternity future...

Now Barbara spoke up and said, "Let's have all the Michaels hug..." I cried. They all, past and future, gave me a huge hug—all the past and future, and then, of course, POPPA, *JESUS*, and HOLY SPIRIT came around to hug from the outside, and Bear joined in...all the generations past and future were there and watched! We had to tap that in...

IHOP-KC Aaron from above: "Those that seek my soul will contend with my GOD..." Jonathan and Melissa Helser: "Raise a Hallelujah," "No Longer Slaves."

11.15.20

13:51: Such revelation from a two-part sermon by Ps. Josh Morgan, exposing the Jezebel spirit. Wow! Was it me, not all the ladies in my life! *Freedom*! Only in the Name of *JESUS CHRIST*. I was Ahab, not the man of GOD I thought I was. It brought such revelation and clarity to the recent HEalings from strongholds of rejection from more than fifty years ago, narcissism, arrogance, pride, acts of service with ulterior motives, need for power and recognition, loss...remember I think it was that lady, who we believe may be my daughter, who was, sadly, never born, said this generational sin, curse, darkness was really bad! It was so cool the way THEY were unwrapping and revealing such revelation and HEaling...I could only cry, and it was more like wailing...

14:01: I believe they just told me that dude Bear took out was one of Jezebel's major eunuchs (we thought he was a high-ranking demon); he's the one that torments pre-b Michael and back down to me standing up to him with *JESUS* next to me. Remember I believed they had said not to be too sure I won't have to cut his head off.

17:36: Remember I think it may have been the day I'm referring to at 13:51 that the female spirit came on me. I wonder if it was Jezebel...I'm Praying about it.

10:08: I believe they are making it very clear that this tiredness and fogginess is the enemy because they know when I'm not sharp, I'm not on my game and not as much of a danger to them...

18:00: I'm feeling very strongly that there is a major Spiritual attack against me...I think yesterday's victory on top of last week's work is causing a lot of collateral damage and loose ends! I'm having a real up, down, up, down day...really strange.

11.17.20: Barbara's Presession Notes

11.17.20: Nine months since I moved out—that's a gestation period! HE is birthing something...

Post-Session Notes

We started, and I immediately was glowing and energized all over. It was so cool and so different, and an angel came out of me. It wasn't Mike but a warring angel, maybe Gabriel, and he let me know it was not good and time for battle. I was wearing my armor and was on my horse, and so was he. I grabbed my sword, said, "This battle belongs to *JESUS*," and raised it, and we took off. We approached the edge of a ridge overlooking a large battlefield that Mike A. was waging war on. It was clear that Mike A. and His angels were fighting this war, and He looked back at me and smiled. Suddenly one of the demons came over Mike A. (I knew that he didn't get past Mike A.) but was supposed to be in front of me, and *JESUS* was next to me on my right. This demon was right in front of me; it didn't scare me. I had my shield and a sword, and my horse snorted at it; it was pretty funny. So here we are—an angel to my left and *JESUS* to my right, and I'm talking to this demon... Barbara said, "Ask its name," and *JESUS* said, "Don't worry about a name—ask him what he wants." Barbara liked that, and I told her, "Then it said we want PB Michaels." And I said immediately, "No, he's not yours; he belongs to *JESUS*!" Then there were a bunch of them, and post-b Michael came riding up to my left when I made it clear and started rebuking them and remembered Barbara said not to do that right away, so I stopped and suddenly felt something. While noticing that, Mike A. appeared between me and post-b Michael and let me stay focused to tune it to that. When I did, it got stronger, and I addressed it. Instead of the flattening feeling, it was different, so I knew it was something different. Then a lady was around, but not the lady, but I couldn't see anything but blonde hair...and then there were a lot of them, and I could see they were demons and actually very ugly because I could see who they were. They were trying to come across as beautiful to trick me, and I could see right through it because of *JESUS*. Thank YOU, LORD. Suddenly, we were at the run circuit just east of the south power line, where all the angels usually hang, and then a big one was there, like the size of the giraffe, and I couldn't even see how tall she was because she was so close, and I accepted her size and stature and asked her if she would come down more toward my size, and she appreciated that and did out of respect. It started morphing and looked a little like a lady from River Church, the singer, and Melania Trump; it wasn't them, but it wanted me to see it like the lady from River Church but having the authority of the most powerful woman in the world. Meanwhile there were a bunch of them, so I asked the main one if she would go for a walk so we could talk, and we went to the bench fifty feet away. Then one of the guys who lived in the same house as I did came home and started cursing about how they were all tramps like my mom. I tried to drown it all and noticed it was part of the session; this thing next to me appeared more like a lady and reminded me that I'd spoken like that to Michelle and worse, and I felt such conviction—it was heavy, majorly heavy, not condemnation but conviction...I felt so bad and cried and cried. I asked her if I could update Barbara, and as always, it was just the ladies, but it seemed most of these spirits liked that I asked... so after I did, I could see hell, the pit of hell opened up in front of me; it was a sea of fire and souls burning and crying...it was awful...then some of them came out and started grabbing my legs and feet, but I wasn't scared at all...and this lady next to me felt comforting, so I held my ground, and Barbara said, "Invite *JESUS*..." It reminded me of the healing I got in March of 2015 and was casting masonic demons out of me because those demons were encircling my feet and legs...I don't know if they were trying to pull me back in—I don't think so—I'm now feeling they were trying to be comforted and relieved of some of the torment and pain (that's what I'm feeling)...so I asked *JESUS*, "What's going on?" And *HE* said they are impurity and sin still in me, and they're mainly from PB Michael and the last Michael that we haven't finished up with, so I immediately took ownership for all of us, repented, and asked for forgiveness...the lady next to me got mad! Especially when I mentioned and took ownership for pre-birth Michael...I really pressed in at that moment. *JESUS* was so excited that I didn't even hesitate. I was in my royal robe and crown, and hell and this lady disappeared. It felt so good but not emotional or glorious as usual, and when I told Barbara, I was immediately back on the ridge in full royalty and on my horse and knew that I had dealt with part of it and now had to finish in the battle. There I was—from left was the original angel, post-b Michael, Mike A., and me, and the last Michael rode up next to me, and *JESUS* next to him. I firmly told those demons they had no authority over any of us in the Name of *JESUS* and to leave now! And they did right away! Then post-b and last Michael came into me, and there we were at the little house in such peace...Mike A., *JESUS*, Bear, and me...then POPPA and HOLY SPIRIT joined us.

POPPA and HS Michael were beaming at me, and when I looked around and saw that we weren't at the place of peace, I knew there was more I had to do, and THEY nodded, encouraged me, but said, "Rest up! There's a lot more..." I asked, "Anything else now?" And it was so cool; THEY reminded me it was Tuesday and we wanted to cut short for Barbara, and I just laughed; of course we did—she appreciated it.

11.19.20: Barbara's Presession Notes

11.19.20: Today is the first day I have felt good in weeks...
I'm reminded of a song by Leeland, "Carried to the Table."

Post-Session Notes

We spent a bit of time talking about Tuesday, the election, rona...how proud I am of President Trump, and I reminded her that he was like a good little schoolboy compared to my narcissism and how humble I see him getting. His last conference he kept on saying my staff, the staff...instead of me, me, and me...I told her I was watching the Bible right in front of me. The battle from Tuesday was like looking down on Joshua fighting with Moses, Aaron, and Hur holding his arms up...

> *Now Amalek came and fought with Israel in Rephidim. And Moses said to Joshua, "Choose us some men and go out, fight with Amalek. Tomorrow I will stand on the top of the hill with the rod of God in my hand." So Joshua did as Moses said to him, and fought with Amalek. And Moses, Aaron, and Hur went up to the top of the hill. And so it was, when Moses held up his hand, that Israel prevailed; and when he let down his hand, Amalek prevailed. But Moses' hands became heavy; so they took a stone and put it under him, and he sat on it. And Aaron and Hur supported his hands, one on one side, and the other on the other side; and his hands were steady until the going down of the sun. So Joshua defeated Amalek and his people with the edge of the sword."*

> Exodus 17:8-13 (NKJV)

Trump's election, our tidal wave of votes where too many for the cheating machines to keep up with, and that's why they had to stop the counting, see how far ahead he was, calculate how many ballots they needed to make, make them, enter then, and then continue counting his...of course that's the case...in the last four years no weapon formed against him has prospered, nothing—the Russian hoax, rona, impeachment...this is biblical. "'No weapon formed against you shall prosper, And every tongue which rises against you in judgment You shall condemn. This is the heritage of the servants of the Lord, And their righteousness is from Me,' Says the Lord". Isa 54:17 (NKJV)

So we started, and I got hit hard, a huge punch in the gut; it was so tight, it actually felt good, but it hurt, but, seriously, it hurt so good...it was that lady, but not a woman—it was the demon from Tuesday. She reminded me that she was a friend but also like Melania Trump, the most powerful woman in the world...she made it clear that she was with the enemy; she's a demon but friendly toward me because she liked and respected me. It's like the guy weeks ago who looked like my friend Bill Durham. He was with the huge dude that Bear took out. We were right back where we were left off Tuesday on the run circuit on the bench. I couldn't see her, but she was a demon...she said that she was here to show me how much women have hurt me, and I have allowed it—how I always looked at the beauty that is skin deep. She said that I had changed and it wasn't important to me, and that was why *JESUS* gave me Michelle, the most beautiful woman in the entire world, but I did think that way and have been taken advantage of...of fallen for tricks because of it...I've paid a huge price...I asked her to please tell me more...but like some of the other women from these sessions...she said that was all she was here for, and she left...like the one that I like so much, who I think is my little girl, the giraffe (which I think is also a female for the same reason). We were at the same place as Tuesday when the open hell came, and the souls were reaching out and grabbing me...I believe they weren't trying to pull me in, and I told Barbara that I got word that they were just trying to get comfort from me from the torment...while I was telling her, I believe THEY told me these were not souls in hell because they wouldn't be allowed comfort; these were souls living the life that would lead to hell, but I was saving their souls, giving them comfort, and saving them from hell...this was all new...

Meanwhile, back at the ranch...that's an old saying. She left, and I felt someone or something else there, and it turned out to be a wolf...he was big, mostly black, and mad. He was in the same place as the lady was: right next to me. We were on the run circuit bench east of the south power lines where all the angels hang...this was where it started getting strange like it did the other week. He was next to me, and I started feeling something going to the left but knew I couldn't take my eyes off him. I was working on it, and, of course, Mike A. came and said, "I'll keep an eye on him..." It was so comforting to have Him in my life...there were a bunch of men to the left; they were big... and I suddenly figured out that the wolf that was on the bench with me was now farther away and down. I was feeling a court or trial. I was not sure. Was I on trial? Was he? But then I saw that I was up in a judge's seat with Mike A., who was next to me. The wolf was down toward the right, and these guys were down toward the left. It was strange, but I figured it out. These guys on the left were like laborers in biblical times, and the wolf oversaw them—there was a dispute. Now Mike A. sent for angels to sit to my left in case these guys got out of hand. He told me I was the king of this territory, ruling over the land...like what? Like the millennial kingdom, we will reign over cities...

CAVEMAN TO PRIEST

Now when He had taken the scroll, the four living creatures and the twenty-four elders fell down before the Lamb, each having a harp, and golden bowls full of incense, which are the prayers of the saints. And they sang a new song, saying: "You are worthy to take the scroll, And to open its seals; For You were slain, And have redeemed us to God by Your blood Out of every tribe and tongue and people and nation, And have made us kings and priests to our God; And we shall reign on the earth."

Revelation 5:8-10 (NKJV)

It started getting strange, and the guys to the left weren't saying much but grumbling, and the wolf wasn't saying much either. So I asked each of them, "What would you like from me?" And they really didn't answer. I didn't know it then, but I guess I told them to come back...it wasn't clear then, but now it is...so we were still on the run circuit, and I could hear the boys on the trail (these are my Spiritual sons Caleb and Joshua and Isaac), and it was so kind and HEaling to my soul...then I started seeing witches, a lot of witches, and they were now filling in toward the right, where the wolf was. Now that lady was back, and she was on the right but above the witches. *JESUS* was now here above all of them and more in the center. She started saying how much witchcraft was in my life, reminding me it wasn't just Joan, the wiccan, which I knew clearly and passively went along with it but also my other sisters with the tarot cards and all that junk...the Harry Potter stuff, masonic temple in my past generations...this was all a continuation of last week with POPPA pulling down all those strongholds of the family from masonic junk and how very strong it was, and Mike A. and *JESUS* agreed.

Then I started hearing and feeling how I must cut all their heads off, like Elijah with the 800 false prophets.

Then the fire of the Lord fell and consumed the burnt sacrifice, and the wood and the stones and the dust, and it licked up the water that was in the trench. Now when all the people saw it, they fell on their faces; and they said, "The Lord, He is God! The Lord, He is God!" And Elijah said to them, "Seize the prophets of Baal! Do not let one of them escape!" So they seized them; and Elijah brought them down to the Brook Kishon and executed them there.

1 Kings 18: 38-40 (NKJV)

I said, "I'm going to have to speak with Barbara," and as soon as I started speaking, my sword was right there and all my armor...she said something like, "Do you have a sword?" And I told her, "It just appeared here," so she said, "Go ahead..." I heard Michelle say, "I'm Praying for you," and I think She was there...I drew my sword. I saw women's faces; I didn't hesitate, and my right hand tightened on my sword like I had never felt before. I told Barbara, "It's like an eagle's talon; it's not going to loosen unless I clamp down even harder." I could see my sword, and it was beautiful, the gold handle, not gory, beautiful, and the shiniest silver blade, and I was ready. I got ready, and it got strange, confusing, foggy... She (that lady) said, "It's the witchcraft that you have been under for a long time." I was standing ready to cut off heads...and it got foggy, dark, and thick. Mike A. was right there, and I was now on my horse. He was to my right, and all His angels were to my left, and we were ready, and I could hear the movement of the enemy.

But I couldn't see anything; we were ready for battle. I still had my sword, and my right hand was tightly gripping it. I was telling Barbara how hard I was holding it, and I seriously couldn't let up on it; it was part of me or under my control. I couldn't let it go; I'd never felt anything like it. I mean it. We were getting close and ready for war! I was on my horse, and I said boldly, "This battle is The LORD's, and I will follow YOUR will, LORD..." Then in my left hand was my shofar. I blew it...and I blew it well with authority...they all fled, the fog lifted, and it was over. They were all gone. The battle was won by *JESUS*...it was exactly as I had always pictured it. When I blew my shofar over water, the Spiritual realm would flee or move...I just remember that I had been blowing it every day since election day until we won. I was still on my horse, shofar in my left hand and my sword in my right. I could now feel my right hand begin loosening, and I put my sword away, or I was going to drop it... At first it was strange, but now I realize my strength was in the left hand with the shofar... not the right in the sword...wow. Barbara said, "Hold on—wait for a call or something," and it got so clear; there we were on the ridge that we were on Tuesday watching Mike A. fighting down below, and here we were now—we fought the battle. The sun was out; it was crystal clear, and THEY said, "This is your kingdom. You have fought well, and all this is yours...it's for your entire family..." Then POPPA was there, and "HE" said, "You did great. Be ready; you're ready. Be ready and trust 'ME'..."

11.23.20 Barbara's Presession Notes

11.23.20: I had a very powerful dream. I was with men in a group but speaking to one individually about what was going on, and he was a man of authority Spiritually, big time... Suddenly, out of the blue, Billy Humphrey, director of GCHOP, body slams me but on top of himself so that he wouldn't hurt me. He was encouraging me, seeing how much THEY were doing in me. It had something to do with Jacob wrestling the angel of The Lord.

Then Jacob was left alone; and a Man wrestled with him until the breaking of day. Now when He saw that He did not prevail against him, He touched the socket of his hip; and the socket of Jacob's hip was out of joint as He wrestled with him. And He said, "Let Me go, for the day breaks." But he said, "I will not let You go unless You bless me!" So He said to him, "What is your name?" He said, "Jacob." And He said, "Your name shall no longer be called Jacob, but Israel; for you have struggled with God and with men, and have prevailed."

Genesis 32:24-28 (NKJV)

Billy isn't an angel, but it was significant, not only because of who Billy is but for what he means to me. It had a profound effect on me physically, emotionally, and Spiritually...

11.22.20

I helped a friend out with a problem with his house. I was leaving, and he hugged me. Then his little two-year-old daughter Amy signaled to hug me. I had to squat and fold myself to reach down to the eighteen-to-twenty-inch cutie and hug her. I cried and cried. I felt like Bear, the giant guy, and my heart melted...I saw my friend the next day and told him.

12.01.20 BARBARA'S PRESESSION NOTES

My proverb (11.29.20, around 08:00):
"Arrogance, superiority, and pride are the fruits of sin." (Proverbs 21:4, TPT).

12.06.20: MY NOTES

A friend (Bobby Humphrey) came up to me after church and told me he had a dream. He and I were in a Send56 Ministry meeting. He turned around, and my hair was brown.

I had a dream last night about a snake, maybe because of my friend Andrew's story. Andrew Faletti's story—that he had a snake in his backyard and went after it with a shovel. Jammed it, but the handle hit him in the nose. Poor guy. In my dream, it was hanging there, and I didn't want it around, so I swatted at it—well, this got it very mad, and instead of leaving, it slid down and started coming after me. Most animals back down from something like this—not this guy. This seemed to me to be a Spiritual match. It was huge, so I started backing up because it was getting bigger and bigger. I didn't think as much as it was getting closer, but it was bigger, and I was giving it space. It was a black king cobra. I rebuked it, and it wouldn't back down. I stood my ground but ended up pulling my forty, and I believe I shot it dead in the face, but I'm not certain. Then it was over.

Post-Session Notes

She had me go to the peaceful place, but THEY had me at the little house. Then it was me, *JESUS* on my right, and Bear next to *HIM* at the fire pit. *JESUS* wasn't disappointed in me at all about the way the dream with the snake went, but there was some correction coming; that was why *HE* had Bear there. I had a dream last night about a snake, maybe because of my friend Andrew Filette's story. It was hanging there, and I didn't want it around, so I swatted at it. Well, this got it very mad, and instead of leaving, it slid down and started coming after me. Most animals back down from something like this—not this guy. This seemed to me to be a Spiritual match. It was huge, so I started backing up because it was getting bigger and bigger. I don't think that it was getting closer but bigger and giving it space. It was a black king cobra. I rebuked it, and it wouldn't back down. I stood my ground but ended up pulling my forty, and I believe I shot it dead in the face, but I'm not certain. Then it was over. I knew Bear had something to do with Mike A. He is such an encourager and comforter. Now I believed THEY were saying, "Don't be too sure it's Mike A.; it may be HOLY SPIRIT or someone, something else!" That came as soon as I wrote "comforter"!

Suddenly, I could sense some commotion in the ravine and the fire. I could see myself with *JESUS*, but I could also see myself over toward the ravine. This time I didn't have my full battle gear; this was a lighter battle gear—my shield, sword, and almost nothing else, like just shorts. Suddenly I was blowing my shofar, and that became part of my gear. I was standing over the ravine, and it became my kingdom, and on the other side (the ridge across the way) were the fiery warriors of Heaven.

> So he answered, "Do not fear, for those who are with us are more than those who are with them." And Elisha prayed, and said, "Lord, I pray, open his eyes that he may see." Then the Lord opened the eyes of the young man, and he saw. And behold, the mountain was full of horses and chariots of fire all around Elisha.
>
> 2 Kings 6:16-17 (NKJV)

Not certain if it was my ridge wrapped around, but it probably doesn't matter. In the valley below, there was commotion, war, unease, turmoil...I was just standing there without my shield up or sword out, and I heard, "Be ready. You're ready—trust 'ME.'" I was standing there, and I could feel *JESUS*, Bear, and Mike A. behind me, and I was standing ready. The junk was still going on in the valley, and sometimes I could feel or sense some of them trying to get up or toward me, but I was not moving or affected by it, and then I felt my robe and crown being put on me! Wow, *JESUS* put my crown and robe on me, and there was only peace in the valley—that junk was gone! *HE* said, "More crown, less sword..."

I was back at the fire with THEM, and POPPA came, and "HE" had King David with "HIM." *JESUS* was telling me, "You're acting in love more, which is what WE want; there are insecurities and hurts that WE are going to work on, but you're working in love more..." *HE* reminded me of what I'd wanted for years: to have a huge guy in front of me, mad, and I just love on him...a warrior like David but a lover like David. A man after GOD's own heart. That was why "HE" brought David. Now it was *JESUS*, Bear, POPPA, David, and Mike A.

I started telling Barbara POPPA was telling me, "Make sure," and POPPA said, "No, not make sure. Let them see your 'crown'; they will know the sword is there." Then "HE" turned into that huge, lovable "lion" and jumped on me with that huge hug.

"They will see it"—my crown—"wear it! Always!"

"HE" reminded me about walking around, especially in Walmart, where so many people look angry, disconnected...and they look at me and smile, especially men, often big dudes...the enemy sees it...they know it...

I started telling Barbara about the offense I was harboring toward someone on Sunday, and it really messed me up until Thursday morning. THEY asked, "How's that going?" I repented immediately and forgave him right there. A weight of heaviness and junk came right off me...changed everything...I can't believe I carried that around, especially after Billy doing a teaching Sunday and Tuesday... She said to be certain to ask myself in a positive way, "How is my anger trying to help me?"

We were talking about how this session was different than any other one... Then, THEY showed me an image and said, "For months the sessions have been mountaintop experiences in Healing, intimacy, *love*, and identity..." Then THEY showed me an iceberg, not much height but a lot of depth!

Wow, I started crying. It was going to get really hard! You have mountaintops, then you have valleys, but then you have icebergs...valleys have nothing; they're empty with emptiness...icebergs have almost everything they have—deep under water, dark, cold, dark! It's gonna go deep! It's gonna be painful. It hasn't been... Barbara said, "It will be all right..."

18:45: THEY gave me. "More than Your sword, count on Your love."

19:38: THEY said THEY needed to get me operating in my identity before THEY could deal with what I was going to deal with now..."Be ready. You're ready—trust 'ME.'" "Wear your crown always. Let them see it—they'll know the sword is there..."

"Have I not commanded you? Be strong and of good courage; do not be afraid, nor be dismayed, for The LORD your GOD is with you wherever you go" (Joshua 1:9, NKJV).

19:55: "For GOD has not given us a spirit of fear, but of power and of love and of a sound mind" (2 Timothy 1:7, NKJV).

20:26: "Fear is a reaction, Courage is a Decision!" (Churchill).

22:00: That's the reason THEY had me in a stripped-down armor, kind of like an Indian, the other day. I was wondering—it was so strange; I kept seeing an Indian, and I kept blowing it off. It was me, nothing but my sword and shield, but I had neither out nor up. This next season is going to be different than the last. I've had my full battle gear (armor of GOD) on noticeably and my horse.

> *Finally, my brethren, be strong in the Lord and in the power of His might. Put on the whole armor of God, that you may be able to stand against the wiles of the devil. For we do not wrestle against flesh and blood, but against principalities, against powers, against the rulers of the darkness of this age, against spiritual hosts of wickedness in the heavenly places. Therefore take up the whole armor of God, that you may be able to withstand in the evil day, and having done all, to stand. Stand therefore, having girded your waist with truth, having put on the breastplate of righteousness, and having shod your feet with the preparation of the gospel of peace; above all, taking the shield of faith with which you will be able to quench all the fiery darts of the wicked one. And take the helmet of salvation, and the sword of the Spirit, which is the word of God; praying always with all prayer and supplication in the Spirit, being watchful to this end with all perseverance and supplication for all the saints.*
>
> Ephesians 6:10-18 (NKJV)

The next season, I believe I'm going to be with nothing much besides my crown... It's strange, back in the beginning of June, I went away to the mountains for around four days, and that seemed to be the major theme—I had almost nothing... This season, I believe, they want me to strip away everything—all my protections, cover... And only let my crown be seen, knowing that it is not mine but what THEY gave me...

CAVEMAN TO PRIEST

Chapter 3

IT'S DANGEROUS OUT THERE

12.10.20: BARBARA'S PRESESSION NOTES

PRE-NOTE FOR 12.10.20

6:18: A roommate walks out the door and says, "It's dangerous out there. Don't go walking around." My response would normally be, "Not without my gun..." But today it was, "Not without my crown!" Kind of strange after my dream and not knowing if I had killed it.

We started with Prayer as always, and she began. One of the first things she said was stillness, and it resonated in me. That's exactly what I'm feeling—so very still in The LORD. I couldn't describe it to her—at 16:23 today I wrote in my log, "Very, very different!" My meeting with her is at 17:00. I don't know, except very, very different. That's what it is: stillness!

We went over every single bit of the post-notes from last time. It was incredible to read it out loud to her. Most of it was from the session, so she knew a lot, but, boy, did the rest of it just blow it out of the water!

Then we started the session, and she did something new. She had me call my parts, and we were on a path. I had to tell them that they needed to stay here while I went down the path alone. I told them I would be back, "But please stay here," and Mary, Frank, and Sal were fine with that. We were on the path to Blood Mountain in north Georgia at the spot I saw Mike A. up ahead at that beautiful little tree; the last time I was there in the Spirit, we had that Heavenly feast with all that food during a session in the Spirit! I walked the path, and then Barbara said, "Ahead is a gate." I approached the gate, and it was locked, but she told me to look through it, and what was on the other side was something like my heart's desire...I don't know if I really got the heart's desire part. Maybe she didn't say it like that. I looked through, and it was the turn to head to the buff, and it was sunny and beautiful...she said, "Now you're being pulled back to the beginning of the path." It was so amazing—immediately

I felt I was falling upward in The LORD...Wow, I've felt it before, but not this intensity, and I still didn't know. You met Mary, the part who used to be the obsessive talker. Frank was the hot-headed defender, and Sal was the arrogant one. I'm back at the beginning of the path with Mary, Frank, and Sal and I just realized that I was looking into Heaven. There was no guilt or sadness, not being able to get in; THEY just told me, "It's not time..." I had to stop and take all that in... It was breathtaking...I really looked into Heaven. Once again I didn't realize it when I was looking, but after upward falling, like the song, I can see it clearly... "Touch the Sky" by Hillsong United.

I was in front of my parts, and I got it. Wow, I was just staring into Heaven! It was so beautiful, and I didn't know it... Then she said, "Ask them if they are ready to go with you on the path, but they have to be different," and Mary was set, grabbed my hand, and was ready, but sadly Frank and Sal weren't. They were mad and didn't want to change—they just weren't ready; they had no grid for it. They didn't say it, but it was like "you two are *JESUS* freaks, and we're not." Then they told me, like Peter jumping out of the boat to run to *JESUS*, how there was no way—the others were gonna go.

Now in the fourth watch of the night Jesus went to them, walking on the sea. And when the disciples saw Him walking on the sea, they were troubled, saying, "It is a ghost!" And they cried out for fear. But immediately Jesus spoke to them, saying, "Be of good cheer! It is I; do not be afraid." And Peter answered Him and said, "Lord, if it is You, command me to come to You on the water." So He said, "Come." And when Peter had come down out of the boat, he walked on the water to go to Jesus. But when he saw that the wind was boisterous, he was afraid; and beginning to sink he cried out, saying, "Lord, save me!" And immediately Jesus stretched out His hand and caught him, and said to him, "O you of little faith, why did you doubt?" And when they got into the boat, the wind ceased.

Matthew 14:25–32 (NKJV)

It was so sad...they just didn't have it in them; they just couldn't do it...they just weren't ready... at this point Barbara said to go back to the fire at the little house, and there we were, and there was *JESUS*. *HE* had Bear with *HIM*...Bear is just the most lovable big lug! He's just so lovable and loving...

It's me. Mary's to my left holding onto my arm, *JESUS* to my right, Frank, Sal, and Bear. The two guys love *JESUS*, but they're just not there yet. *JESUS* grabs Frank's hand, and Bear takes Sal's itty-bitty hand in His ginormous hand! His claws are bigger than Sal's hand. Sal grabs Frank's hand, and they all start Praying with *JESUS*. Suddenly Bear picks both of them up like they're rag dolls and puts them in His lap, His huge, furry lap, and just starts loving on them. *JESUS* moves closer and begins laying hands on them and loving on them. It is a huge lovefest this side of Heaven...*HE* starts pouring the oil of intimacy on them—I mean pouring it on them; it's getting all over them and Bear.

All they can see is *JESUS'* Heavenly eyes and smile... Then I'm on Bear's right leg next to Frank and Mary next to Sal...Bear pulls a huge hug, pulling me and Mary in, smothering all of us. This is the warmest, softest, oil-of-the-LORD lap. All Frank and Sal can hear is Bear's huge bass drum heart, boom, boom, boom; even Mary and I can't hear anything other than His heartbeat, and we can only see *JESUS*'s beautiful face, eyes, and smile. This melts the four of us together. We're now on the run circuit, just after the bridge, just before the first hump...and the three of them start overwhelming me with what is going on in their hearts. I say, "One at a time, I wanted to hear every single bit of what each of them had." I don't even know if parts have hearts. Frank cries and cries and cries and says he is sorry for all the rage he is responsible for... Oh, how much rage he is responsible for—he just keeps crying and asking for forgiveness...it is the exact scene as me a few months ago, at the base of the first hump, not having the rage, the fuel, to make it up the hill...Then Sal, the exact same thing ...I just cry so much...He says he is so arrogant, narcissistic, and apathetic...and causes me and so many other people pain, just like Frank. Then Mary starts crying and saying how she won't shut up and thinks what she has to say is so much more important than anyone else... They are so broken, repentful, and genuinely remorseful in such a GODly way...then POPPA, HOLY SPIRIT, *JESUS*, Mike A., and an extreme number of angels are there...they give me the word when one single soul is won, all of Heaven rejoices..."Likewise, I say to you, there is joy in the presence of the angels of God over one sinner who repents" (Luke 15:10 NKJV).

Then Barbara starts mentioning the path, and they have just showed me as she is speaking—the top of the second hump (hill) is where Mike A. hangs waiting for me. Then it looks like it continues from there and connects to the path, and I can see Heaven just on the other side. It is amazing...my circuit connects right to the path to Heaven. We start to go to the path; THEY are just unbelievable... THEY are so GOD! There we are, and we're looking like the *Wizard of Oz*...you just can't make this stuff up. I'm crying and crying...Mary is Dorothy, Sal is the Strawman, Frank is the Tinman, and that makes me the lion, but I'm confused and think my issue is the heart! Suddenly it hits me hard! No, Sal has no brain and is arrogant, Frank has no heart and is rageful, Mary is just too gregarious, and I, the lion, need courage. It hit me like a ton of bricks. I'll be running an unofficial Sprite Triathlon on this circuit. I called it a Strawman, Triozathon...I had no idea and didn't even put this together until writing this book! I am crying my eyes out.

"Have I not commanded you? Be strong and of good courage; do not be afraid, nor be dismayed, for The LORD your GOD is with you wherever you go" (Joshua 1:9, NKJV).

19:55: "For GOD has not given us a spirit of fear, but of power and of love and of a sound mind" (2 Timothy 1:7, NKJV).

Can you believe this? Then Bear says, "I'm Toto!" I can see this ginormous, big old bear trying to get into Dorothy's (Mary's) basket. I'm splitting a seam...like Bear is splitting the seams of the basket...and we start skipping down the trail...the five of us—well, Bear isn't skipping 'cause He's in the basket... We get to the gate, and I'm not making this up: the three of them completely disappear into me, whole, Healed, and now one! Bear jumps out of the basket and starts hugging me, and now I'm just getting this huge welcome *Home*! We're not even inside the gate yet—we're in the gate, and He is welcoming me *Home* whole...all I can feel is His soft, furry, huge, muscular, strong belly and chest and smell all that oil of intimacy from *JESUS*...I'm in HEaven...We're crying and crying and crying...

It was so very humbling in such a kind and gentle way—I could only describe it as meek!

12.15.20: Barbara's Presession Notes

12.14.20

09:17: I'm Praying and wishing I had gotten this counseling done much earlier in life. THEY lovingly said, "You weren't ready; you didn't love with intimacy, and you never loved like you do now. Now you can love US and others well." Not a moment too soon or too late. Thank YOU, LORD.

"You will enjoy the fruit of your labor. How joyful and prosperous you will be!" (Psalm 128:2, NLT).

10:01: True sorrow brings remorse...true remorse brings repentance...true repentance brings humility...

True humility brings wisdom, intimacy, and love...

12.13.20

09:45: I'm driving, and THEY remind me to put my crown on. It is strange. I can see and feel myself putting on my crown; it is so cool. Seconds after that, someone confronts me in the Spirit; they're big and mad. My Spirit grabs my sword and cuts off their head. I don't even move physically, and I'm at peace. It is unreal and happens so fast; it is my Spirit. I can't explain it, so GOD! Thank YOU, LORD.

12.12.20

16:45: I started feeling rejected, and I immediately said no! *JESUS* Healed me of that. "I rebuke you in the Name of *JESUS*. Emotions, you don't lead me. Get behind me in love."

I told her that I didn't have any plans at all for CHRISTmas, and most probably, I would not see any of the girls or other family. We addressed being alone, loneliness, sadness, and depression...I told her that I was really feeling okay with being by myself for CHRISTmas (I'm never alone because THEY are always with me!) and really didn't have or want to make plans. I want to be completely open for what THEY want for me.

We did something different today. I closed my eyes, and she asked what I feel when I hear the word "alone." I felt absolutely nothing. She said, "What about 'sad'?" I felt something very lightly and said, "Saddened or sorrow." I'm finding sorrow is good. I'm beginning to fellowship with sorrow, not enjoying it but recognizing and acknowledging it...very different for me...Then she said "rejection" and that I felt or experienced manifestation on. It was in my lower legs, but just the shins, and then it wrapped around to my calves and up toward my knees. It wasn't like a vine or root or bad; it seemed to be alive, excited...I started speaking to it and then thought I should ask Barbara; she said no, and it disappeared. It was funny; I believe it wanted to talk, and I guess it didn't like her saying no. So we went back into it, and, sure enough, he came right out, different than anything else. Not like my parts or any other things, but it appeared in front of me. At first, I couldn't catch a shape, but it reminded me of that monolith. Then a man with black hair and blue T-shirt. I don't know. He said he was angry that I rebuked him the other day, but he made it clear he wasn't angry. He was upset and hurt, not mad or angry. But he really started getting big, huge. I looked up in the natural, and there was Bear on my big screen. I believe He looked at us and said to me, "Do you want to take care of him?" I didn't know what to do but said, "No, I've got it—thanks." I told Barbara, and we laughed...I just love You, Bear.

We started talking on the bench on the run circuit where Mom and Dad hang. I was firm that I wasn't going to apologize for rebuking him, but Barbara said that I should because I hurt his feelings, so I immediately apologized because I felt bad. "I didn't mean to hurt your feelings; I wanted to be firm with my emotions." He appreciated that I apologized, and when I turned to tell Barbara about him, I turned back, and he was smiling and looked satisfied. He then began to shrink and disappeared.

After explaining all of this, we went back into it. At first I could tell it was a lady with raven black hair—that was all I could see. She was then beginning to morph a lot and got really tall. I had to put my chair back to be able to look up at her—I mean tall! Like the giraffe...I asked her if she would please sit down so we could talk because I couldn't keep looking up that high. I mean, she was like fifty feet if not much bigger...she did come down but was still morphing. I asked, "Did I hurt you?" She said, "No, I hurt you," and that was when I noticed Rejection was back on my right on the bench. It was getting confusing like it had a while ago. I didn't Pray to bind the enemy and lose clarity because Barbara did but will next time even if she does. When I told Barbara about the confusion, she said, "Have them talk," and she jumped right over there to talk with him. They began speaking and seemed to get along, maybe even well...so I waited and tried to be patient...he turned to me a few times, and it seemed to be going well, but I couldn't hear or see anything. After a few minutes, I let Barbara know what was going on. I think I said, "I don't know what's going on, but it seems good." She asked if I was good with it, and when I said yes, she said, "Sit on it, and we'll address it next time."

12.16.20

These are emails a client sent to the deputy director while I was doing my Trader Joe's ministry.

08:37: "Can someone please help me out with this? I need an answer back before noon today."

08:51: "Once again, these are in no way 4 story buildings. Please redline the plans with exactly what is indicating to you that these are 4 story? Can someone else on this email also review the plans to help me out. This is absurd."

11:37: I'm absolutely "fit to be tied, smoking!" While writing the email below, my arm muscles are shaking, not me or my arms, just my muscles; they're flexing, which, of course, is due to an email reply that a deputy director says needs to be done in twenty-three minutes, and the man doesn't have a clue... There is a huge difference between a three-story and four-and-above-story building. Four and above are considered commercial.

I write, "Sir, Please look at your coversheets and read '4 Story' in the Building Code Analysis (pictured below). This phrase is also on multiple sheets which I referred to in our phone conversation last week."

12.17.20: BARBARA'S PRESESSION NOTES

06:30: I had a conversation with my feelings and asked, "What was going on yesterday that you got so angry?" I tried yesterday and didn't hear anything. I think he was still upset...he said, "Well, Wednesday mornings are very stressful." I had to get up and get as much work done as I can. I couldn't run; then I started my ministry at 08:15, which I loved, but I had to drive forty-five minutes to Trader Joe's, and it was cold...I enjoyed talking with my three new friends: Bob, Forest, and Hal. I had to sort through around twenty to thirty boxes, set up three to four boxes for others, load the van in the cold rain, drive back forty-five minutes, sometimes unload by myself, and get back to work ASAP...I read an email from the deputy director that I had to respond by twelve, and it was 11:30! I needed to stay calm, but I was smoking...I said to him, "Wow, that's stressful. I'm sorry that it's so overwhelming for you on Wednesdays. Is there anything I can do to help?" He said, "No, but thank you for listening, acknowledging, and asking if you can help." Then he shrank and disappeared with a smile on his face.

07:00: I'm writing the above, and my boss, Mike, calls me. He says, "I've got to say"—inside I hear, "Here it comes—you're in trouble"; I say, "Shut up!" Mike continues—"I'm proud of you for not allowing your emotions to come through in that email yesterday...you remained calm and made a fool of the guy by staying professional, providing proof with pictures of why he was wrong and not allowing him to drag you down to his level..."

08:23: "HE" said, "'I' know it's been tough, but WE had to send you into the desert to work some things out in you, but that 'forty-day' season is almost over...WE're proud of you..."

13:08: Yesterday Ali and Cate replied to texts about getting two feet of snow...it did good for my soul!

POST-SESSION NOTES

Started as usual, but there was nothing but peace, nothing, so I went back in and the same thing. When she mentioned rejection, that dude instantly appeared in front of me—he didn't come out of me but was right there. Once again, he had thick blue strips or something blue on him or around him just like last time.

When I mentioned this, she said, "Ask him about it." I did, and he said, "Blue means sad, color of my eyes, the stones in my shield, crown, and sword (sapphires)." Then I asked him if he was part of me, but he wouldn't answer me...I asked if he wanted to sit down. We were on the run circuit, and he said yes. I said, "You can hold my shield, but I'll take my sword." He was rather quiet, and it was moving very slowly... He was really admiring my shield, and suddenly *JESUS* appeared. It's unreal the way *HE* comes in like that. *HE's* absolutely beautiful...GOD...*HE* told me that this guy is part of me. *HE* gave him a sword and a shield and Prayed over him. Then we were at the little house sitting at the fire, and the ravine turns into my kingdom... It was sunny; it was my GODly kingdom. Then just as fast, I was in South Hempstead, New York, the village I grew up in until twelfth grade, on the side patio—Pop Pop, Mor Mor (my dad's mom and dad), and the rest of the family were there. I was little; it was the '60s, and here came my kingdom. I saw the backyard, with our clubhouse...and my kingdom overtook it all, and that guy was nowhere...then it went to my Upstate New York house, which I described a few chapters back with the back deck. Then there was Dean's Creek and the school I went to for twelfth grade.

The only way I was able to explain it to Barbara was that my kingdom, GOD's kingdom, took over my entire Long Island and Upstate life. I was feeling, thinking...and told her, "My first pre-marriage life... That's what I got, like THEY HEaled me of the entire time period all the way up to 1988." Barbara said that sometimes after major HEaling, THEY come back and do more of a blanket or net HEaling, cleaning up a lot of little things at once. THEY reminded me of an iceberg—it was not as majestic or as grand as a huge mountain, but it was vast, deep; that was what they were doing now. Going deep!

12.22.20: Barbara's Presession Notes

I'm cutting my hair. I start with the sides of my head with a quarter-inch guard and pull out the one-and-a-half-inch guard, and my phone buzzes (no pun intended). I guess I get anxious and start the razor at my right eye and diagonally across the top of my head. I see a huge bunch of one-and-a-half-inch hair hit the sink and realize I didn't put the one-and-a-half-inch guard on! I couldn't do lap a three-inch wide, one-and-a-half-inch trench. Do lap: brush your hair over your bald spot. Some old guy's part was halfway down their head. We called it a do lap! So it all came off.

Post-Session Notes

We tried something new. "Sad" was the word that was resonating with me. I said, "It's foggy. I can't see where I'm going, and I'm confused." I was speaking about being confused about what HE had next for me. I didn't know what was next exactly. There were three or four paths in front of me. I was waiting on clarity for which one, but since Friday I'd been in a fog. I think she asked something like, "What will happen if you can't see?" And I said, "I may fall off the path..." I saw this vast cavern immediately. Wow, it was enormous, like no way to see the bottom. I couldn't take my eyes off it and kept looking farther and farther down it the whole time she was talking. I was beginning to not fall but travel, sink down in it, maybe even float...I was going farther and farther, deeper and deeper. Then I was sitting on the bottom; it was dark, but I was okay. It was not bad, but suddenly evil and darkness started covering me, enveloping me...I told her, "I won't rebuke it, but it's taking over most of me." She asked if sadness was there, and I said yes. She asked when the first time was I felt like this. I started to go back and back, and there was pre-birth Michael. I could feel that he was in the same type of space as before the HEaling. There he was—it was so good to see him. We began talking and sharing how I was feeling and what he had experienced but didn't anymore. I started telling Barbara, "This is what he experienced—dark, deep sadness and the enemy tormenting and enveloping or casting over him, clutching at him." We both knew—no more in the Mighty Name of *JESUS CHRIST*! We both felt such freedom...then I stood up because the darkness was completely gone. I could see that it wasn't just a chasm or cavern, but it was a church, a underground, magnificent church. Like I've heard of in Turkey and other places. It was beautiful with arches, and it was bright...especially over my left shoulder, but now immediately around me was getting gray or dank, and now over to the right was satanic. It was like the counterfeit or satan's church...disgusting, orange, black, evil. I was standing in front of it, not tempted or desiring it at all! Suddenly I had my crown and sword, and I was waiting on *JESUS*' lead. *HE* was behind me in all *HIS* Glory, which was on my right before. I drew my sword, and it was almost as tight in my hand as a few weeks ago. It wasn't a talon like the other time, but it was very secure in my hand. It was comforting to me. I began to fellowship with it, kind of like fellowshipping with *JESUS* in my sorrow but different...I had it more backhand to my left rather than front-handed to my right...and I could see wolves from hell, and they knew not to come close, or they'd be toast! *JESUS* was right behind me, and they knew I was just waiting on *HIS* lead. I could hear someone or some people inside, and they weren't happy, like they were in torment. Then I felt it was time to go in, so I started walking, and they moved right out of the way. Then I saw a man on my right, and the wolves were around him, if not even over him, and it was bad...I stopped and asked *JESUS* what I should do, and *HE* said, "Keep walking." I felt bad, but I couldn't, wouldn't question *HIM*...

HE has all knowledge, power, wisdom, and *love*...so I kept walking, and I could see Glory just on the other side, but it looked like I was seeing it through windows, and there were walls all around. I kept walking, and suddenly there was my "palanquin" like Solomon's. Why would I have a palanquin? "Of the wood of Lebanon Solomon the King Made himself a palanquin: He made its pillars of silver, Its support of gold, Its seat of purple, Its interior paved with love By the daughters of Jerusalem" (Song of Solomon 3:9–10, NKJV). I put my sword away and got inside, and it started moving forward. I was by myself inside and didn't know how we were moving, but we were moving forward into Glory. I could see that we were heading into the golden Glory, and I came right into the Glory. It was breathtaking with a shine. I was looking out my window, and I saw what made me think of what John saw in Revelation: a door. "After these things I looked, and behold, a door standing open in heaven. And the first voice which I heard was like a trumpet speaking with me, saying, 'Come up here, and I will show you things which must take place after this'" (Revelation 4:1 NKJV).

I could see now that my palanquin was drawn by horses, beautiful, white, powerful horses. We turned around and headed back through the same way we came, but there was no darkness now! I didn't know if I was still in the palanquin or now on my horse, but suddenly I was at the peaceful place...it was beautiful, peaceful, gorgeous... It was me, *JESUS* on my right, and HOLY SPIRIT, Bear, and Mike A. on my left around the fire, and *JESUS* made it clear; this was where "you are," not the little house but here at the peaceful place, and I could hear POPPA say, "Remember who you are, wear your crown, and let them see your crown."

12.26.20: 02:15

19:07: I like this sensing my emotions, conversing with them, asking what you are trying to protect me from, acknowledging them, thanking them, and then asking them to let me handle it from here.

12.29.20: Barbara's Presession Notes

12.27.20: I wasn't doing well, just in a funk, and had a conversation with Loneness; unfortunately I sat in it for around an hour. While in the funk, I wasn't certain who it was, so I asked, and, of course, it made sense, and he shared that insecurity was there as well. I asked what was going on, and he shared how much he was missing Michelle. When I asked, "What do you miss most?" he said, "Just having Her around, seeing Her, hearing Her, knowing She's there."

Is there something deeper? He said, "She never loved or took care of me; maybe I shouldn't have married Her." I said, "I'm sorry that you're having such a hard time—do you feel this way often?" "Not always, but yes." "What causes you the most pain?" "When I think about perhaps She never really loved me or wanted to marry me...I believe that She heard from GOD to marry me and was convinced it was HIM but never really liked or agreed with the idea. We spoke about it many times, especially sharing with partners, sharing what GOD has done. I know that we're supposed to be and will be together, but I don't know if She is ever going to love me." I asked, "Have you ever felt loved by Her?" And I believed, sadly, he said no. There had been so much deep pain, and as She had said many times, there was almost no memory that didn't have pain, arguing, or sadness involved with it. I knew this but didn't really believe it. I sent Michelle hundreds of pics last year for Easter, and that was what She said...now I felt and believed it...

I said, "Do you remember what She did for our fifty-fifth birthday at the Air Force Museum?" He said, "Yeah, that was so kind and caring, but do you remember the fight when we were there? We turned it around, but, boy, was that bad." I said, "Yes, you're correct. It was." I said, "What else are you feeling?" He said, "Abandoned, abused, humiliated, judged, rejected..." "That's a lot for you to carry. I'm so sorry that you feel abandoned, abused, humiliated, judged, and rejected... What can I do for you?" "Just what you're doing—recognize and acknowledge me, listen to me, and don't try and encourage it away. All of this stuff really actually happened to me (us); you only felt it in rage and didn't deal with it. I had to feel it and carry it, and I appreciate you finally asking me about it and wanting to experience it with me, be there with and for me. I'm really glad that we've begun doing this."

"Is there another time that you want to share about?" "Yes. In Highland you didn't do as well. I thought the door was going to fall off the car after you slammed it—then for you to walk an hour home before letting Her pick you up, thanks to Wayne and Sherry. You just stuffed it down and said it was physical, so it wasn't bad. It was bad, Mike…" "Yes, I can see how all that would have hurt you tremendously. I remember now how sensitive you are. I allowed my heart to harden, but you couldn't; you had to experience it head-on, fully exposed. I'm sorry you had to do that on your own; I'm sorry I wasn't there for you to nurture you, listen to you, console you, or take it to *JESUS* with you. Let's do that right now, can we?" He said, "Yes, but I want to mention a few more things." I said, "Okay, perhaps I was trying to stop the bleeding, the pain in my heart; you obviously need more time with me first. Please go ahead."

"There were so many times She said She was going to remarry." "Yes, I can remember that and feel that… If it did happen, what's the worst thing?" "Probably what it's done or is doing in Her heart." "Yeah, I agree. I Pray it didn't or isn't, and I appreciate that She is the first one you're concerned for…

"I'm so sorry that you've gone through this and still are. Will you allow us and agree to put it in *JESUS'* hands and not take the weight of it on unless we find it out true? And then we'll really need *JESUS*. Can we do that?" He said okay; he'll try, and that is all I can ask.

In the beginning I asked him to forgive me, and he did, and it was nice; he took a while because it really hurt him, but he knew that I meant it, and he understood that we wanted *JESUS* defending us. "Thank you for forgiving me.

"So hang in there—let's keep trying, get HEaling, and Pray for reconciliation soon. I'm proud of you and all you have and are doing to become whole. I can't do it without you and all of my feelings, parts, and mes. Let's be strong. I don't mean to encourage or blab you out of your pain, grief, or grieving period. I just want us to become as much like *HIM* as we are physically able to be as soon as we can be.

"Is there anything else hurting you, anything at all, even if it doesn't involve Michelle or our Marriage?" (I missed the "i" in Marriage, and it was sweet to be reminded that "I" am in the Marriage…) He said no.

19:11: All of me and my feelings came into alignment. I could become one and then one in my heart, get their permission to speak, forgive Michelle, and ask *JESUS* to completely bless Her and help us by wiping it all, what we mentioned and didn't. I even gave time for anyone else, and no one came forward. Thank YOU, LORD.

Something I need us all to ponder in our hearts:

Do you remember all the ways we hurt Her?

How She took care of us during the kidney stones?

My fifty-sixth birthday at the Cinci Restaurant.

How could we have been better to Her and actually loved Her?

POST-SESSION NOTES

I felt something right away in my very lower stomach, not my gut, a few inches below the belly button. I don't think I've ever had that, and it took a bit, but then it came right out. He was a little, not tiny, but not a huge, powerhouse of a guy. He was ripped and in black, tight workout sweatpants. He was running around, like making me dizzy. I asked, "Are you part of me, and can we talk?" He said, "Real short, I'm Anger, and that's why I'm running around. I'm upset!" So I let him keep running around. We gave him time, and he was still running. I noticed we were at the run circuit, so I asked if we could run together. I said, "I haven't run lately, and I miss it and need it." He said, "Yeah, I know, that's another reason I'm mad." This was the first time he said mad. We were running, and somehow, we got from the usual spot near the Heavenly hosts and were now immediately at the base of the first hill. I didn't know why or how, but we were taking the first part of the first hill, and he was moving...I said, "Dude, I can't keep up; you're going to have to slow down." He did, and we were talking, but he was not big anymore, but he was stacked, like a little Hulk—not seven feet tall but closer to my size. He had huge arms and a V-shaped chest. We took the first hill, and now we were crossing the powerlines to the north and getting ready to see Mike A. I was excited and smiled, and he kind of just blew Mike A. off. We took the next hill, and, of course, we got to the powerlines; he was excited to see the angels, which was kind of odd since he wanted no part of Mike A....I waved to Mom and Dad...and then it was over.

01.05.21: BARBARA'S PRESESSION NOTES

12.30.20, 05:30

07:32: I just got so weepie just thinking about how good THEY are to me...I can't explain it—I'm nobody! Why do THEY think I'm someone? I used to know I was somebody, but it was all me—arrogant, disgustingly arrogant. It took so much to be someone in my own strength. Now I'm nobody, and it's just so peaceful... Thank *YOU, JESUS.*

"I am the vine, you are the branches. He who abides in ME, and I in him, bears much fruit; for without ME you can do nothing" (John 15:5, NKJV).

I'm going to explode! My heart is going to explode. You think Disney exploding would make a beautiful mess—just wait. Disney is worldly colors; my new heart is full of Heavenly colors. I've seen them; they are going to make a gorgeous Heavenly mess. Mike A. is smiling and nodding. Yes!

8:20: I had a conversation with Anger and Rage, letting them both know that I appreciated them and we were all going to be working a lot together. I told Anger that I was enjoying our conversations and how it was all going. I let Rage know that I appreciated him. I knew he was trying to protect us, "But please be very aware. Unless our life is in imminent danger, hang tight, speak with me, and let's be clear before proceeding."

20:00: "Anger and Rage, you're not in trouble. I've got to be the one in control in *JESUS*. You both must clearly speak to me and get my okay before you react. Do you understand this is new to all of us? It's just like when Anger felt I didn't protect us in the past. GOD is completely in control, not me.

"Even if I make a mistake and tell you to stand down or even force you to stand down incorrectly, THEY will cover us. We are THEIR best friend. I need you all to understand that and trust me. We're talking GOD here. Do each of you understand and agree to this?

"Rage? I mean this in love, but I'm very serious—do you?" He said, "Yes, I understand, trust you, agree, and promise you not to react without speaking with you and getting clear instructions on how to proceed. I will submit to your authority in *CHRIST*. I trust that you hear and follow The LORD." I hugged him with tears in my eyes and told him how much I appreciated that.

"Anger, what about you?" "Yes, Mike, I'll speak with you, wait for clear instructions, and not react unless you say so..." It was the same thing; I hugged him with tears. I can't even write this right now. (All of this is being edited and worked on with them again at 20:00—it's even more powerful.)

I asked, "Is there anyone else we need to speak to?" Immediately Rejection, Impatience, Insecurity, Doubt, Hurt, and Defensiveness all jumped up to speak, "Okay, thank you, each of you. I appreciate you all and want you to know how important you are to me and us. You all have a vital role to play in our life, and I want us to love, honor, and respect each other. You are all equally needed to me and us."

I spent a lot of time with Rejection. It seemed that was what The LORD wanted first. When I first started speaking with Rejection, I couldn't see an image. I saw an image of me as a little guy. I was glowing and looked beautiful, but then that stopped immediately. I saw nothing but knew it was beautiful, and then I felt a female but saw nothing. I don't know if Rejection is female.

When I asked if they had a name, they responded right away with Bobby; we spent time together and bonded. Everyone else was there as well...

"Rejection, Bobby, I think it's important THEY choose you next. You're my newest feeling coming off that powerful Healing, and I am excited to be speaking with you." We sat together in my big chair. She seemed very sweet. We sat together, talked, and cuddled. I asked Rage if he had a name, and he said firmly, "Rage!" When I asked Rejection, she said Bobby. What's so sweet is the HOLY SPIRIT said I could call HIM BOB (Big Old Buddy).

12.31.20

LORD, my heart is meek before you. I don't consider myself better than others. I'm content to not pursue matters that are over my head—such as your complex mysteries and wonders— that I'm not yet ready to understand. I am humbled and quieted in your presence. Like a contented child who rests on its mother's lap, I'm your resting child and my soul is content in you.

Psalm 131:1–2 (TPT)

LORD, I receive this as a prophecy today, the last day of 2020.

08:42: Wow! This is so cool! I know cool just doesn't do it, but you know what I mean...I get ready to run, and there is Rage, right there with me, all set to run. I am excited to have him but make it clear: no disrespecting anyone. I am not mean but very firm. He agrees, and we run. He is "anger on steroids," and the other guy is anger on wisdom—does that make sense? Anger is not a sin, but rage is... We're running, and he's fit. I let him know that I'm not as fit, "so just hang," and he is fine. I think the other guy wants to be part of this, and I say, "I'd really like to spend alone time with him—do you mind?" He is a little disappointed, but I believe Rage appreciates that I want alone time with him. We make it up hump one, and I ask him, "When was the first time you felt you had to take over for me?" He doesn't have an answer; we're heading for the power lines, and I ask him who the boys are. I say, "I know they mean something to you," and again, he isn't ready to talk. I let it go and say we have time...I remind him that when we get up a bit. I hug Mike A. He is good with it, and Mike A. loves it. I introduce him to Mike A., and he is good with it. Now it's time to take the big part, hump two, and he is having a tough time. I look at him and say, "What?" He explains that he is the one that pushed me during the Triozathon, but I was the heart that carried us! It's like wow! I cry and am truly taken aback. We top the hill; this is where Michelle is, so I remind him, and there She is! I ask him again,

"Do you have a name so I can introduce you?" And he says Gary. Here's Michelle. My heart drops—I mean, down, down, down deep. She is glowing. I huggggg Her! And just hold Her. Wow, is it exactly what I need, need and want! Oh, do I miss Her. I think our hearts touch and huggggg as well. Then I look at Her and take Her in; it is very different, real! Powerful, nurturing, consoling, overwhelmingly satisfying...She and I stay there for such a long time...it's reminding me of May 29, when *deep cried to deep*... The last day of 2020—I don't know what this means, but I think it means something...I look over, and Gary is different. I introduce him, and he's kind. I say, "We're gonna get back to running," and Michelle really wants to come. Oh, do I want Her to come. I look at Gary, and he is willing, but I know in my heart, even though I want Her so badly, that no is the right answer. I say, "I'm sorry. I would love, love, love for You to come, but I need to spend time with Gary. Could we get together later, say around 4:00? I really want to see You and give You Your alone time. Would that be okay?" She hesitates, looks at Gary and back to me, and says yes. I must tell you when I was speaking with Gary about his name, and...I said, "Now remember, this is Michelle's Spirit, of course, so She will most likely know who you are either way, and I think that's what was going on here..." Her knowing that I'm fellowshipping, developing a relationship, and working with Rage!

How, oh how, does that make any sense? Except to a spirit...I am so disappointed not to have Her running with me—oh to have Her next to me! But running, wow! She is like a magnificent, gorgeous, strong, meek mare, oh such a mare in beauty and Gracefulness...when She runs! I can't explain it; it's Heavenly...we start running, and he is very much different...I let him know that She would have blown our doors off...he starts sharing about my heart; he says, "Mike, I don't have a heart, and that's why I'll do anything, anything, to be one with you and part of your heart." He's crying so hard. We get to the angels, and there's something with him and the angels...I don't know what, but they are special to him. We go down the hill, and you can hear and see the boys through the woods. I start crying and just run...there they are, and I grab them both and squeeze them, a huge group bear hug...I'm melting; my heart is actually melting all over these boys, and they are just gushing back...it's different. I can't physically see them, but they're real. I'm hugggggging and squeezing them...I'm telling you; my heart is going to explode, and once again it's going to be a huge, gorgeous, Heavenly, colorful mess! I don't know if I explained this yesterday; when Disney blows up, it's going to be a Technicolor, beautiful mess, and when my heart explodes, it's going to be a mess with Heavenly, gorgeous colors. The colors don't exist here—well, they do, but we can't see them. They are out of our range of understanding and sight...I've seen them in my new shoulder-tip-to-shoulder-tip heart when they gave it to me and filled it. My new heart goes from my outside shoulder tip to my outside shoulder tip; it's huge!

So we're back to running, and Gary starts explaining that he wants to continue feeling this way and knows the only way he can is to be right with me. If he's "rage"-filled or going off and causes me to be rageful, he knows I'm not happy with him and will disconnect with him, and, therefore, he won't experience my heart. He said he'd absolutely work with me to only react if it's absolutely necessary and only with my permission...I mean, come on! Is this GOD or what!

We're driving home, and *JESUS* is there in the van. Gary is sitting on the console with no seat belt, and it's okay. You don't know, but I've always been the seatbelt nazi. Ask my girls. *JESUS* is in the passenger seat. *HE* starts telling me how proud *HE* is that I chose correctly (it is like what *HE* told Martha about Mary. "But one thing is needed, and Mary has chosen that good part, which will not be taken away from her" (Luke 10:42, NKJV). *HE* knows how much I want to be with Michelle and that I'm completely comfortable and happy being number three, *HIM*, Michelle, then me. I have in the past put Michelle before *HIM*, which is wrong and is part of what we're going through now. I now know that, but *HE* is speaking with me about humbly being number three doesn't mean that everything to do with Michelle is more important than me. Yes, She's more important than I am, but not everything about Her is more important than everything about me...

16:00: I had a wonderful date in the Spirit with Michelle. We played pickup sticks! She whopped my butt all three games, 26–15, 27–14, and then 32–9! She usually beats me at everything, and I miss it so very much. We had some blueberry/lemon sparkling water, raw peppers, and a rare Angus ribeye...the date lasted until around 18:30. The visit (Spiritually) soothed my soul and heart. Thank YOU, LORD. I really needed it!

01.01.21

Gary (Rage) came running with me and reminded me how important running is. He wanted to let me know—not boast, though that's how he used to be: very strong, explosive, high, gigajoules (units of energy, 10^9 [9 zeros or a billion times]), mega (10^6 [6 zeros or a million times]), if not gigawatt, strong dude. But he said to me, "I'm extreme power, terawatts (10^12 [12 zeros or a trillion times]), all torque." I'm having trouble writing this next word. He said meekness, way, way power, but, under control, there is so much power to use, but nothing compared to the power of restrain. That's what intrigues him...I've allowed him to take over in my hurts and woundedness. He was saying he knew that and actually took advantage of it because he thought I was weak—instead of me trying to use restraint. I thought the same thing about my dad. He wasn't weak, but he was the meekest man I've ever known; he was a WWII army staff sergeant who was on the Rhine River in Germany for VE Day (Victory in Europe). I now know he was loving...I thought he was letting Mom walk all over him; no, he was loving her...and us.

I was weak in my insecurity, brokenness, and rejections. I thought, *But that's weakness*. I caused so much pain and allowed such pain by not controlling him (Gary) in my selfishness and brokenness. Therefore, he will submit to me, actually *JESUS*, because he sees it's not me. He told me that I've always been logical, wise, and calculative (in a good way), and he's been able to take advantage of me with his explosiveness. But he says, "No more!" He has too much respect and reverence for *JESUS* and me. Thank *YOU, JESUS*.

01.02.21

11:07: One point five miles out of one point seventy-five. Gary R. didn't start with me but joined me before the first hill. He looked great, really fit, but not like on steroids. Cut, defined. We hit the first hill, and he told me, "I don't have it in me anymore, like you." The intensity was gone! I was excited to run, but I didn't have the poison, the rage.

I was so excited. I cried and said, "Thank you for not only sharing that but also what you said the other evening." While running I told him, "Either of us sets the pace. If one's tired, that sets the pace, even if the other wants more and faster." We got to Mike A., and I hugged and kissed Him for all He did in 2020. "I wouldn't have made it without You..." Then Gary shared with Him, but I don't know what he said.

We started running again, and THEY gave me a beautiful pic of us being equally yoked, the two of us, and now, of course, it was a three-way yoke with *JESUS* in the middle. We got up a bit, and, of course, there was Michelle. I think he was thinking he wanted to share with Her, so I said, "Please let me speak with Her first." I gave Her a huge hug and said, "It wasn't mostly Gary; it was my rejection or insecurity. I take full blame for everything I did. No excuses. I'm sorry that I hurt You and abused You emotionally. Would You please forgive me?" She immediately said yes. Then Gary spoke; once again, I don't know exactly what he said, but it spoke directly to Her heart. I said, "Okay, we're gonna get going," and I hugged and kissed Her, and we were off. Suddenly She came running and asked if She could join us; when I said yes, She grabbed my right hand so lovingly. Gary grabbed my left, and there we were. I suggested that She get in the middle, and She did. It meant so much to Gary. There the three of us were, and we came to the angels! It was so joyous! Then we started heading down the hill, and Gary said he wanted us to be alone and took off. It was just Michelle and me holding hands, and we started running while holding hands. We came down the hill and could see the boys, not my boys but our boys, our boys in the Spirit! We started running and came around the bend, and there they were, and were they excited! "Mom and Dad," they said! They started screaming! And we had a four-way hug fest! I grabbed Caleb, and She grabbed Joshua, and we took a selfie! And the four of us were off running. Me, Caleb, Joshua, and Michelle; then Caleb came around to my right and Michelle to my left, and we were having such a loving time. We got back to running after I took a selfie with all of us. Caleb was next to me in the middle, and I grabbed him by both hands and ran with him in the air, then Joshua, who was next to him, and then Michelle; of course, I couldn't grab Her by the hands, but I lifted Her up gently and lovingly and ran with Her. We all laughed and had such a good time. We were getting ready to leave the woods, and THEY put a walking stick right at Mile Marker 0; the post right next to the stick said, "Mile Maker 0." The beginning…I'm crying and crying. You just can't make this stuff up!

21:00: After the four of us, Michelle, Caleb, and Joshua, in the Spirit, had a delicious dinner and a movie (*Heaven Is for Real*), they all left. I didn't even get a hug or kiss, but the entire day was amazing.

01.02.21

I was supposed to run yesterday, but it rained all day! Here the four of us were in the Spirit at Mile Marker 0 with a new walking stick. It was a lot like the walking stick I had the first week of June in the Northern GA mountains. That was when THEY told me about Caleb and Joshua. It was so sweet the other day with Michelle holding my left hand, and each of the boys, our boys, was on my right on either side of the walking stick, walking all together into 2021 from Mile Marker 0. Hallelujah! Once again, you can't make this stuff up or outdo JESUS!

They are all still here with me while I write this.

14:10: We're all still together spending the day together. It's so rewarding and comforting to just all spend the day together. We went to the Quarter Thrift store. All the stuff starts at $2.50, and each day the price gets cut in half until it's $0.25. We love the store. And I bought Michelle so many beautiful pairs of pants! And a Chico's top. Now we're at Walmart, and then the plan is to go home and wash the van together.

01.03.21

I'm feeling that I'm being called into consecration (for the last week or two) and a life of a Nazirite (today).

I'm beginning to possibly understand that the shaved head wasn't an accident. LORD, what do YOU want of, for, and within me in consecration?

THEY made it clear, and loudly THEY ratcheted things up! The last few months were getting me strong in my identity as a "royal warrior king." Well, today, you know JEHOVAH Sneaky—that's what we call "HIM"—said, "Now you're ready for what we really want of and for you. You weren't ready to even hear it before the Nazirite (Holy) Warrior King." I told THEM clearly, "I'm not ready!" THEY said through Jeff Lyle, my pastor, "You thought you shaved your head two weeks ago by accident, and, of course, you know there are no accidents," but I had no idea what a mighty prophetic act or statement it was!

Now this is the law of the Nazirite: When the days of his separation are fulfilled, he shall be brought to the door of the tabernacle of meeting...Then the Nazirite shall shave his consecrated head at the door of the tabernacle of meeting...This is the law of the Nazirite who vows to The LORD the offering for his separation, and besides that, whatever else his hand is able to provide; according to the vow which he takes, so he must do according to the law of his separation.

Numbers 6:13, 18A, 21 (NKJV)

01.05.21, 07.10

We received a special gift (check for $150) from a partner in the mail addressed to IHOP-ATL. I'm thinking maybe it's The LORD nudging me to officially become a part-time missionary with IHOP-ATL. It's funny—I just reached out to around twenty-five third-party plan review companies on CHRISTmas day about part-time contract work. Maybe they want me to be part time with IHOP instead. YOU know that's my heart's desire. I've been Praying about it for a few months now.

01.07.21: Barbara's Presession Notes

01.07.21: "That the world may know that I love the FATHER, and as the FATHER gave ME commandment, so I do" (John 14:31a, NKJV).

THEY have been echoing this since Sunday. THEY didn't punish me, but it has been brutally severe, and that's why I've gotten such Healing in the last year.

"When you are punished severely, you learn your lesson well—for painful experiences do wonders to change your life" (Proverbs 20:30, TPT).

01.06.21: Today is day three of a water fast (water fast means only drinking water), and I'm having a horribly tough time with it.

Barbara said a lot of people with ADD suffer from rejection sensitivity.

She wanted to do it a little differently today, so we invited Rejection (Bobby) and anyone else that wanted to come, and here came Mary. Barbara said, "Please ask Bobby why she came as a woman." She said that I would be able to relate more with a woman with the feelings of rejection from how much I've been rejected by woman. It was like in the movie *The Shack*. POPPA was a sweet, warm, kind, heavy-set black woman until it was time... then "HE" was a man, an American Indian man, warm and friendly but firm and strong...

Then Mary said she came as a woman because of the stereotypical gabby, chattering, bobblehead woman...

When we invited Bobby to sit down and talk, I saw her, though I hadn't yet, just her hair, black hair with a middle part. She ran away immediately. I couldn't see clearly, but I thought she got mad when we invited her to sit down and turned into a raging fire, which seemed to be over her head. I stayed curious and waited...the fiery rage came and scared her off. There it was, looking down at me. I asked it if it was part of me, and it didn't answer. I asked it if it would sit down, and it did. It turned into a "Michelin Man" with rolls of fire, not huge but big around. It started getting odd again. I think at this part there was darkness to the right side. I saw a woman, and there was black all around her, but I could see her face. The blackness enveloped her, like closing in, triangulating, like a V, and then completely covering her. It was sad; suddenly it was back up to a raging fire, and there was a man in it being tormented. Barbara said, "Invite *JESUS*," and when *HE* showed up, we called Bobby to sit down. I couldn't see her but knew she was there. It started a wave of fire like lava, and it came over her. *JESUS* said, "This fire is purifying her." Next was a water baptism, and *JESUS* said, "New life." We decided to let Bobby spend time alone with The LORD.

01.12.21: BARBARA'S PRESESSION NOTES

I'm feeling vulnerable just before the session! I felt great yesterday.

PRESESSION

01.09.21 11:10: I'm on the trail; it's cold! I get to the north side of the power line, and there's Mike A. It's so good to see Him. And there's Gary Rage. with Him. Gary says, "Do you want me to come?" I say, "Yes, unless you want to hang with Mike A." He decides to hang.

I said to The LORD, "Is that why *YOU* didn't have me take my glove off? Because *YOU* knew I wasn't going to be taking a picture, eh?"

THEY said, "WE, of course, knew you weren't going to take a picture but left the decision to you, and you made a wise decision." *B.*

I said, "Okay, thanks for leaving it up to me and letting me know I was wise." *C.*

THEY said, "Yes, you make wise decisions; if not, WE have your back." *D.*

I said, "I love YOU all so very much." *E.*

THEY said, "WE know you and how much you love US." *F.*

I said, "Thank YOU for telling me that. I needed to hear that." *G.*

THEY said, "WE know." *H.*

I said, "Yes, of course. YOU do," and that was it. *I.*

It was so cute! Did you get it? Where I come from, Canadians say "eh" and pronounce it "a." THEY are so much fun!

01.11.21

19:16: I believe THEY just let me know our first separation. I learned to wail, deep groans of anguish from the bowels of my soul. This year, I learned sorrow, deep gut-wrenching sorrow, but most importantly, how to fellowship with THEM in and through it! THEY just said, "Well done, but it's not over! Be strong, trust 'ME,' and believe 'ME'..."

01.12.21, 09:28

POST-SESSION NOTES

We started differently; she had me walking down the shoreline like I always did with POPPA. I was feeling the breeze, smelling the air and seawater. She said that there was a bench. "Picture two people next to me on either side." One of them was the spirit of the world on my right, my power side, and on my left, my heart side was a Spirit of GOD. I couldn't see either of them clearly. The one on the right was a spirit like the whole arrogant worldly dude. "We're going to eat Trump and all you CHRISTians up." It was so dark and ugly on the right side. It was funny there was this Plexiglas sneeze guard (you know, like at the salad bar) between us. He was ranting on about bla, bla, bla, and the peace on my left was incredible...then she asked that the three of us sit in a circle, and that changed everything. The dude on the right changed; he could see the peace in me but really see the guy on my left. He couldn't see him when he was sitting on my right, and he wanted what was in us! We started holding hands and Praying. Here came *JESUS. HE* sat down in between them; we were all holding hands, and the peace was overwhelming. *JESUS* let go of the Heavenly Spirit's hand, held the other guy's hand, and put *HIS* right hand on my heart and poured into it to rid me of my anxiousness about what was going on. *HE* knew I was good with the entire worldly thing, but *HE* wanted me to be great with it. I now knew deep in my heart persecution was coming, but that meant that we were going to be that much closer to *HIS* return. Yes, persecution but an open HEaven where our Prayers will not be hindered! Hallelujah! Such peace.

She said, "Let's check in on Bobby," and here she came. I saw black hair, and she was in a black gown with a black vail like death. Now I was concerned and trying to stay calm, curious, and patient, but I was concerned, but I heard this was the end of Bobby's (my) rejection. I couldn't actually see her or hear her because *JESUS* said she was not ready. I looked at her, and I heard she was excited...

When I explained this to Barbara, she said, "Go back and make certain..." I looked, and she was nowhere; it got deathly insecure. *JESUS* was nowhere to be seen or heard. Bobby wasn't around, and it was dark and evil, dark, dark, dark...it was bad! I got hit in the upper gut—bad, strong! I was talking with it, and it was different...it was tight and sucking my upper gut into my chest...I asked it to please come out, and it did. It was a really arrogant dude; he was amped up, fired up big time... he was disrespecting me to my face big time, jumping around and telling me he was going to jack me up...I was staying curious, calm, and patient asking him if he was part of me. He immediately said, "I'm not a part of you, you piece of turd." I said okay...I was now having a tough time staying curious, calm, and patient, dealing with this guy! Barbara told me to ask if he was part of me, so I kindly asked again, and he said he was not a part of me 'cause I was a turd. She said, "Ask him what he's mad about." I went back and found out that he was a part of me. He was the driven, 100-percent-task-oriented, push-push-push-kick-down-doors me. Barbara said, "How long has he been around and mad?" He said, "You wouldn't have had all that money, the BMW, the house...without me. You were fine with me even when you knew *JESUS*. I was still strong in your life, even when you were out raising partnership the first time. You wouldn't have been funded without me. Then you disrespected me, but you still needed me until last week." He said, "You still wanted me around; you would say you didn't, but I still had you until last Sunday when The LORD told you you were a Nazirite warrior...

"I know you; I know that is what happened, and I know you now don't need or want me at all...you are now holy, and you're now disrespecting me..." He was beginning to compliment me but still mad by the way he'd been treated by me...he was calming down and talking more clearly...she said, "Ask him why he's hurt." He said once again that I benefited from him but disrespected him and how that really hurt. I asked him, "How could I have treated you differently and not hurt you?" He said that I should have spoken to him like I was speaking with and working with my emotions and parts, be kind to him...I said, "I appreciate you and how hard you've always worked for me, and I'm very sorry for being mean and calling you a fool. I'm sorry I hurt you. Would you please forgive me?" He really appreciated that and knew I meant it. He said this was powerful, that he was at peace with me, and it was so good, but then he just disappeared.

01.13.21, 04:40: I believe THEY are testing me to see if I'm going to live in what I hear THEM tell me face to face or believe what I think I see or hear afterward!

01.14.21: MY NOTES

10:52: Our seventy-sixth (month) anniversary. I was on the run circuit. I ran two-thirds and saw Mike A. and then Michelle! Our hearts and souls touched and joined. After I left Her, She came running up; we ran to the power lines—then I just wanted to walk with Her, and that was what we did. We walked down the final hill; She stumbled and wrapped Her arm around mine as well as held my hand, and it was so sweet. She told me just before where the boys would be that She lost them—I don't know, but it felt real...we cried and cried...I shared with Her how much the trail means Spiritually and physically. I got most of my HEaling here, and then I said, "Would you please share? I have always just blabbed." She said, "Would you continue? I've missed you so much"...I told Her how much that meant to me...

Then She said She loved me...I couldn't say anything...

11:11: I wonder if that's why the boys aren't around.

01.19.21: BARBARA'S PRESESSION NOTES

Presession—POPPA and I were walking down the shoreline like "HE" and I used to and haven't in forever! It was tender just walking with "HIM." Suddenly "HE" grabbed me, threw me up on

"HIS" shoulders, ran into the water, and dived in. "HE" came up and said, "It's been really serious lately, and 'I' just needed to do that for you, Mike!"

I lost another dear friend to "c," and it messed me up! I shut everything down and left...

Post-Session Notes

I get a different sensation in my gut, right square in the middle, not intense but there...this little dude with a pot belly slides out. He's tiny, so I sit down, and we're on the run circuit near where the angels are. He's pleasant and cute! I ask him if he is part of me, but he won't say, nor if he has a name. He lets me know two things—he's self-conscious about what people have said about me being fat and that I have a problem or attitude with people who are heavy. I console him about that, acknowledge his (our) pain with it, and receive the part about my attitude. Then he tells me his name is Jim, and I feel something about the boys. Barbara asks when he first came, and it is clear the first marriage. She asks, "Is he a protector?" He says that he is more of a comforter or soother. Back a long time ago, he would have me drink a lot of beer and vodka and other stupid stuff. He says, "Then you stopped the drinking twenty years ago; you've stopped eating all starch and now all the gummies and sweets." He isn't mad, but not happy. Then he talks about the molestation. He starts getting big! Huge like the Michelin Man, not fat, big, and he is mad, thinking about what he went through. We are at the side of the Southern State Parkway on Long Island, New York! I thought he was looking for Wilber because that's what Michael wants, but Wilber doesn't appear. I can see the whole place clearly, and he starts kicking all the scrubs, trees, fences, just clearing the whole area. Then it turns into a clearing around the lake; it is beautiful like a lake beach...he grabs me—remember he's huge—and we're suddenly at Jones Beach, and it is such a sunny day. Here comes *JESUS* out of the blue and sits down next to me. *HE* puts *HIS* hands on me, and Jim starts getting smaller and smaller and comes into me as *JESUS* is Praying over me.

Then Bobby shows up with the black gown again, takes it off, and is wearing jeans and sits down next to me. I know it is her from her hair. Then Barbara asks if she's part of me, and she gets hurt and says, "Mike, don't you remember me? I'm Bobby, Rejection," and she really gets hurt and emotional. I reassure her, and Barbara asks, "What about what Jim did at the lake?" And she says he did that for me (her). So Bobby is good with what Jim did, but I am feeling deep sadness. I feel it strongly, and then Sadness comes out of me. It is a shape, not a person, and it knows that I, Michael, and the rest of us are healed but is still sad. I was experiencing it as well, just deeply sad, almost painfully sad for Michael. We believe he's with *JESUS*; we are both sad for me because, of course, I went through it as well...Sadness is on my left and engulfs me while Bobby is on my right with such joy about the lake...

Then Barbara asks, "When did sadness first appear?" Sadness brought me through when the next-door neighbor's cat got to my guinea pig and killed it in about third grade. Then when Timmy bent the gear shift on my brand-new green Schwinn Varsity ten-speed bike, when I got hit in the head by the ladder from an attic at my uncle Vinny's house (it made me look like a rhino; maybe that's why I like rhinos—my corporation is Rhinobeck, Inc.), and when I was hit by the car, jumping all over the place... it just wanted to be sad for a bit and hang out with me in it, which I liked and wanted. It is strange, cool...there is Bobby, kind of oblivious to it in her joy. I feel strongly to just hang, and we stop there.

01.26.21: Barbara's Presession Notes

01.21.21

19:32: I broke the fast from sweets yesterday, and I'm having some Swedish Fish for the second time—last night was the first! I took a small handful, and they were so good! I ate the handful and decided to grab another, and I could hear Jim say he was very happy! So I grabbed a third one, but no more!

01.22.21

08:30 (starting around 07:00): Just downright mad! Rageful! So after an hour or two, I finally ask, and, of course, it's Bobby. She says, "Are you serious! Come on! We could probably take all the parts of the hill on the run circuit in under a six-minute mile! Even if Mike A. weren't there right now!" Yes, the furnace is back, and Gary is stoked! He is huge and pumped; you think he was wired before! He is bouncing off the walls like "Bing Bing Ricochet Rabbit"! It was an old TV show in the '70s. Even Frankie Boy is involved, and I think Bobby would beat us all up at once! She's bigger than Gary. Look out! We are all laughing now, which is good—boy, do we feel better! Mary's not mad because she's too wise to be, but she is giggling at us all. I think every one of my mes, my parts, and everyone else in me is laughing. I guess that's a good thing. Oh my! Boy, did we need that!

01.23.21, 07:00

13:00: I'm making lunch—grass-fed Angus! I believe "HE" said, "'I'm' sorry it's not time to be on staff or officially in the ministry..."

My relationship with POPPA is so extremely, very painfully good. It's the only way I can explain it. Especially lately, some of these times with "HIM," I can't even breathe from "HIS" smothering *love* of and for me...I know I've told you over and over, but I'm going to explode... "HE" spent at least an hour on Wednesday morning saying over and over and over, "Hey, Mike, do you know how much

'I' *love* you?…have 'I' told you how much 'I' *love* you? Hey, Mike, have 'I' told you that you're 'MY' favorite best friend over and over and over…?" "HE" still keeps doing it. I can't breathe writing this, and "HE" keeps saying it and saying it! I'm fogging up my contacts… "HE" is fogging my contacts; I can't even see.

20:00: I'm realizing why Michelle would be so absolutely bewildered… How could I go from a credit score of the low 500s (around three years ago) to a score within 10 points of a perfect credit score and be pre-approved for a $300,000 house? We've been separated for basically two years. Have you heard of my GOD, *JESUS CHRIST*? Hallelujah, *JESUS* loves me!

20:39: Do you call that a Cinderella story? The Frog and the Princess…?

01.24.21, 06:45

06:55: THEY had me lying down across all of THEIR laps, and THEY were moving THEIR legs like a wave. I'm fifty-seven years old, and GOD is rolling and playing with me like I'm a very small child on THEIR laps. There is nothing better than this!

01.25.21, 05:15

20:17: Edited email from Barbara: "I'm glad to hear you have had such a powerful encounter with GOD. HE is really pouring into you in a mighty way. I'm sure it is hard to contain!"

Thank you. "HE" won't stop, and I don't want "HIM" to. Someone from church yesterday said something like, "It looks like lightning is striking me, and joy is exploding in the room." It's going on all day every day. I'm going to explode! It's coming from every angle and side! Top, bottom, left, right, front, back, above, and below! All I can do is cry! There's nothing better.

01.26.21, 05:00

07:00: You don't get relationship; you earn it… That was my problem—I thought Marriage meant I automatically got relationship; it doesn't, and, therefore, I took advantage of it.

She wanted to see if there was someone who was hiding or showing themselves as happy and not. We went right into it, and there somebody was, all the way in the bottom left corner of my belly. It was like Sadness from the movie *Inside Out*. I couldn't see her, but she seemed to be intelligent and confident but shy and reserved. Barbara asked, "Is she a memory or a part?" "I believe it's a part." Then she asked if it was protecting me from something. I clearly saw a big wolf behind a door, and she immediately slammed the door on him; she was very strong—maybe she was part of the bad...I didn't know, and she let me know it was really bad. I felt it was major, something bad we hadn't touched yet. I felt like it would make everything else look small. Then it morphed—it wasn't clearly a woman or a figure, but I knew it was there; it wasn't strong but still there. Then it got clearer—it was fear of a prostate problem if anything happened. I started crying...Barbara said, "Invite it to sit with *JESUS*," and it did. It sat at the table, and there was *JESUS*, but I couldn't see clearly...there was a pretty, sunny field and valley behind it. *JESUS* was talking to it; I couldn't see much but a sunny scene and a pretty yellow and orange glow...Barbara said, "Just sit and watch..." I did, and *JESUS* was definitely talking to it. I didn't know for certain if it was still that female, but I thought it was. After a bit, *JESUS* got up and said, "*I* want you to fellowship with her and become one." I tried, but I didn't know how to become one with it.

Chapter 4

REVIVAL'S IN THE AIR

02.02.21: BARBARA'S PRESESSION NOTES

02.01.21 (2121), 16:00: I started listening to the songs below and just ball and ball and ball...it was a disgustingly beautiful mess!

The song "Revival's in the Air" by Bethel Music and Melissa Hesler and "Abba" by Jonathan and Melissa Hesler.

10:32: Someone leaves me a pound cake, and THEY remind me that as a kid, that was my favorite cake. I invite friends home from junior high school for some birthday cake. They are amazed that I would choose pound cake, Plain Jane, boring, no opinion pound cake! I've always said growing up, I never had an opinion—after engineering, I got an opinion, and maybe that's why I've drilled my opinion so strongly and became such a narcissist!

02.05.21: MY NOTES

12:08: THEY let me know that I'm working in Grace. You can't know or work in Grace without doing what is impossible in the flesh!

POST-SESSION NOTES

Strong feelings, like unresolved feelings, toward Wilber. He wouldn't show up when Michael was mad and called him out; I believe *JESUS* said he was in hell, which was sad, but there were still feelings...

She had me sit in a room by myself in a chair, and then *JESUS* came in and put *HIS* arm on my shoulder to assure me. Then Joan, the two guys who mugged me, and Wilber came in and went to the left. As soon as I closed my eyes, I could feel something very strong. I didn't say anything...

I invited it out of me, and it turned out to be Pam, and she was upset. Each and all of these people had hurt me and us, and suddenly it was Frankie and Bobby, and they were upset. We Prayed and gave it time, and Mary joined us, knowing we needed wisdom. She'd become so wise. *JESUS* made it clear *HE* was an observer, and Barbara agreed. She asked if anyone felt like forgiving them, they should step forward. Mary did and said she forgave them all but was still hurt. Then Frankie did the same thing, expressing how each of them hurt us tremendously, but he forgave each of them and walked away. Pam wasn't bending; she was mad! More hurt than mad but still mad...so we gave her space and time. I acknowledged her feelings and, more importantly, her right to feel that way. I told her I wasn't going to make her forgive them, especially since none of them looked like they were remorseful. I did tell her that they don't have to be remorseful in any way for us to forgive them even if they are not asking for it. But in no way was I going to make her do it.

Barbara asked what would make her feel 10 percent better, and she immediately said, "A hug." I went right over to her and hugged her. Remember we only met her last time, and I rebuked her hard! So the hug was really nice on both sides, like the melting hug that Bill Durham gave me on Sunday. I was telling Barbara all of this, and I could feel something going on with Joan. I didn't know what, but she came right up to Pam and started talking with and connecting with her. I think she saw me showing love, compassion, and empathy for someone and thought that was so foreign for me. She wasn't looking at me or connecting with me, but not disrespecting me either. They really connected; maybe she knew that Joan didn't know *JESUS* and probably hadn't gotten any Healing and really needed it. They wanted to spend time together, so it ended here.

02.25.21: Barbara's Presession Notes

Forty-day take-me-up meatless fast.

Post-Session Notes

I must have said I didn't want to get stuck in the weeds; she said, "What do you mean by that?" And I immediately saw me heading into water (like the HEaling) from the land (like the place of the problems), and the weeds were the mucky, taller grass, vegetation that prevented me from walking smoothly onto the water or HEaling...that was where we started, and I felt something. I was trying to walk into the water, and there was resistance, not strong but resistance. I asked my other parts, and they said they'd seen everyone else HEaled, which was cool, but they were not ready. They knew I was not going to push it hard, so they weren't pushing. We talked, and suddenly ponytail Mike (me from Adopt-A-Block days, 2005) came out with one or two guys, and they left. I was not able to keep up and feel that I was not supposed to. I stopped, called to them, and said, "It's okay." I looked, and there was the water, and I felt I was supposed to walk to it. I walked, and there was no resistance, so I walked right in. There was ugly evil or something in there, but I was okay; that was what the parts were afraid of. I moved around, walked in, and started swimming, and there was junk (not garbage but bad) grabbing me, but it couldn't hold on, and then I was walking back toward the shore. I was talking with The LORD and feeling fine but didn't know what was going on...

I started swimming again and heading out a bit—then there was a boat. I climbed up the ladder, and there was no one there, but I could feel The LORD, and HE said, "Start sailing." I was not that certain on how to navigate a boat around, and HE said, "Start sailing..." So I started sailing; there were people and boats around, so I took it easy and got around and away from them. Then suddenly, I was not at the wheel, and it was someone else.

They didn't look good; they looked evil in black and not nice. I knew Barbara was not going to want me to rebuke them, so I stayed curious. We were in open waters, and he started gunning it. I believe that was what *JESUS* had just told me; he wouldn't be allowed to sail around people. That was why I had to sail away from them. He was rocking the boat, and I could hear Barbara in my head, "Stay curious..." I said to it, "Okay, do I know you?" "No!" "Okay, are you part of me?" "No!" He said something like sharks, and I said, "We're in fresh water." He went, "Oh..." and continued to race.

I started feeling something inside of me, more toward the gut, and, sure enough, it was Pam...she was scared of this guy, and I still didn't know who he was. I had Pam sit to my left, and this dude was on my right, steering the boat. He was still not slowing down, and Pam was very uncomfortable. She said to talk with Barbara, which I thought was too funny...I thought maybe Pam had a little talk with the dude, and he was slowing down by the time I got back. I asked him if he would come over and sit with us; he hesitated but did...things were calm, and suddenly Pam called Joan up from below—she sat down on the far side of Pam. There was no discomfort or coldness, not joy or happiness but no problems...the four of us were sitting in chairs in a circle, and I felt to tell Joan I was sorry for the pain I caused her. Pam told me to speak with Barbara first. I thought she knew I was going to invite *JESUS*. I told Barbara about my saying sorry, and I asked her what to do; we decided I would just go back. I got back and realized there was Pam, who we believed was a part of me, but we really didn't know her. Joan was there, and also one of my mes (possibly during the first marriage but didn't know where he ended—we saw ponytail Mike on shore—or he wasn't too long after the divorce, but I believed clearly probably shortly after). They started talking because I still felt funny about saying I was sorry. The three of them started bounding. Mes started shrinking in a good way, like through HEaling, and disappeared into me with such peace. I breathed it in, and suddenly Pam got thin; she complained about being fat and defending me. She was thin and started shrinking and came into me. I thought to myself, *I hope it's not just Joan and me*, and Joan disappeared…and there was such peace. I was on a boat in the sun out in the middle of a big lake, and I was soaking it all in. Then I heard The LORD say, "Take it out…" So I started cruising, and it was nice. I'd always wanted a boat…then I started fishing. I cast, and the peace quickly left. A shark came after the fish that hit my hook, and other sharks hit him, and there was a whole lot of junk…at that point I started talking with Barbara, and she said often water has to do with sexual abuse…

POST-SESSION NOTES

There was something that started as peaceful, and then it got firm. Not mean or aggressive but firm. I saw what looked like a little girl on a tricycle; it looked like Delaney Collins (my niece). It was going back and forth and not very clear, and there was Michael from last week on the boat, but he was calm. There was a whole lot more going on, but I couldn't figure it out. I think the little girl, Delaney, was scared about Michael. Barbara asked something like, "Is there another Michael, maybe two, one who's not good and the other who is?" We went with that, and two came out, but I couldn't see them. I believed it was Michael on the boat—maybe pre-saved, and the other post-saved. We asked them to sit on either side of me, which they did, but I still couldn't see them. Then Pam came out and was with Michael on the boat, and he was very peaceful. When I asked Pam if I could come on the boat and talk, suddenly, I couldn't see her or anything; it seemed I was seeing less and getting more impressions than visuals. I thought she was skinny now; she was heavy and said it was because she took on all my hurts…I could see Pam and Michael. He was peaceful, which he hadn't been. Barbara said, "Who is this big Michael?" And I think he said the fool Michael. Someone or something was smoke screening to distract or pull us away.

I clearly saw Pam, and then I saw a very clear image of me—approximately three to five in front of the garage in South Hempstead. I looked really happy and peaceful but then had thoughts of the guinea pig that the neighbor cat killed! But this Michael was the whole Michael from kindergarten who got HEaled, and he wanted me to know about the other Michaels who weren't HEaled. Barbara asked, "Is the big Michael a protector to the other little Michaels?" Little Michael said no—because he was HEaled, he (little Michael) was trying to show me the other Michaels who weren't HEaled; they wanted to and needed to be. Barbara asked if they could show me the other Michaels, and suddenly they or someone started calling out different Michaels at different ages. Michael getting the hair cut from Dad (Dad accidentally cut a chunk of hair out with the electric razor), guinea pig Michael, Michael getting the hair cut from Patty Sue (which I think didn't go well because of Dad's haircut experience, and I cried, which really hurt her, sadly). Then I heard junior high Michael, high school Michael, college and married to Joan, after married to Joan, and then I clearly heard after that the married to Michelle and now...I started crying badly being reminded that I was still such a mess. I thought big Michael turned around and said, "See? It's not just before *JESUS*."

So we went to the earliest Michael getting the hair cut on the side patio from dad, and he was smiling with teeth missing; he was so cute. I hear "Pollyanna." I think poor little Michael getting the hair cut had something inside behind that smile. It was so sad. Immediately the dark evil came—there was this ugly goat, and it was horrible. It was rude and taking advantage of female goats; it was dark, evil, and confusing, and I couldn't see Michael anymore. This goat was violent and very bad! I started understanding the Spiritual end of it, and it was bad. I believed it was the masonic temple bad, maybe knights of columbus...the goat was a man with the goat's head and big. I wasn't scared Spiritually at all, but neither was he...he was bold, not intimidated, and didn't back down. I didn't want to challenge or rebuke him yet, but he was challenging me and made it clear he wasn't intimidated by me. Then I saw an image that it wasn't just female goats he was domineering and abusing; it was little Michael, me...it was really clear, and I started crying...it seemed clear that it was Spiritual—maybe a man, a boy, a girl. It seemed bad. I couldn't see Michael. I looked, and it seemed that the image of the goat was still there, and maybe it was where Michael was—burnt out of a picture. I could see more of the evil and the goat behind the picture of Michael. Barbara asked, "Do you see Michael?" And I couldn't. Suddenly I could see him kind of jump up from behind the evil, behind the picture...it was so good to see him, and he said he was all right. Dad was there with him, and then Uncle Norman came over as well...but the goat was still there as a reminder.

03.09.21

18:00: While speaking with Ben, one of my mentors, I started talking about the delta wave problem in my brain—almost 100 percent delta wave activity 100 percent of the time. The problem is that my brain is in REM sleep all the time. People talk with a man (me) all day long, and my brain is in REM sleep 100 percent of the time... Very odd! And I believed The LORD shared that it is/was the poison in my heart that has been and is still causing this problem. "Continue seeking 'ME' and your HEaling, Mike," is what "HE" just kept saying.

Post-Session Notes

It started very oddly. There was this heavy, flat feeling on my gut, and it lifted. Then it was a breeze, a warm, gentle, blanket-like breeze. There was something else very strong clinging to my gut just under my right ribs, and it was different; it seemed to be on the outside of me. We were clearly on the run circuit over where Mike A. hung, and this thing was like a starfish—sucker thing clinging on very tightly.

Then the gang was there—HEaven hosts and my parts. Then we figured that it was Pam. She was scared because she was found out! Then she was sitting on my lap but didn't really have shape but then was the shape of a person. It seemed evil had called her back or something. She was gone, but the empty shell like a cicada was there...it was sad and astonishing all at once...I heard and saw this guy over where Mike A. usually was, and he was shouting very excitedly, "Push it off, push it off," but he seemed too scared or foolish for me to listen too...and there was this hollow, empty shell of me over there near him...

JESUS was off to the far left on the hill in the sun alone with POPPA, and I could feel part of me go over there, but not most of me. It was very sad, like I wasn't allowed to come over completely, like I was in trouble. *Did I do something wrong?* Now I was thinking like I was impure...I cried. Then I could see that it was my Spirit with *HIM*, and I was stuck with these three—very disappointing, sad, and painful. I believe *HE* said, "*I* am going to spend alone time with your Spirit." There I was without *HIM* and felt very alone. I thought I heard *HIM* say something like, "I'm going through a lot right now and weighing down my Spirit." I cried like I was unworthy, worthless, and dragging down my Spirit...I felt like I was going into a desert period like *HE* did alone. I was crying..."Then Jesus was led up by the Spirit into the wilderness to be tempted by the devil" (Matthew 4:1, NKJV)

Wow, it was bad—at around 18:45, *JESUS* was with my Spirit. I was with the three of them, and *HE* said, "I'm gonna go it alone," which made me very sad, and I cried and cried...then, it was so *JESUS*. Suddenly I felt something touch my lips, and I was in Heaven...not my Spirit, not the sin, not the empty hollow guy or the anxious in-between guy, me...so I was up there, and it was so weird 'cause Barbara was in the session with me, but I was in HEaven. It was a different feeling than ever before. I was being lifted but not lifted—floating but not floating. I guess, like they say, upward falling...I was in HEaven. My Spirit was with *JESUS* down there, and I felt heaviness, anxiousness, and worldly thoughts falling off me.

I wasn't in The Throne Room, but I was in one of my mansions. I couldn't see well around inside, but I could see the streets of gold and *Glory* outside like through the windows. I could hear POPPA, and I started feeling like I was being called out up above the mansion.

> *In My Father's house are many mansions; if it were not so, I would have told you. I go to prepare a place for you. And if I go and prepare a place for you, I will come again and receive you to Myself; that where I am, there you may be also. And where I go you know, and the way you know.*

> John 14:2-4 (NKJV)

I could see halfway to The Throne, but I was in between. I started somewhat telling Barbara goodbye and noticed it was 19:03, but I wasn't here...with all of that I was still in between but not heading for The Throne. I was clearly in HEaven, and "HE" kept saying, "Relax, enjoy, walk around. Yes, you're with 'ME' in HEaven..." I was still in my chair. I got up and went to bed. I was still walking around HEaven...as I was walking, I would think about something like work, and it would fall off me, back down to earth, where it belonged—thoughts, feelings, they would fall off me and float down to earth, sort of like what it looks like when a rocket heads to space and drops its engines or something. It's funny—I had some work papers on my bed, and they fell off the bed at the same time, and it felt like work was falling off me. I thought to myself, *Oh, I'm supposed to pay a bill?* And I felt it fall out of Heaven. It was just like a huge part of me, like a lot of anxiety and pressure falling off of me. It was so big, I thought it was actually me falling back to earth, but it wasn't. "HE" said, "Keep going, keep walking, enjoying...'I' am peeling you down to your Priest, and more and more is falling off." I didn't think I was getting smaller—I think purer...

I was still walking, floating. Stuff was falling off me, and I was getting lighter and lighter...I was still in HEaven, but not in The Throne...I was being told now that what touched my lips were the kisses of *HIS* Word purifying my tongue, lips, and me on my way up like the coal from the Altar in Heaven. "Then one of the seraphim flew to me, having in his hand a live coal which he had taken with the tongs from the Altar. And he touched my mouth with it, and said: 'Behold, this has touched your lips; Your iniquity is taken away, And your sin purged'" (Isaiah 6:6–7, NKJV).

I looked up, out of my bed, and there was the picture of *JESUS* on my big screen reaching down below the water. Like the Scripture, "Then Peter got down out of the boat, walked on the water and came toward Jesus. But when he saw the wind, he was afraid and, beginning to sink, cried out, 'Lord, save me!' Immediately Jesus reached out *HIS* hand and caught him" (Matthew 14:30–31a, NIV). And it was 7:47, of course—19:47. It was so clear and peaceful. I heard THEM say, "Just rest with US—let the kisses of *MY* Word wash, purify you, and let the world fall off." This silence fast doesn't mean you don't speak, but you don't share about what you don't share about...with anyone...this is the time for you and you alone to work with the True Mike (my True self) without the help of your Spirit while WE speak into and strengthen your Spirit...

Someone, a man, was here last night,
kind of like the first time Mike A. was...

Post-Session Notes

Barbara is not happy that she keeps talking to this upbeat guy all the time. She says, "I want to talk to someone else; close your eyes, and let me speak to someone..." I close my eyes, and I hear "control freak," so I tell her. I don't know who said it, and no one will admit to it. I look down. I see all my parts, and it's not them. I look farther down, and it looks like a brick way, way down. My parts are about near my gut, and this is down like at my feet, but it's not like that...I don't know who it is, and no one is saying anything. It's clearly speaking; it's not mad...I see a silhouette, and it doesn't seem confident. She's speaking with me. I'm the one who, like, has confidence and knows and loves *JESUS*...but she wants to speak to the other guy. I tell her, "I'm who I am." I ask, "Can we speak with the other guy?" And I can see that silhouette of a guy way down there, and that brick is a chest. He's sitting on it. Suddenly Mike kind of unzips and falls off me. He doesn't fall, but he comes off me so that the other guy can talk...I can't take him off or make him come off; he decided to come off me so that the other me could talk... How does this stuff happen? So here's Mike, a big bag of muscles lying on the floor behind and around me...a bag of muscles like a big jacket that I just took off...it feels so good, like a huge weight just fell off me. Mike feels the same way; he is just lying there and relaxing like he has never been able to do before. Here I am, and I can see that the silhouette is little Michael, who was getting the haircut on the side patio with the big missing tooth and innocent smile—Dad was shaving his head a few weeks ago. I'm him, and/or he is me. I start talking and explaining that we love Mike—he's confident, smart, loves *JESUS*, gets along with most people, and is liked by most people. He's really nice to us and protects us. Barbara asks, "Is he Gary?" We say no, and she asks about the other two guys on the left from last week, and I start saying that it seems like Pam was never a part of us 'cause I remember when she exposed herself, which I believe now she did on purpose because she loved me and wanted to be caught for who she was but was scared of all of them, that she tried to get inside me. She turned into that silhouette and sat on my lap until evil called her back or took her back. I think she tasted love and didn't want to keep hurting me or us and allowed herself to get caught, but sadly I think she's back with evil. At least now she knows what love is. I'm hoping and feeling good that something good may come from her...

Barbara says, "Is there someone that Mike doesn't like?" I can immediately hear him say, "That yappy fool over to the left from last week and the empty, hollow guy." I don't know if they are a part of me or something like Pam, which is external...so we continue, and Mike is still really relaxed and comfortable and completely lets me continue. I now know what happened, and I let innocent Michael speak. Everyone loves me/him as well; it's just that Mike has been like a big brother protecting us and making us look good. Mike feels good and sits up on a rock ledge seat below next to me, and the parts are still down lower. Barbara asks about the chest, and no one knows anything, but I can see it down there, and there appears to be a golden paved road to it, but it seems to be surrounded by darkness. Remember two weeks ago when we were wondering about Pam? Now, the darkest of all darkness showed up around her, and she was down and in front of us. Now, the darkness was mocking me like pre-birth Michael. It was bad; it was saying, "Just you wait," and it was huge! Then Mike A. came screaming in from the left driving Glory and covered all that up down there. What could we say but wow! That was Mike A.! The chest seemed to be connected to that darkness. I don't have my Spirit because he's with *JESUS*, so I can't tell what's going on with the chest, and I don't even have Mike... The last two weeks are just really being woven together here; it's amazing...

I feel that I am supposed to leave Mike and all my parts and go down to the chest. I believe I have to go, so down I go, and I am completely on my own. I go past my parts and continue down. I don't get to the bottom—I can hear POPPA say clearly, "Remember you always have your crown and sword, but don't use them..." I continue down, and I get down there, and it's dark. I know there's evil because I heard and saw the wolves on my way down, but I'm okay...I can't see the chest and have no idea where it is. I start walking, and I think the darkest of the dark is over to my right, and I feel I'm supposed to go to the left—sure enough! I go to the left, and what's out toward the left but HEaven! THEY sent me down all alone into darkness. I accepted it, and I'm on my way to HEaven again! I'm walking in HEaven like I was last time, not The Throne, not one of my mansions but that place where POPPA kept on saying, "Relax, enjoy, walk around." I don't hear or see "HIM" or anyone, but I'm in HEaven, so I don't care about anything...I keep walking, and it's like Scotland...a huge, beautiful mountain. I think of work or something, and, sure enough, it falls off. I know I'm in HEaven. I keep walking, and I can see *Glory* off to the left and up; not certain what to do, I keep walking toward there.

There are some distractions ahead and to the right, but I'm not letting them affect me, and it's not the HEaven I was in. I go to the next level—I'm walking next to the sun; it is *hhhuuuuggggeeee* and briiiiight. It's burning away parts of me. Remember I'm not Mike. I don't have the worldly confidence, the overconfidence, the arrogance! The sun is roasting me, but it doesn't hurt; it feels so good, and I'm in *Glory*...I can see and hear some people around me, but not clearly. I just keep on walking, relaxing, and enjoying, like POPPA said. I can hear "HIM" more, not clearly, but I can hear "HIM" doing "HIS" business—you know, running the entire universe...I keep walking, and this is Heaven.

It's not The Throne, but it's bright and crystal clear and maybe even almost The Throne Room, but not yet! Here comes another sun on my left, and I start getting it again, and I hear something like I'm processing, but not processing...being sanctified...I hate to even say it, but that's what I believe I heard, and the sun is way, way bigger than the one we know, and it's cooking me! Roasting me like potatoes! Wow! I'm now on the other side, I'm not going through the sun but through the side of the sun...and everything is different; it's now like a cloud, no, not clear, cloudy, but I can't see too much walking space—like it's time to float.

I look up, and there is POPPA just above me and in front of me. "HE" is riding, sitting, throning on in a cloud. I don't know if it is Ezekiel's cloud with the four living creatures.

Then I looked, and behold, a whirlwind was coming out of the north, a great cloud with raging fire engulfing itself; and brightness was all around it and radiating out of its midst like the color of amber, out of the midst of the fire. Also from within it came the likeness of four living creatures. And this was their appearance: they had the likeness of a man. And above the firmament over their heads was the likeness of a throne, in appearance like a sapphire stone; on the likeness of the throne was a likeness with the appearance of a man high above it. Also from the appearance of His waist and upward I saw, as it were, the color of amber with the appearance of fire all around within it; and from the appearance of His waist and downward I saw, as it were, the appearance of fire with brightness all around. Like the appearance of a rainbow in a cloud on a rainy day, so was the appearance of the brightness all around it. This was the appearance of the likeness of the Glory of the Lord.

Ezekiel 1:4–5, 26–28 (NKJV)

I don't want to make something up, but that's the only way I can describe it. "HE" is getting closer and closer. I can reach out and touch "HIM," but I wouldn't dare. I know POPPA Loves me, and I probably won't get in trouble, but I just can't and won't. I let "HIM" know, "Just call me, and I'm there," but it's such peace. It's okay! "HE" floats by me, clouds and throne right by me, and it is amazing. I'm in Heaven now, no doubt. I believe POPPA's throne just passed by me close enough that I could touch it and "HIM." I keep walking, and I'm telling you—I'm running out of whatever I'm walking on. I look to the left, and I can see the heavenlies—it's like the upper Heavenlies opened and showed themselves to me. It reminds me of the first time I was in HEaven with POPPA, and "HE" showed me the universe from Heaven. I saw the Cat's Eye Nebula...and then I was sitting on or in HEaven...

07:38: Ezekiel's vision of GOD.

Now it came to pass in the thirtieth year, in the fourth month, on the fifth day of the month, as I was among the captives by the River Chebar, that the heavens were opened and I saw visions of GOD. On the fifth day of the month, which was in the fifth year of King Jehoiachin's captivity, the word of The LORD came expressly to Ezekiel the priest, the son of Buzi, in the land of the Chaldeans by the River Chebar; and the hand of The LORD was upon him there.

Then I looked, and behold, a whirlwind was coming out of the north, a great cloud with raging fire engulfing itself; and brightness was all around it and radiating out of its midst like the color of amber, out of the midst of the fire. Also from within it came the likeness of four living creatures. And this was their appearance: they had the likeness of a man. Each one had four faces, and each one had four wings. Their legs were straight, and the soles of their feet were like the soles of calves' feet. They sparkled like the color of burnished bronze. The hands of a man were under their wings on their four sides; and each of the four had faces and wings. Their wings touched one another. The creatures did not turn when they went, but each one went straight forward. As for the likeness of their faces, each had the face of a man; each of the four had the face of a lion on the right side, each of the four had the face of an ox on the left side, and each of the four had the face of an eagle. Thus were their faces. Their wings stretched upward; two wings of each one touched one another, and two covered their bodies. And each one went straight forward; they went wherever the spirit wanted to go, and they did not turn when they went. As for the likeness of the living creatures, their appearance was like burning coals of fire, like the appearance of torches going back and forth among the living creatures. The fire was bright, and out of the fire went lightning. And the living creatures ran back and forth, in appearance like a flash of lightning.

Now as I looked at the living creatures, behold, a wheel was on the earth beside each living creature with its four faces. The appearance of the wheels and their workings was like the color of beryl, and all four had the same likeness. The appearance of their workings was, as it were, a wheel in the middle of a wheel. When they moved, they went toward any one of four directions; they did not turn aside when they went. As for their rims, they were so high they were awesome; and their rims were full of eyes, all around the four of them. When the living creatures went, the wheels went beside them; and when the living creatures were lifted up from the earth, the wheels were lifted up. Wherever the spirit wanted to go, they went, because there the spirit went; and the wheels were lifted together with them, for the spirit of the living creatures was in the wheels. When those went, these went; when those stood, these stood; and when those were lifted up from the earth, the wheels were lifted up together with them, for the spirit of the living creatures was in the wheels. The likeness of the firmament above the heads of the living creatures was like the color of an awesome crystal, stretched out over their heads. And under the firmament their wings spread out straight, one toward another. Each one had two which covered one side, and each one had two which covered the other side of the body.

When they went, I heard the noise of their wings, like the noise of many waters, like the voice of the Almighty, a tumult like the noise of an army; and when they stood still, they let down their wings. A voice came from above the firmament that was over their heads; whenever they stood, they let down their wings. And above the firmament over their heads was the likeness of a throne, in appearance like a sapphire stone; on the likeness of The Throne was a likeness with the appearance of a man high above it. Also from the appearance of HIS waist and upward I saw, as it were, the color of amber with the appearance of fire all around within it; and from the appearance of HIS waist and downward I saw, as it were, the appearance of fire with brightness all around. Like the appearance of a rainbow in a cloud on a rainy day, so was the appearance of the brightness all around it. This was the appearance of the likeness of the Glory of The LORD. so when I saw it, I fell on my face, and I heard a voice of One speaking. And HE said to me, "Son of man, stand on your feet, and I will speak to you." Then the Spirit entered me when HE spoke to me, and set me on my feet; and I heard HIM who spoke to me.

Ezekiel 1–2:2 (NKJV)

08:26: Where Zeke concentrated on the four living creatures, my interaction was more about The Throne. It may have been because that's what "HE" is focusing on in my life. I was in HEaven, and The Throne wasn't being transported down to earth? It also seemed very peaceful...I don't know—I have so many emotions about it; it's tough to write down.

11:28: I've been guilty, if not worse than Adam, for not being a priest and letting the enemy steal my Wife. I was a caveman, and cavemen are no threat to the enemy. The enemy is no threat to a true Priest. Dear sweet and Mighty POPPA, I repent for being a caveman and not defending and protecting my Wife, Michelle, and family. Please forgive me and return a thousandfold what I have lost, in the Mighty Name of *JESUS*.

14:02: I decide to lie down with a nice blanket and listen. Okay, Mike is still letting me, Michael, drive—this is me talking as Michael for all of us, and that's why no one is telling me that they're talking. They want me to figure it out. Spend time, slow down, and figure it out. Mike would have just drunk a Diet Coke 'cause this is a deep one and wait, but maybe not long enough to find out.

I'm back in HEaven; it seems that here it's like zero gravity, but I'm not floating. It's much easier for distractions, interruptions, anxiety, rushing...to fall off. *JESUS* is here, and I believe *HE's* telling me that's why *HE* has me here—to train me on allowing these things to fall off easily and quickly. *HE* wants me to learn not to allow all that to cling on or attach themselves to me to begin with. I believe *HE's* saying that some of the problems the Mikes have had, hurts, wounds...he and I have allowed us to disconnect from the rest of us, become disenfranchised, and fall out of fellowship, and we were easier to be attacked by the enemy. It made us more easily distracted and not care. No more! We're going to slow down, take things in, think, dialogue, and make wise, informed decisions, not snap decisions without thought. Please help us, LORD.

04.05.21: My Notes

06:45: I've met Grace—as Pastor Dustin says, Grace I wish I didn't know. The world doesn't want you to meet Grace because then you learn in Grace not to strive and do it in your own strength. Grace is the power to do GOD's will in GOD's strength.

You can't know Grace, like you can't know Agape. Grace can only be experienced when you do something that is impossible in the flesh—that's Grace...

Chapter 5

I Go Up for the Fourth Time

10:05: I'm at my doctor's, and I go up again for the fourth time. I'm waiting for impurities to fall off, and I'm in one of my mansions. POPPA is talking to me, and "HE" says, "Yes, that's a good desire—keep working in Grace on that. Like 'I' did with the Israelites—'I' didn't remove all inhabitants; a small amount of the enemy keeps you strong and on your guard. Don't fellowship with them like so many have."

> *Now these are the nations which the Lord left, that He might test Israel by them, that is, all who had not known any of the wars in Canaan... And they were left, that He might test Israel by them, to know whether they would obey the commandments of the Lord, which He had commanded their fathers by the hand of Moses. Thus the children of Israel dwelt among the Canaanites, the Hittites, the Amorites, the Perizzites, the Hivites, and the Jebusites. And they took their daughters to be their wives, and gave their daughters to their sons; and they served their gods.*
>
> Judges 3:1, 4–6 (NKJV)

"Be strong and courageous always." Then "HE" shows me an ant. "HE" says, "Look at the ant—he's always working; keep working hard in Grace only." "Ants—they aren't strong, but they store up food all summer" (Proverbs 30:25, NLT). I know it is POPPA, and I say I don't know what an ant looks like playing, and we laugh...it is clearer in HEaven, and the upward falling is so cool... Thank "YOU," POPPA. "HE" says, "When you fall, not if, remember what Dustin shared yesterday. You're forgiven immediately and completely. Get up. 'Cleanse me with hyssop, and I will be clean; wash me, and I will be whiter than snow' (Psalm 51:7, NIV). You're clean, Mike, like it never happened! Because of the Blood of *JESUS*."

This fast, forty-day take-me-up fast.

It's been powerful, painful, and rewarding.

I've been taken up to HEaven at least four times.

It seems the flow between earth and Heaven is less hindered. Maybe my access has been granted at a higher privilege. My security clearance is higher. Making the approach time and procedure smoother, faster, effortless, streamlined. Having high-priority access to the King. My worries, anxieties, heaviness, and stinking thinking fall off with ease and float back to earth.

04.15.21 Barbara's Session Notes

She asked me to close my eyes and asked, "Who is sad?" They all said me! We asked my feelings that were longing and yarning to please give me separation:

» Loneliness

» Sadness

» Dread

» Unbelief

» Doubt

There was such comfort, ease, relaxation, and love. All the feelings came out of me; some of them were stubborn, but they all came out. Two came out of my head—then my gut or core. It was so relaxing and comforting, peaceful and loving to have so much weight taken off me when each manifested and came out...sometimes they would just come; some didn't manifest, like anger and unforgiveness, but others did. Some were harder than others. They were all right next to me on the run circuit near the regular place where all the angels hung.

Barbara said to ask which of my parts wanted to go speak with them; they all said that would be me. The entire time, I could see them all. I couldn't say exactly what each looked like, but I could see them. They were like a pile, a crowd, or something while each of them gave me space. But now, when I went to speak with them, darkness came in. Evil, a few wolves, not as intimidating as it had been in the past—more like in *The Passion of Christ* when satan would slither around, not with power but just evil, disgusting, filthy evil and sin...and it looked like a big cardboard box of emotions.

04.16.21: My Notes

21:27: I woke up at 03:30 this morning, and I had a very busy but productive day until 15:30. I was tired and knew I wasn't going to bed early. I washed three loads of laundry, which included the bedding, wrote up a lot of yesterday's session notes, and had a good night. I was heading to bed and asked POPPA, "Why do I feel so good?" And I believed "HE" said it was the HEaling last night. So I asked "HIM," "I know we dealt with a lot of feelings, but what did we do?" I believed "HE" said "HE" removed much of the "emotional baggage." It rang so true in my heart, soul, and entire being.

05.06.21: Barbara's Presession Notes

I was talking back and forth with someone and Barbara. He was tough-sounding, gruff, and pompous. Barbara asked a few Qs, and when I started asking him, he began to cry and asked, "Why didn't you protect me when I got mugged?" I didn't try to do this or hurt him, but he just fell apart and cried and cried and said he was afraid and that he was all talk and became this puddle of tears. I felt so bad; he was insecure...then we thought maybe we should bring some of the others. There seemed to be a great divide between them all. He was on my left, and they were on my right, and it wasn't crossable or something...he didn't want to see Frank or Gary. I think, even more so, he probably didn't want them to see him. He said he knew them all, but they didn't know him. We didn't know what that was about, and he couldn't really talk; he was such a mess. I asked Mary, and she jumped at the chance, and then Bobby wanted to come. They didn't know him, but he supposedly knew them. He suddenly started to morph into this huge silvery thing, and I could tell that the ladies were scared, so I called them back. When I spoke with him, he started coming back down slowly. I think it was Bobby, something like "she's pretty," and he got funny about it and blew up, not angry but maybe tried to hide his insecurity...*I don't know*...once he was back to the puddle, we decided maybe Mary should come alone; she's a lot older, wiser, and very kind. It reminded me about what a dear friend of mine, Inger Beisner, would always say. She was attractive and felt funny hugging men until she got older; she said she was more of a grandma and could...

I invited Mary back, and she was perfectly fine—then Bear showed up. I loved when Bear showed up! I really had to make sure it wasn't me. I just missed Him so much, but it wasn't me. I could see that pic of Mary spoon-feeding Him honey, and it was Him. He let this dude know if he messed with Mary, He would eat him. Kind of like someone else in the past sessions. It was big ol' Bear, and it was so good to see Him. Once again, I missed Him so much. But He left as quickly as He came after threatening the guy. We decided to let Mary and this guy spend some time together.

05.07.21: I checked on them today, and he said his name is Harry. I just cracked up—Harry and Mary, of course! I don't make this stuff up. I can't—it's just too good…

15:01: I said, "Does anyone have anything they want to say?" Quinn Michael, my baby girl who was never born. She has been the beautiful young lady who always had the goldenness around her, and I believe she's the sweet giraffe looking out for her dad. She said, "I love you, Daddy!" And said She was excited for me to see Her yesterday.

Restoring the Foundations Ministry—Gaining much insight, especially at a heart level with all of Mom's stuff, her family, but also all the death stuff in Dad's. Wow!

It was strong—the bottom left of my gut was speaking and getting my attention, but then another part (top right) started. I thought that was the pure part; he kept on saying, "I'm you, Mike," and I would say, "Okay. What part of me are you?" And he kept going on and on. We found out that the impure part was actually Sal. Remember Sal? He was the arrogant part that just about completely disappeared when everyone else fell in love with *JESUS*. The last few weeks we'd been calling him and looking for him and thought maybe he got pulled away with Pam. He'd been hiding from everyone because they loved *JESUS* and had changed, and he hadn't.

They were not wrong, but we all need HEaling from it. Then we concentrated on the earliest memory, and that was when it went to little Michael stretching out Sean's blue sailor suit. He is number seven out of nine and not, as Mom always said, as husky as me.

05.27.21: Barbara's Presession Notes

Friday 05.21.21, 08:00: I read the divorce paper at my run circuit and died! Cried and ran…worst day of my life. I'd never hit a floor so deep, so hard.

09:00 I believe I heard "HIM" say, "'I' have heard your Prayers, especially this morning with a pure heart and righteous intentions, and your cries. 'I' will teach you to love Michelle, and 'I' will also teach Michelle to love you well."

11:31 Hopelessness is chasing me down, and I'm getting tired.

11:38 I believe "HE" said "HE" can't resurrect what isn't dead. "Have faith, Mike! Trust 'ME.' You do trust 'ME,' Mike, right?" Yes, I trust "YOU," POPPA. Thank "YOU."

Saturday 05.22.21: Continued worst day of my life, then POPPA spoke to me at around 14:00, "'I' gave you Michelle; no one will take Her from you, not even Her." Went and walked part of the circuit backward (the circuit backward, not me) and thought, *Wow, I've been in the desert more than thirty, even forty days, actually sixty days.* I wondered, *Will it be ninety?*

Sunday 05.23.21: Cate's twenty-third birthday. POPPA speaks, "'I' know you know this, but when the enemy was attacking you, 'I' whispered in your ear yesterday, which was a 'thus saith The LORD' moment..."

Up, down, up, down, down, down, and even farther down and then sometimes up. Then sixty-six days after March 18, when *JESUS* said I was going into the desert without my Spirit, *HE* took him aside, and I went up to HEaven. Today "TM," True Mike, took over, and I don't know how we would have made it without him.

Around Monday or Tuesday, Michelle wrote, "There is nothing you can say or do to make me reconcile with you or not divorce you." I started tightening my gut for that shot, and TM said, "No, we don't react!" Just like when She said to me on the phone, "I never expect to ever see you again," POPPA put "HIS" hand out, stopped the arrow, and said, "Glad 'I' have a better plan." TM has and is saving us, but I don't know... "The Spirit is strong, but the flesh is weak" (Matthew 26:41, NIV). He was helping us not to go where we often have gone before he took over...

05.24.21: My Notes

09:39: 'HE' is telling me (me, my emotions, my mes, feelings, protectors) I'm allowing my Spirit man, True me, T, to run things. There's such peace; he, my Spirit man, is like HOLY SPIRIT. He is not HOLY SPIRIT because I am not GOD, but he is my Spirit from GOD. It's like I'm beginning to be more like JESUS CHRIST every day. I'm not JESUS CHRIST. He's a gentleman and won't take over without permission. It was sixty-six days ago, since 03.18.21, that *JESUS* took my Spirit away and told me I was going into the desert alone; it scared me to the core. Then, almost immediately, *HE* took me up to HEaven for the first time of the take-me-up forty-day fast. I felt something on my lips as soon as I started ascending. I thought it was the coal from the Altar of Heaven. "Then one of the seraphim flew to me, having in his hand a live coal which he had taken with the tongs from the Altar. And he touched my mouth with it, and said: 'Behold, this has touched your lips; Your iniquity is taken away, And your sin purged'" (Isaiah 6:6-7 NKJV).

09:56: HE has an applicant call me. I decide to answer, which I'm beginning to not do often. It is this man, Joseph Ahlzadeh from Persia, not Iran but Persia, and he opens up with words directly from POPPA. I don't remember what he said, but I cried and said, "Do you know those aren't your words?" and said that all came directly from GOD. "You don't know what I'm going through right now." What an amazing man! We talked for twenty minutes. I couldn't help him, except give him a number for watershed. What an absolute Blessing. Thank *YOU*, *JESUS*!

06.03.21: BARBARA'S PRESESSION NOTES

This last weekend I believe "HE" clearly said, "No more jumping through hoops." No explanations!

Yesterday, 07:20, we took a nap, and all had a peaceful talk. Sal shared...I started to say something, and Mary jumped right in, spoke directly to him lovingly, and smiled at me like "are we okay?" Then Frank shared lovingly as well...

Today Harry was mad! It was different. I only comforted him. "It was just not fair" is what he kept saying. I said, "I know; it really isn't, so we just don't know anything, except 'HE' has always been so good to us and always will."

07.08.21: BARBARA'S PRESESSION NOTES

07.05.21

11:00–11:30: I lay down for a nap, and I asked, "Who wants to hang out with me?" Immediately I was back in The Throne in my favorite spot. I was holding onto POPPA's left leg. The Throne was in front of us along with the entire universe. It was absolutely stunning; I saw the Cat's Eye Nebula in all its astonishment. Thank "YOU," POPPA. "YOU" knew that was my favorite. I asked, "What's 'YOUR' favorite?" and "HE" said the whole thing, and I said, "Of course, POPPA." "HE" explained, "Mike, you see myopically, and that's how 'I' designed you. The Cat's Eye Nebula is magnificent; 'I' see it all in as much magnificence. One day, you will use your entire brain, eyes, ears, and Spirit and will see, experience, and hear things like that. I said, "Wow, I'm excited for that day, but very gracious for what 'YOU' have given me." I said, "What's special to 'YOU' right now?" And "HE" said, "You, Mike, just the way 'I' built you and what you just said!" I cried...

Then *JESUS* was on "HIS" right, HOLY SPIRIT (BOB) on "HIS" left, and the entire Throne took off—like I can only imagine what Zeke saw. "And above the firmament over their heads was the likeness of a throne, in appearance like a sapphire stone; on the likeness of the throne was a likeness with the appearance of a man high above it" (Ezekiel 1:26 NKJV).

That was why Quinn Michael could now speak and share more clearly. She couldn't be completely open because of my demonic influence; it always hurt her heart.

I asked her what her favorite part of HEaven was; she said, "Your heart, Daddy," kissed my cheek, said, "I love you, Daddy," and left. Then I woke up. Thank "YOU," POPPA!

15:45–16:15: Another nap. I was taken up again, not quite as dramatic as on 03.18.21 but cool, and Quinn Michael came to see me again. So, so nice—we just chatted. I asked if she thought she would have looked more like Ali or Cate. She said she didn't know but knew she'd look exactly like Quinn Michael. We laughed and agreed; she has a sense of humor like my Cate Mike. Ali has a great sense of humor, but that sounded more like Cate.

I asked her what she thought would have been nice if she had been born. She said graduating HS in Rhinebeck. I asked why, and she said, "That's what both my sisters did." I said maybe things would have been different if she had been born—maybe we wouldn't have divorced; maybe it would have worked out; maybe we wouldn't have moved to Rhinebeck…

I asked her what she thought she would have done after HS, and she said definitely college and an engineer like her Daddy. She said either computer or electrical—definitely electrical…I smiled and asked, "Are you serious?" She said yes and said it probably would have also been with photography.

I told her very intimate, sweet stories of each of the girls, and Quinn Mike really enjoyed hearing all this. It was so comforting to talk intimately with someone, and here it was, the first time ever, and it was with my daughter in HEaven. Thank "YOU," POPPA.

She also said how she enjoyed watching me play golf and how very proud of me she was for running the Triozathon. She said she was right there with me; I just didn't know it. She hugged and kissed me, and then suddenly she left, but I could hear her say, "Bye, Daddy. I love you, Daddy." It moved my heart to be called Daddy and to hear "I love you, Daddy," even just to hear "I love you" right now…"HE" and she knew how much I needed that…thank "YOU," POPPA, and thank you, Quinn Michael. I love and miss you soooo. Thank you for spending so much time with me today; you filled my heart overfull.

07.08.21

10:15: While running, Quinn Michael joined me just before the north power lines. I said, "If you need to stop, we can stop." Then she said, "Can we?" I said, "Are you joshing?" (she's a Spirit); she said no. When we stopped, she asked for a hug, and my heart melted!

I asked her what was her saddest memory of earth, and she said when her heart stopped. I cried and cried and cried!

She asked what my saddest memory was. I said March 16, 2021, when Michelle told me She was divorcing me, and the day I was served. She didn't feel my pain then because she wasn't in my heart then; she said she was kind of glad because it probably would have torn her apart.

Then she asked my happiest in recent years, and I said, "First my Triozathon, then Restoring the Foundations Ministry."

She said she was very thankful that I did the masonic Prayer today. She let me know that they were mounting up and had been setting a major battle against me and to be prepared, "but you're ready, Daddy." We ran together and had such a great time.

My right knee started hurting bad; she kneeled, laid hands on it, and Prayed, and it felt better! Hallelujah, *JESUS*. My daughter Quinn Michael laid hands on me and HEaled my right knee in *YOUR* Name. What's better than that?

12:55: I think I heard Quinn Michael say, "I'm going to have to start talking to my stepmom. You know I can have the same relationship with her as you, if not better! Keep Praying, Daddy."

06.30.21: My Second-Year Spiritual Birthday

06:15: I felt and heard a word of discouragement, so I took it captive. "For the weapons of our warfare are not carnal but mighty in God for pulling down strongholds, casting down arguments and every high thing that exalts itself against the knowledge of God, bringing every thought into captivity to the obedience of Christ" (2 Corinthians 10:4–5, NKJV). But then asked if everyone was okay. I didn't hear anything, so I asked Mary, and she said, "We're okay—just trying to figure this new life out." I said, "Thank you, and yes, we're all doing that." I thanked them all and told them how proud I was of everyone. I especially thanked Frank, Gary, and Harry for not getting upset with an applicant yesterday. I told Sal that I was really proud of him. I praised True Mike and let him know that there was no way we would be here without him. Then I thanked Bobby and congratulated both for a job so well done.

07.06.21, 04:44: My Notes

19:51: Quinn Michael reminded me how excited she was that there were no demons oppressing me, and, therefore, I was 100 percent *JESUS*, POPPA, HOLY SPIRIT's and Hers! "And God will wipe away every tear from their eyes; there shall be no more death, nor sorrow, nor crying. There shall be no more pain, for the former things have passed away" (Revelation 21:4, NKJV). She was so lonely, not sad because there were no tears in HEaven. She was with both Her grandmas and Pop Pop and not at all with her mom or two sisters.

One of my Restoring the Foundations Ministry Prayers is to take my fixations and obsession off of Michelle. That is taking a tremendous amount of anxiety from me. It's all part of "casting down arguments and every high thing that exalts itself against the knowledge of God, bringing every thought into captivity to the obedience of Christ" (2 Corinthians 10:5, NKJV).

Post-Session Notes

We went into the session, and, boy, did I need it. I immediately felt something, and here came this huge dude. I mean, a lot bigger than anyone else. He looked like the cartoon character Genie in *Aladdin* but real! And he was mad! He fingered me in the chest. I said, "I'll respect you, but if you do that again, there's going to be trouble!" He was very upset about purity, and I asked him if he was part of me. I already knew the answer...I acknowledged him and his feelings, and he just shot right down to a normal-sized guy. It was amazing! I mean, the guy was a hundred times bigger than anyone else. I was kind to him, and there was a 180-degree shift. He didn't like the idea of me going hard on him about the whole purity thing, but it turned out that he was my creative part. The reason he came out now was that CD artwork I was making for Michelle's birthday. He was the one behind a drawing of the broken heart I gave Michelle on our first CHRISTmas...it was so good to meet him. I said, "You don't have to worry about getting thrown out. I love you!" He appreciated that so much. It was so rewarding to meet him after how bad the beginning of the meeting went. He said his name was Joel.

What was happening was he was so enamored by Michelle's beauty in a creative and artistic way, but Sal and Harry would fixate on the physical part of Her beauty. He was the creative part of me, and we were now working together well.

07.15.21, 13:00: I lie down for a nap, and there I am with The Three of THEM, and WE're admiring the cosmos, and I think Mark would Love this, so I invite him. Boy, does he love it. He sits down in Quinn's place, and I say, "I don't mean to be controlling, but that's Quinn's place." POPPA says, "Some people may think that's controlling, Mike, but you have such fondness and admiration for that little lady, that 'I' think it's okay!" Who am I? Now Quinn wasn't in her place until POPPA said this, and then there she was. At what time do you think I'm writing this? It's 4:44! Well, Mark sits next to Quinn, and I'm thinking, *I should probably see if anyone else wants to join us*, and of course, they all jump at the offer. Frank jumps on POPPA's lap like a little kid, and he's not a kid. Gary jumps on JESUS' lap, same as above. Mary so gently and kindly sits on HOLY SPIRIT's lap. Bobbie, of course, sits on HOLY SPIRIT's lap. I'm hearing or sensing The LOVing, gentle, kind HEart of HOLY SPIRIT. Sal jumps on POPPA's lap. Harry looks disappointed, and I say, "HE's GOD; there's plenty of room on POPPA's lap—go ahead!" T sits on JESUS' lap. We're all looking in amazement, and I ask Mark, since he's the newest, what really captures him, and he said, "Mike, I know the Cat's Eye Nebula because you are so fond of it. That's my fav, and it's astonishing to see it for myself and especially from HEaven!" Then I ask Harry, since he's the next newest, and he says, "A black hole." Suddenly, we're all on a field trip to a black hole; it's crazy! I'm wondering as we get closer, "Are we going to get sucked in?" And POPPA said, "You would if you were in a ship, but not with US." So we go in, and it's amazing, but then I get bombarded by bad thoughts, and I have to battle, and battle I do. At first it is sad because we are all having such fun, but now I'm hearing I did good; that's most important. "When the enemy comes, take him out!" is what I just heard POPPA say! "That's 'MY' Royal Warrior King, Mike!" Who am I?

07.29.21: Barbara's Presession Notes

07.26.21, 05:20

07:20: My dad, in the Spirit, told me about the tough, tough times ahead, "But Mom, Norman, Brien, Quinn Michael, Ralph, Derek, and I are Praying for you! Also, Grammi knows you're a good man and interceding for the right thing with Joan. You're ready!" He reminded me of when he was a kid in the 1920s with his homing pigeons and shoeshine kit, which I have now, and my Pop Pop's AA baseball games with Mor Mor.

07.27.21

"HE" says, "You deserve it, Mike, and you did the hard work. You broke shame, rejection, and insecurity."

08.31.21: Barbara's Presession Notes

Dr. Cantor. The brain mapping was gloomy! I used the word, and he agreed and repeated it.

When we started, Barbara was saying how proud she was that my parts seemed to really be trusting me and getting along. She said all my parts were getting along, agreeing, and thanking each other and me. It was such a good confirmation.

Then I started feeling someone on the right side of my gut. But everyone was there, and it was very comfortable. I waited, and it was a young blonde girl. She came right out, no manifesting, no trouble. Barbara and I believed it was because I didn't have the demonic oppression causing trouble and blowing up at me...She came out quietly. I was gentle. She had this beautiful horse with her, and she was hiding behind it. I said hi and started walking toward the bench on the run circuit as usual. She came right over quietly with her horse. She was a part of me that missed, longed, and yearned for Cate, Ali, and Michelle. There weren't any females for us to communicate with—no personal female, no sisters, moms, aunts, friends. She started wailing and crying at the bowels of her soul, and I joined her. She was so sweet and hurt and so very alone...her name was Jane—it was so sad...she (Jane) said, "I'm so hyper guarded about communicating with women," and it's not right; she gets no female interface at all.

Barbara asked if she was depression, but she said, "No, that's a big dude," so we left that there... then Barbara said she'd come up a few times before and that she was going to have to speak with the religious part of me, but she got scared. I comforted her, and she felt better—then he was there. She and I were on the bench, and he was across the way dressed in full armor! She started speaking lovingly to him, so I just backed off; it was so cool. I sat back and watched her talk kindly, lovingly, and directly to him. She said, "It's okay; you're safe here. You have nothing to be afraid of or on guard about." I reassured him, and he sat down, put his sword and shield down, and took off his armor. There was no hoopla, just like her, no manifesting, blowing up, or anything. Wow, that was so different; he wasn't even huge! She continued speaking with him, sharing her heart about needing some woman just to talk to. She said, "I know we've been hurt by so many women," and she was sorry for all the hurts. We were not insecure, rejected, or messed up—at least not as much as we were—and she smiled. He got comfortable with her and agreed. "Maybe you don't have to be so rigid, overly protective, and isolating with all women." I think he got it; his heart started melting, and I believe he felt loved and began letting down his guard.

Then, another guy came, and he was the overly protective, pure guy. He wasn't as strong and intimidating as the religious guy but equally as religious. His name was Paul, and the other was Peter; they talked and then spoke with Jane. It was so cool to have the parts handle the entire thing. They all agreed that Peter was to relax and both would only protect us from a woman who was trying to harm us physically and emotionally. They both were to love with POPPA's *Love* (Agape *Love*) and not be overly protective.

10.07.21: Barbara's Presession Notes

I spoke with both girls, and it was so nice—sad but so nice.

I felt a huge tightness in my gut; it was getting tighter and tighter. They came out, and I saw this blonde running to the right, down the hill of the circuit and into the woods. There was a big guy right behind her, and he went to the left. She wouldn't come out, and he wouldn't say a word! She eventually came out, but I couldn't see her at all, except her hair, and she was not speaking. I asked Mary and Bobby to hang with her, and there was Bear; it was so very good to see him. I cried and cried, like always—I just love that guy! He came out and knew both of them but stood next to him. The guy started talking and said his name was Bob. I said, "Wait a minute. We have BOB (HOLY SPIRIT), and I still don't know if Bear is HOLY SPIRIT, a manifestation of HIM, or what." But this guy said it was Bob, and he got along well with Bear! The girl smiled and said she loved Bear also, and her name was Helen (we all smiled because it sounded like Heaven; I don't know; it did—maybe it was one of those "you had to be there"). We found out that Bob was hurt and a bit upset with Michelle. Helen was a major fan of Michelle, and that was why they didn't get along. He shared kindly how Michelle hurt his feelings by saying our sin was worse than Her sin. I listened to him, nodded in acknowledgment, and told him I understood and appreciated his vulnerability and honesty. Then I asked her what her feelings were, and she explained very elegantly how Michelle sinned against us as much as we sinned against her. She explained it was our deep-seated narcissism and spirits of death and dumb that were the destructive root and the ultimate cause of the failed Marriage. We listened well and acknowledged her. I asked Bob if he remembered that, and he said yes. He wanted to be heard and allowed to share. Everyone was feeling loved, appreciated, and heard. We all enjoyed the intimacy that we were feeling. I started crying thinking that I was (we were) beginning to feel and appreciate intimacy and how it may be too late for us to share and feel this way toward and with Michelle sadly.

This was amazing. Bob started feeling so overwhelmed by the love and intimacy that he started manifesting, and the religious spirit got broken out of him. Hallelujah! He was the one who harbored this spirit, and suddenly this huge ship chain and anchor—I mean huge—fell to the ground and off of all of us. Hallelujah! It was huge and weighed a ton! We were all feeling weightless. Bear reached over and threw it into the lake of fire in the Name of *JESUS CHRIST*. We all basked in this new freedom in *CHRIST* from the religious spirit in *Love*. Helen waved goodbye and left. Barbara said she was a messenger, and suddenly Bear came over and hugged me, and He left. I was so excited to have been broken of the religious spirit. Thank *YOU*, *JESUS*, and Hallelujah!

Then the most amazing thing happened—THEY gave me back my Spirit! After 203 days since 03.18.21, two days after Michelle told me I was going to be served, She told me on the 16th, ten minutes before my session with Barbara. I just cried and cried through the entire session. The 18th is when THEY sent me into the desert without my Spirit. Hallelujah, the desert was in Heaven! I had forgotten I hadn't had my Spirit since then, and POPPA said, "'I' didn't want to remind you, Mike." Then THEY gave me back my crown, sword, shield, robe, ring, and sandals, which was absolutely amazing. Then THEY gave me my "belt of truth" and "beastplate of righteousness."

Finally, my brethren, be strong in the Lord and in the power of His might. Put on the whole armor of God, that you may be able to stand against the wiles of the devil. For we do not wrestle against flesh and blood, but against principalities, against powers, against the rulers of the darkness of this age, against spiritual hosts of wickedness in the heavenly places. Therefore take up the whole armor of God, that you may be able to withstand in the evil day, and having done all, to stand. Stand therefore, having girded your waist with truth, having put on the breastplate of righteousness, and having shod your feet with the preparation of the gospel of peace; above all, taking the shield of faith with which you will be able to quench all the fiery darts of the wicked one. And take the helmet of salvation, and the sword of the Spirit, which is the word of God.

Eph 6:10-17 NIV

Now I had my entire armor of GOD! What's better than that? Thank YOU, LORD *JESUS*, POPPA, and HOLY SPIRIT!

Then Mike A. (the Archangel) came. Boy, had I missed Him. He gave me a great big hug and was looking at me like He used to, at the table of the feast and The Throne. Then, He completely blew me away by giving me His sword. I said, "No, I can't..." He said, "Yes, Mike, you're ready to wield two swords, and it's My honor for you to have My sword. I see how much you love Me and GOD." This was the beginning of my baptism of royalty ...

Then, POPPA took my sword, and Mike took His. POPPA was on the right, and Mike on the left and ordained me with the swords...I heard ordination, graduation, and Marriage...

Ordained into HEavenly royalty. Graduation into Kingship.

Marriage of my Spirit and me.

While all this was going on, I saw Michelle, Ali, and Cate looking on, and they were so excited and honored for me. I also saw my mom and dad, Kathy and Mike, and Michelle's mom and dad. Then Michelle gave me an amazing hug. I could actually feel Her, and She kissed me. POPPA gave me an "eternal Ancient of Days hug," and I couldn't remember Michelle's hug anymore, and "HE" said, "That's right, Mike. I know you love Her and should; 'I' gave Her to you, but remember! No more worshipping Her, anyone, or anything!" "HE" was deadly serious. I'm trembling now about it. But "HE" was soo loving...

Then *JESUS* and HOLY SPIRIT gave me a huge hug, and Bear came running back for another hug too!

Then satan came. I wasn't scared; I was more annoyed. I looked up at POPPA, and "HE" nodded, so I knew it was all right. I told him he wasn't welcome and had to leave now in the Name of *JESUS CHRIST*. He went into the lake of fire and took back his big old ship chain and religious spirit. I shouted at him, "It's not coming back in the Name of *JESUS CHRIST*," and he left...

Michelle grabbed my hand and held it so lovingly...then She was on my left. I was at the head of a huge banquet table. Cate was to my right, and Ali was on Michelle's left; at the other end was POPPA, *JESUS* on "HIS" left, HOLY SPIRIT to "HIS" right, and Mike A. to *JESUS'* left. Then the entire Heavenly and earthy family were on the sides of the table. I had a huge prime rib, a big old ham steak, baked macaroni, mashed potatoes, and asparagus. I was finally eating starch! Heavenly starch, which is different than earthy starch! Thank *YOU, JESUS*. Then there was a huge slice of pumpkin pie with Heavenly whipped cream! I felt so loved, honored, cared for, and at peace.

This was like one of the old sessions! Thank "YOU," POPPA. "YOU" always know what I need and what's best for me.

Then we tapped the breaking of the religious spirit in before we closed the session.

Chapter 6

My Green Royce Union Stingray

We went into the session, and I really had peace. Something started on the lower part of my gut like never before; it wasn't strong but definitely there. I waited, and I was on the corner of Irene Street and Central Ave in South Hempstead, Long Island, New York (the house I was born in and lived until around 1979). Where I grew up and spent the first sixteen years of my life.

I was standing on the corner looking around, still at peace. Here I came on my green Royce Union Stingray with the white banana seat at probably ten years old, and it was summertime.

Me with my green Royce Union Stingray that I turned into a chopper by cutting forks off of three other bikes and sliding them over mine. Then I bolted them so they wouldn't fall off. Especially when I pulled a wheelie or rode off a ramp. That's what we did in the late 1960s and early 1970s.

I was coming down from Maude Street racing to pass the house and skid on the tar spot in front to the south of the Emo Cacedo's house (my next-door neighbor to the south). He didn't even see me; he was just having fun without a care in the world. I would do that over and over and over for days and laugh just as much the 10,000th time as the first. It would make this cool rubber on tar skid leaving a mark and making a loud skidding noise!

Then here I came. It was wintertime, and I was probably twelve, and I was *skitching* up Irene Street (this is when you grab the bumper of a car—usually the driver didn't know—and you ski without skis) toward Grand Ave. This was what you did in the '60s and '70s. For some reason we almost never went the other way; maybe we didn't want to pass the side of the house. I would think it was easier for Mom and Dad to see out the front door, but who am I? I, of course, wore my cowboy boots because they worked best. I'd freeze my toes off because they were too small for me, but I loved them and wore them all through high school and junior high, from about sixth grade. Maybe even into college! Maybe that was why I had such small feet, like the old-world Chinese girls who had their feet bound. Once again he didn't see me there.

Now here we came sailing west on Irene Street in the blue plastic boat after one of probably a half dozen golf-ball-sized hailstorms that hit the area as kids. We were having a blast, and they didn't even see me. I was just standing there enjoying the fond memories and being, as Barbara always wants me to be, inquisitive…

Then, all of a sudden, the memories became darker and more sinful. No shame, no condemnation or conviction, just the listings of my sins there in South Hempstead. Like *JESUS* was just lovingly showing me all my sins, one after another, not holding them against me…this went on and on until we were in Upstate New York…here I was in twelfth grade (Upstate New York) through fourteenth grade in liberal arts at a local community college until 1983 then back to Long Island to SUNY (State University of New York) Farmingdale (1983 to 1987 electrical—I started aerospace [that's why Farmingdale instead of Temple University in South Philly, Pennsylvania], but I switched during my second semester to electrical). *HE* was doing the same thing. Now I'm realizing *HE* was taking them from me. Once again, I was not feeling any shame, condemnation, or even conviction…it was the oddest thing…repeatedly everything I'd done wrong—all my sin…gone…not the fond, good parts of memories themselves, just the sin, pain, and heartbreak…

Then, it was my life after the first divorce; that was a huge pile of sin—more and more and more sorrow on my part for all the sin… That was when I met *JESUS* and thought I was saved but sure didn't act like it. So, so sad. All the people I've murdered emotionally and verbally…so, so sad…

Then, I met Michelle, and, boy, did I feel the sorrow for all the sin and pain I caused Her, my beautiful butterfly. I realized not only was *HE* taking them from me but HEaling me of all the negative emotions, taking all the sorrow and pain, and I was seeing HOLY SPIRIT with *HIM*. THEY were lovingly removing all the negative emotions and letting me know that I'd already repented of them all and had been forgiven. Now THEY were taking the negative emotions, pain, and scares and removing them as far as the east is from the west... "As far as the east is from the west, So far has HE removed our transgressions from us" (Psalm 103:12, NKJV).

I remember that I did my Prayers to break the curse of Catholicism yesterday and today at 14:06. I Prayed to unmask and break freemasonry from my life. Today, I begged for a pure heart and clean hands ("The one who has clean hands and a pure heart, who does not trust in an idol or swear by a false god" [Psalm 24:4, NIV]), and here were *JESUS* and HOLY SPIRIT removing the filth and stains sin left on me after I repented of it. During my Prayer today, I could feel HOLY SPIRIT or angels or someone actually cleaning, scrubbing all of my organs. It was the wildest thing (I didn't even realize it); there was someone inside me, cleaning all of my organs when I was reading the Prayer unmasking freemasonry. There was some slight manifesting in the lower part of the upper gut with the higher orders of freemasonry. Toward the end of the Prayers, I could feel Spiritually all my organs being cleaned, all through my torso, especially my heart, stomach, and lungs.

Then I could feel my legs and feet being cleaned, but then each of my toes meticulously being cleaned. Hallelujah. After that, my arms, hands, and fingers, followed by my brain, head, throat, neck, nose, ears, and eyes. They were being scrubbed clean of all demonic and false GODly filth. I could feel POPPA give me clean hands and a pure heart in the Mighty Name of *JESUS CHRIST*. Amen and hallelujah. Thank "YOU," POPPA. Now, here I was, just two hours later, having the inside of all of me scrubbed again of the filth.

You just can't make this stuff up... Every session THEY blow me away...

I was explaining all this to Barbara, and I thought we should probably Pray to make sure we filled this clean home with HOLY SPIRIT, and we continued talking.

> *When an unclean spirit goes out of a man, he goes through dry places, seeking rest, and finds none. Then he says, "I will return to my house from which I came." And when he comes, he finds it empty, swept, and put in order. Then he goes and takes with him seven other spirits more wicked than himself, and they enter and dwell there; and the last state of that man is worse than the first. So shall it also be with this wicked generation.*

> Matt 12:43-45 NKJV

She reminded me that she said in the beginning to make sure I opened all the way up, open my chest and heart completely, open my hands to receive fully...

"Search me, O GOD, and know my heart; Try me, and know my anxieties; And see if there is any wicked way in me, And lead me in the way everlasting" (Psalm 139:23–24, NKJV).

I was explaining all of this and realized it was like I was telling someone else's story; there was no pain or sorrow, no negative emotions, no sin, no condemnation or guilt. "HE" had taken it all away from me…I remembered it all, but it felt as if I was talking about last night's dinner. There was no sorrow or anguish for all the pain and sin, no condemnation or guilt. Thank "YOU," POPPA.

Then Barbara said, "What about Prayer?" and I was immediately back into it with *JESUS* and HOLY SPIRIT. THEY were filling me up with the fruit of the Spirit. I was watching and feeling THEM fill me up with liquid fruit of the Spirit, my feet, ankles, up to my knees, and it kept going, my waist, belly, and suddenly it got to my chest. THEY said, "It's going to take a while to fill that big beautiful new heart of yours, so just be patient," and, sure enough, it took longer to fill my new heart than the rest of my entire body…then the heart was full, and the level started heading up my neck and throat, past my mouth, and then I could see it filling my eyes; it was the coolest thing. Liquid fruit of the Spirit was filling my eyes, and I could see it just begin, halfway, then full, like little waves, as THEY poured it in and filled me up. Then the rest of my head, and as soon as it hit the top, my ears popped. Like I said, you just can't make this stuff up. Thank *YOU, JESUS*. I was afraid it would flow out my ears or nose, but, of course, THEY had it covered, and it sealed my ears, causing them to pop numerous times…the entire time I was hearing, "Love, joy, peace, patience, gentleness, kindness, goodness and self-control…" Over and over again.

I heard, "Liquid *love*…"

I asked, "How many fruits are there?" And we don't really spend time on it because it is just so absolutely amazing…

After we hung up, I checked, and there were, of course, nine fruits, I think, *Man I missed faithfulness. How come faithfulness was forgotten?* And immediately POPPA said, "You didn't miss or forget faithfulness. You were already full of faithfulness. WE didn't have to fill you with it, Mike." I was just crying and crying… "But the HOLY SPIRIT produces this kind of fruit in our lives: love, joy, peace, patience, kindness, goodness, faithfulness, gentleness, and self-control" (Galatians 5:22–23, NLT).

How and why do "YOU" keep doing this to me, POPPA?

11.04.21: Barbara's Presession Notes

I'm doing better but still sad, sometimes dark. I'm allowing myself to stay there a bit, even shared with *JESUS* while I worked with *HIM* building my new table in the garage. Which reminded me of *HIM* in the movie *The Passion of Christ* when *HE* built a table!

I shared my regret of having the vasectomy, being all alone…just comforted my heart and soul…

The demon was still there, and Barbara said, "We will have to deal with it," so I tried to talk with it, and it seemed to be afraid or keenly aware of my authority or something. She said to ask *JESUS* to deal with the demon, and, of course, *HE* was right there…I looked at *HIM*, and *HE* was shining *HIMself* and everything around *HIM*, *Glory*. *HE* didn't even look at the demon and was just smiling at me. I asked, "Do I need to do anything?" And *HE* said no…*HE* came up to me and started ministering to my heart and soul for these losses, and still all that was going on, just deeper and deeper ministry, oh my… Then there was Ali. She was so sweet, LORD; that was my Ali…I could only imagine what she went through and still has to be carrying. Then there was my amazing Michelle. I didn't know if She went through this or what, but there She was in all Her absolute beauty… Then *JESUS* started ministering to Ali's heart, and Michelle held my hand, and I just melted…*HE* was loving on my Ali and HEaling her…I was holding Ali's hand and Michelle's hand, and *JESUS* was just loving on Ali… then *HE* started ministering to Michelle's heart. Boy, was that incredible to see—*HIM* loving on Her. Suddenly *JESUS* was behind Ali, just hugging her; HOLY SPIRIT came behind Michelle, and POPPA was behind me—it was a big individual but group hug! Then we, the three of us, started dancing a Davidic dance, and the three of THEM were dancing in a circle behind us!

Then here came Catie! I was holding Ali's hand. Cate came between Michelle and me and started holding both of my girl's hands. Wow, the four of us together. That hadn't happened since CHRISTmas 2015… Then *JESUS* started ministering to Catie's heart. *HE* was HEaling the four of us…then Cate started talking with Michelle, and I was not holding their hands anymore. Then Ali started, and they looked like they were apologizing and making good… Suddenly, I heard a noise in the physical outside, and I felt like I got shot right in the forehead. Michelle and the girls were still talking and loving on each other, and I was shot…I didn't know what to do, so I said something to Barbara, and she didn't know…I was back in it, and I was dead. Michelle and the girls were still together but different now, and I was laid out dead…they looked like they were getting ready for my funeral or something; it was very odd…I talked to Barbara and explained about Michelle's dream or vision of my being taken away and my signaling "I love You," pointing to me, pointing to my heart, pointing to Her. About the girl in Columbine—how she couldn't see herself in college or the rest of her life… It was odd. I wasn't scared but feeling odd. I went back, and it was the same, and now there was something in front of me, like a spirit, but not a demon or death, but I was thinking it was death…I was tracking with it toward the left, and it kind of disappeared, and I called out to *JESUS*, and then everything kind of went dark, not black black but more like the universe, with some light, but not bright. I called out to *JESUS* and nothing…I didn't know what to do, so I asked Barbara. I felt better when she thought maybe it just meant that Michelle and the girls would be there together with me when I died…that helped my soul…

11.30.21: Barbara's Presession Notes

I'm an ordained minister and have my first financial partner.

12.16.21: Barbara's Presession Notes

We did something different today, something like ideal parents. She had me relax and think as early as I could remember in a peaceful place. I immediately went to the little house by the fire at around five years old with my bare feet on the warm, smooth, hot rocks. I could smell the fire and the fresh-cut grass and hear occasionally a car drive by and Rufus barking. Rufus was our German shepherd/Doberman mixed dog. It was really peaceful, and I could feel it in my core. The road above the yard (around thirty feet), then the ravine (around thirty) down to the water/wood. She had me stay there for a bit.

Then she asked something like what it would be like and where I would be if I could be anywhere at five. I really felt that I was there! No place better than at the little house in the summer at the fire! The little house basically was a shack in the Catskill Mountains in New York State; it was about 150 miles north of South Hempstead, Long Island, New York. We, at least four or five kids, would pile in the 1970s station wagon and drive up at least once a year. Then she asked me what the ideal parents would be like, and I could see they were young, around twenty-five to thirty. Mom had blonde hair, and Dad was strong and handsome. They were young enough to play with me big time, chase me around, and take me on hikes. Then we were at the fire, and I was lying on Mom's lap; she was hugging and holding me so tightly, firmly, and lovingly. I could smell her, and she smelled incredible between her perfume, her hair, and her skin. I was just lying there, and she was loving on me and filling me with love. I had my legs on Dad's strong legs, and he held them in his powerful, loving arm. I thought for a second that it would be nice to have my feet on the warm rocks, and he suddenly wrapped them up in a blanket and held me tight. It was so cool.

They both just gave me 100 percent of their attention and adoration and doated over me. Mom was so pretty and nurtured me, and so did Dad. I could see we had a bullmastiff. I was only around five, and he was huge; he was fawn with a black muzzle, of course. They just kept loving me and loving me! My tank was so full; it kind of reminded me of how I felt loving the girls. I was not saying I did it well, but I sure did love helping Ali learn to ride her bike and roller skate and playing in the snow and leaves, the beach...then Catie riding that bike the first time on the Harlem Valley Rail Trail to Millerton and back, playing in the snow and leaves, Sims, and Barbies, baking, and cooking...

It was all such an awesome place to be, such peace, love, and comfort. I thought about how much I missed Michelle but thought about how much Richard and Dustin were loving and pouring into

     Caveman to Priest

me and how much the guys, Wesley, Coby, John, Gee, Joel, Tony, Robbie, Dean, Daniel, Andrew, Andrew, Jonathon...were loving on me, wanting me to mentor and love on them. How I was HEaling, and now instead of just needing and needing Ben and Dustin, I was beginning to pour out and be there for them...

She reminded me of how these parents gave me approval, acceptance, attention, and affection. I remembered Mom and Dad did, but they weren't young and had so many of us, but they did a great job. I remember at least a few times just Dad and I having a baseball and football catch, working in the woodshop. When he, Sean, Terrance, and I flew the kite! Mom loved on me well, rubbing my back when it was so sore as an early teen, getting me that green Schwinn ten-speed bike when they didn't have the money.

She now let all this marinate for the next two weeks. I was very excited to hear this because I didn't get much time with my parts anymore. They really seemed to be HEaled and at peace.

12.30.21: Barbara's Presession Notes

We chatted a bit about my excellent day yesterday, CHRISTmas, and my best gift, the call from Michelle.

Barbara wanted to go back to the earliest experience and check in. We went back to pre-birth Mike; it was so good to see him, but I kind of overwhelmed him. I backed up and said, "Great to see you" and waited. He remembered me and said he was okay, but he was very lonely...I listened, let him speak; he said the enemy left, and there had been no more tormenting, but he'd been lonely—there'd been no one to speak with. I acknowledged that it must have been tough and asked him if he wanted to talk. I just loved the idea and spending time together, and we immediately hit it off again. Then Barbara asked, "Has he ever heard Mom's heart?" I believed he wasn't in the womb anymore because we had that birth experience, but he wasn't post-birth Mike either, so it was an in-between state. He wasn't being tormented but not really in the womb either...he wasn't really birthed but sort of; post-birth Mike met *JESUS* and got HEaling with Mom and Dad, and he watched it happen but was in a limbo state...

So Barbara said to have him go back in the womb—I'm thinking of Nicodemus (Nicodemus said to Him, "How can a man be born when he is old? Can he enter a second time into his mother's womb and be born?" [John 3:4, NKJV])—and see if he could hear Mom's heart. Sure enough, there he was, being HEaled, and he smiled hearing Mom's heart. The enemy wouldn't allow him to hear it or anything else. All he could hear was Mom saying how exciting it was going to be to hopefully have a girl this time and the torment from the enemy. He could now actually hear and feel Mom's heartbeat and her talking and Praying with and for him. This was so, so good; he was beaming; he could feel Mom touching him from outside, as well as all the boys and Dad! The fluid around him was so warm, and he was floating and being loved on like never before. We just loved it and soaked it in. He felt loved for the first time. He saw post-birth Mike being loved, but unfortunately, he had never felt it until now! Wow, could he feel it and Mom and Dad talking, singing, Praying with and for him was unbelievable...so we sat there and took it all in, and Barbara said to tap it in, which we did, butterfly taps, and I could feel them tapping the love directly into my heart! "Tap it in" is a phrase from EMDR. You either do eye movement, tap your arms in a butterfly position, or do something that has a right-left movement.

Then Barbara said, "Let's have him birthed," and I could immediately feel him tense up—like "I've been in hell for around fifty-eight years, now at peace, and she wants me out?" It was kind of funny, and I didn't know how to tell her that, so we just went along; it was so funny. It was kind of like the operation after post-birth Mike had to face and if I asked him to face it again! As always, she was right on; he came out and met Mom. I could feel her holding me, hugging me, and kissing me and caressing me; she kept telling me how much she loved me. Then Dad came in, and he was holding my feet and rubbing them and my legs, arms, and hands. I could feel the sense of touch and love. We needed this so, so much... Then Dad grabbed me; he held me out so he could see me but realized I needed to be held close and hugged, and he did...he kept kissing me and hugging me, and now Mom was rubbing me, and they were both telling me how beautiful I was and how glad they were to see me. The boys were so excited to see me and hugged and loved on me...it kept reminding me of me holding each of the girls and loving on them—so sweet! Then she had me meet post-birth Mike. He was sort of stuck in that world as well; he met *JESUS* and was HEaled with Mom and Dad but was so happy to see me (pre-birth Mike), and the two of them were HEaled and whole. What a beautiful, kind session— both of my earliest mes felt Mom and Dad love on us, and *JESUS* HEaled both of them and put them together with and for each other and me. We tapped this in...

Then Barbara wanted us to meet two-year-old Mike—there he was in Sean's little blue too-small outfit with Bridgette (she is my oldest niece; she's nine months younger than me and my oldest sister Eileen's daughter) and Sean on the chair in the back yard in South Hempstead. He was so happy, joy-filled, and secure! He knew he was loved by everyone...he always had a huge smile on his face; he was chubby, or as Mom would always say, even when I was fifty, "Not chubby, husky," and we would laugh so hard together! He was walking and crawling in the grass. I could feel the grass; it was so tactile; all the feelings were so vivid, and Mom and Dad were there loving on me. Dad picked me up and threw me in the air, and I was screaming with laughter, and there was Mom. So we tapped this in, and it was fun! Once again, now pre-birth, post-birth, and two-year-old Mike became HEaled and whole; it was just incredible...

Then Barbara said, "How can we make sure you keep in touch with them all?" And they all ran up and hugged me and let me hug on each of them. I was holding them all, but especially two-year-old Mike, against me, and his little arms were wrapped around me, hugging me. He was so much wiser than his age; he told me how much I needed him, and he was the innocent one that I wanted to be. He said, "Don't look ahead—this is innocence; let's stay here for a while, and we'll deal with the others later." Then I believe The LORD showed me a beautiful pre-plowed field; it was the richest dirt and no rocks at all. This was life for pre-birth Mike, post-birth Mike, and two-year-old Mike. A gorgeous field that was going to have a wonderful harvest soon! She had me tap this in as well, and there was so, so very much peace and love!

This was a most wonderful way of ending 2021; it'd been such an excruciatingly difficult and euphoric year, and now I had such HEaling in my heart and the first two or three years of my life. Thank *YOU*, *JESUS*, for another so Godly session...

01.13.22: BARBARA'S PRESESSION NOTES

Day five of a twenty-one-day liquid fast (drinking only liquid).

I felt great after sharing and getting it all off my chest. Then the dogs next door started barking (hollowing)...so I started feeling something intense in my head, but it stopped when I shared about the dogs. I felt something around my feet, ankles, and lower shins, like what I felt and saw when I received deliverance back in March 2015 in PTC (Peachtree City, Georgia). I asked it to give me space, which it did, and it flew out of me. I could see a little girl and maybe a boy toward my right, maybe even on bicycles. They were right there with me; there were woods behind them with a path and a white house in a clearing on the other side of the path. I wasn't sure if they were a part, a me, or a demon, but I believed it was a demon. The house was big and looked nice from where I was, but as I approached, it became very dumpy, abandoned, and broken down. So I approached with caution and was curious (as Barbara always wants). It was dilapidated, and I was not going to stand on that porch. I stood there looking around and knew he was inside. I saw a firepit and chairs over to my right, so I decided to start a fire and sit. Suddenly the place cleaned up right in front of my face; it was beautiful and pristine. I could see a heavy-set grandma walking past the screen door like she was serving dinner, so I felt a bit more comfortable about approaching the door but was still hesitant in my Spirit, as well as in the physical with that porch. I Prayed about it and decided to go up to the door. I didn't think anyone let me in, but I felt it was appropriate to enter after saying hello, and there was the creature. He was big, black, and clearly a demon in the room on the left, which was the dining room. I approached him and said, "It's okay. I'd like to talk." He didn't say anything, so I waited...then I asked him, "Are you a part of me?" Still nothing, but he was warming up to me. An angel came out of nowhere and wielded his sword, and the dude freaked out and left the room. He headed for the living room. I said to the angel, "It's okay," and it turned out to be Mike A. I said thank You. I said, "I believe it's okay. I want to try and communicate with him. Please stay here, and if I need You, You'll know." I went out to the living room and asked him again if we could talk. I said, "I'm not here to hurt or rebuke you. I want to know who you are and what I need to learn from you." He opened up to me because I believe he felt comfortable. Then he started morphing into more of a man-like being and reminded me how much I'd been cursed by two of my roommates. There had been a lot of Spiritual cursing directed at me. Even some bad thoughts and feelings from a third...basically all three of the guys I lived with... he was a part of me, so I guessed not a demon, and he was troubled by all of that. I guessed it was originally demonically oppressed, but Mike A. rattled him so deeply, and when I approached him in love, in my authority in *JESUS*, the demon left. Thank *YOU*, *JESUS*, and my man, Mike A. He was very troubled by the Spiritual attacks, and he started thinking about finances and really wigging out about all of it. He'd been worried about all the Spiritual attacks that we'd been under for decades, especially all of it from Joan and others in New York, as well as here in Georgia, from the infection in my tooth and the attack on my feet. I believe The LORD clearly told me the attack on the feet was the enemy trying to trip me up. He was attacking my feet because of the advancement I'd been making in my life—also a lot with one of my roommates here the last few weeks; that was the final straw and why it was so bad. The LORD gave me:

> *How then shall they call on HIM in whom they have not believed? And how shall they believe in HIM of whom they have not heard? And how shall they hear without a preacher? And how shall they preach unless they are sent? As it is written: "How beautiful are the feet of those who preach the gospel of peace, Who bring glad tidings of good things!"*

Romans 10:14–15 (NKJV)

He was very upset, so I asked Barbara, and she suggested asking *JESUS* to come in and help, so there *HE* was! And we sat at a table, and immediately there was such peace holding the hand of the Prince of Peace, but he was still so troubled. "For unto us a Child is born, Unto us a Son is given; And the government will be upon His shoulder. And His name will be called Wonderful, Counselor, Mighty God, Everlasting Father, Prince of Peace" (Isaiah 9:6 NKJV).

I just looked with such love at *JESUS*, and when I looked back, chubby Michael (2yo) was sitting on my part's lap, and they were loving on each other and playing. It was so funny; my part was kidding and turned into something and swallowed 2yo Michael's head like a cartoon. You just can't make this stuff up! It was so comforting to see 2yo Michael, but to have *JESUS* bring him and then for him to love on my (our) part...I felt such peace. We decided to let my part and 2yo Michael hang out.

02.03.22: Barbara's Post-Session Notes

Barbara asked if I thought I was ready to deal with some of the hurts from Michelle. I really Prayed and sought understanding from GOD, and I got such a comforting, warm, and kind of bubbling feeling, but then it completely left, and I couldn't see it, feel it, or anything. We never really had a session on healing from my time with Her. All of the healing so far has been before Her. It was strange, so I sat with it, and nothing...I immediately thought it was perhaps that smoke screen or something. The part that's hiding from us, we call it the smoke screener. So she started asking questions and probing if someone was hurting, and, sure enough, Frank spoke up. He was hurting and wanted to share, but oddly, he didn't want to share as much about Michelle...what happened but more about what he did, the hurt he caused Michelle, but he wanted me to know how he protected me. I'd always been upset with him as being a hot-headed, cold, mean part of me. He let me know how many times he was hurt emotionally to protect me. It was him that really got hurt for me, so I could not retaliate against Michelle. If it wasn't for him standing in taking it all, maybe I wouldn't have been able to not defend myself. We just cried and cried...I had him so wrong—now he did overreact sometimes, of course, but he truly protected me. Then Bobby stood up and reminded me that the worst would stop if I truly cried from being hurt and trying so hard not to argue back and lash out at Michelle, and this was her. She was and is so much like Michelle and loved and loves Her so dearly. She was saying if perhaps Michelle saw herself in me—Bobby with the same intellect and feelings as Michelle—Michelle would stop. Then Gary stood up and said that he would sometimes have to stand up with and for Frank when it was too much for him and how he protected me as well. I just broke down—how mean I was to both of them for what I thought was their temper and how I didn't know any of this at all. Then Mary shared her part—how badly she was attacked for talking so much and being a flake, not only by Michelle but me in the sessions. She took so much as well, head-on, for me and us... here were four giants that protected me in such a kind way and protected Michelle by isolating me...

Then Bobby mentioned Tim. (T: True me with I in the middle—Tim!) How he and she kindly and lovingly worked with Michelle to come up with resolve that saved a lot of pain and damage. So it was actually five of them that protected me, and I didn't speak well of any of them, except maybe Tim (True me), but I didn't know he was around at all due to the false me. False me was the hurt, broken, narcissist old me whom Tim (True me) finally threw out.

I could see all five of them, and they seemed to be on a stage, and then there were all the other parts to the left, not saying anything. I asked if they wanted to say anything, but they were quiet... suddenly it was a graduation—Frank, Gary, Bobby, Mary, and Tim were graduating and actually getting medals for a job well done protecting me and Michelle. None of this could have happened if Michelle hadn't truly and humbly repented the other day on the FaceTime call. Frank is the one who really had me crying. There they all were so healed from such hurts. We both agreed at the end to let all this sink in and be celebrated.

It was so, so good and kind of POPPA to allow such HEaling of my core parts and me. "HE" told me that the other parts are being mentored by these five core parts.

02.17.22: Barbara's Presession Notes

We talked for around thirty to forty-five minutes, and then she tried a new technic called flash. She asked me to close my eyes and see where my feeling was. Immediately I felt something in my belly, not my gut but my belly, and it seemed to be big. Then she asked when was the first time I'd felt this. We were back to the summer before seventh grade when the guys said I couldn't come on the boat because there were not enough life jackets. They waited for me to finish helping prepare the boat. I believe the feeling was about a seven; she had me look into the camera and start blinking my eyes rapidly for what seemed like forever, and then she said to take a deep breath. It felt better (around a three), and we did it again, and it was gone!

The next time was me, five to seven, sitting on third base in Grand Ave Grade School, crying because I couldn't get my four-blade ice skates on. I was sad and upset. Why couldn't Timmy or Sean help me? They weren't far. It felt like around an eight, so there we went blinking again. Did I tell you my eyes were hurting all day and that I was wearing contacts? The memory started fading visually, and the feelings lifted a bit as well to about a three. We did it again, and it lifted completely both visually and feelings. Thank *YOU, JESUS.*

Next was my having trouble tying my sneakers at three to five. I still have trouble bending over, not being able to breathe well, and I get dizzy. I do remember my sisters Kathy and Patty helping me sometimes. They said many times that I would have so many knots in my sneakers. I felt frustrated and sad. Why couldn't someone help me? I started blinking again, and it started getting hard to do, but it was working well. Sure enough, the belly lifted completely, and the memory faded completely! Thank *YOU, JESUS!* I felt great! I love my trauma counseling! I've said to myself many times, "I [*JESUS*] am the vine; you are the branch...apart from ME you can do nothing" (John 15:5, NIV). And I used this as an example; often

I can't even tie my sneakers without *HIM*. I ask for help, and, sure enough, *HE* helps me. There are also so, so many other things, even just something stupid like tying my sneakers without *HIM*, that don't work!

03.03.22: Barbara's Presession Notes

We talked until 18:00. I didn't want to, but she asked questions, and we kept talking, which was good.

18:05: She asked if I wanted to try and address the part or whatever was hiding. I remembered the chest from weeks ago.

About a year ago (I believe exactly a year ago when we did the forty-day take-me-up fast), it was one of the first times I clearly went up to Heaven. There was a chest that we started heading to, and we were distracted. We jumped right in and were off running. No tightness or anything like usual, but the chest had something to do with Frank, and he jumped right up and spoke! He and I went off to find it, and everyone else stayed on the road to the left. We remembered it was in between two roads. We headed down into a low and started searching; he seemed to know where he was going, so I let him lead. We were looking and looking and couldn't find anything; we even asked everyone else if they could see it—nothing. Then Barbara asked if there was another part or someone, and, of course, there was a dragon-looking thing to my left. He was, as you probably already know by now, a big dude. I stayed inquisitive and curious...he was big, and I asked who he was. Nothing—he wasn't mad but tough, and suddenly he morphed into a blonde...I couldn't see her face, but she had long hair and was wearing a sleeveless black turtleneck. I could only see her shoulders, neck, and hair. She didn't stick around long and left...we were wondering if he morphed so he wouldn't scare Frank and me...so we waited, and she turned into a man like a broadcaster. Suddenly he was like the Wizard of Oz...like the broadcaster hiding behind the curtain—weird! He came out, and we were walking down this road; behind us seemed to be a horse pulling a big old wagon, like the movie.

I checked in with Barbara, and she said, "Stay with it. Is he a part?" When I went back, he was nowhere to be found; we spent some time waiting. There were a few odd little things, but nothing really real...then a witch appeared and kind of disappeared as well. I started getting the feeling this was all HEaling that was going on with Frank, and, sure enough, it started making sense. Frank was getting HEaling from Joan's witchcraft, all the shame from the court case, having no money, spending all the money and losing it all to her in the court case..., the shame of smothering and being overbearing to beautiful Michelle. The Wizard of Oz phenomenon: feeling dumb, heartless (apathetic), all the fear, and not feeling at home...the mogging, molestation, getting hit by the car...I turned around, and there was Frank sitting in an Adirondack chair receiving so much HEaling...

the acne, getting in trouble in school, the teacher yelling at me and my lying about it to Mom, Mom leaving me at kindergarten—Frank still had all this junk; it was all getting pulled out of him; it was amazing! Frank was being HEaled of all the stuff I thought I was HEaled of, but he was still too tough and didn't surrender it.

Here he was now, sitting back and allowing *JESUS* to HEal him like *HE* HEaled me. I was watching a part of me getting Healed. I couldn't feel it because it was a part of me, not me or so... but it was a part of me being Healed. He was looking so relaxed, peaceful, HEaled...everything I've been HEaled of. I was watching him get HEaled of...no more old Frank. *JESUS* was putting peace and wisdom in him—no more rage, uncontrolled anger, arrogance, pride...he was at peace and sitting there. Then I saw this big old dragon breathing in his face, and he was not moving, not losing his peace...then there was a wild boar or something trying to stir up trouble, and there was no trouble to be found. Frank wasn't moving or feeding into any of it. Only *JESUS* could do that. Then I saw Mary and Bobby there with him, and they were loving on him. He used to still check them out a little—no more. He had a taste of what they had—purity. Thank *YOU, JESUS*...

There were Gary and Harry looking at him like he used to look at me—like what...? It was amazing. I was just crying and crying...then I saw the four of them with *JESUS* in Adirondack chairs, and there I was; now there were six of us, and *JESUS* had *HIS* hand on Frank's heart, sealing it all in. *HE* put *HIS* right hand on my heart and had *HIS* left hand on his heart. *JESUS* was sealing all the HEaling in both of our hearts. Then get this—*HE* changes Frank's name of Francis...no more tough guys, Frank. It's sweet, peaceful, wise, loving, patient, GODly Francis...

Chapter 7

STANDING ON THE SEA OF GLASS

03.24.22: BARBARA'S SESSION NOTES

We started IFS; it took a bit, but someone was pressing on my left side and went straight across to under my right rib. They wouldn't talk or move. Barbara thought maybe I was being frustrated or impatient, so I apologized to them and asked for forgiveness. They started moving, but not very quickly, so I tried to be even more patient, and it paid off. They came out but were very quiet. It was shy, almost timid, and it felt like a woman. When she came out, she seemed to immediately run behind a tree and hide. I tried to be curious, inquisitive, and patient, and once again it paid off. Barbara said, "Ask her where she would like you to stand," and she said, "You can come to the tree, but please don't look around it to see me." I said, "Would you like me to close my eyes?" I felt like it was like Michelle beginning to trust me. I wasn't sure, and she came right out and grabbed my hand. She was beautiful; it was my Quinn Michael. I just cried and cried…she was my middle girl who was in Heaven due to a miscarriage, and she led me to a bench. I asked her why she was timid, but she didn't answer, so I dropped it. It was so kind and loving to be with her, and she was so different than all the other times. I believe she was telling me, "Now that it's me, who's so different?" And that's the difference.

I asked her if she had to tell me something or warn me, and yes, that was another reason it was so different. She first wasn't sure because I was so different, but she knew it was bad… She told me I had to go alone again, and it was going to be bad! I felt fine with that and said, "Yes, I'm ready and excited to do it." I remember saying, "Come what may." I knew *JESUS* would be with me, even if I was going alone. I was sitting on the seat in a roller coaster or train, trolly, and it was going straight into darkness. I heard Quinn Michael say, "I love you, Daddy! I'm proud of you, Daddy…" Suddenly Mike A. was there; I hadn't seen Him in sooooooo lonnnng. Boy, was that great to have Him around, and then I had my sword, my shield, and crown! It felt good, not as much for protection, but I hadn't had my armor and crown on for so long…then I had Mike A.'s sword on my right, and there we were next to each other like a roller coaster going deeper and deeper into darkness. I felt secure on my own, but there was Mike A. I had my left arm in my shield, but I wasn't touching either sword, and I felt good. Then suddenly I could feel something like sin, vines, or roots entangling my feet, ankles, and calves. I didn't get scared or concerned or even bowed up. I looked at Mike A., and He was fine, so I just hung. I looked for POPPA and didn't get any signals, so I sat tight. The sin kept going higher and tighter, but I felt I was to just sit tight. I knew I could just swing Mike A.'s smaller sword with my right hand and end it immediately but felt I needed to be curious and wait. I saw a huge guy out front in the dark. I called out, "Are you a friend or foe?" And he didn't answer. I was patient and didn't do anything; suddenly it all disappeared, and the guy was an angel, and he called me out of the seat. I looked at Mike A., and He nodded, so I got up, and this dude was huge! We started walking forward, and suddenly I saw Glory. I started crying. He was taking me into Glory. As soon as we got out of the woods, he had me take my sword off, stick it in the ground, and hang my shield on it to mark the territory. I looked, and here was POPPA running to me. "HE" grabbed me and gave me the biggest hug I'd ever felt. "HE" was kissing and kissing and kissing me...then *JESUS* and HOLY SPIRIT came right behind "HIM" and did the same thing. I felt like the prodigal son. I was coming home after doing so well.

> *And he arose and came to his father. But when he was still a great way off, his father saw him and had compassion, and ran and fell on his neck and kissed him. "But the father said to his servants, 'Bring out the best robe and put it on him, and put a ring on his hand and sandals on his feet. And bring the fatted calf here and kill it, and let us eat and be merry.'"*
>
> Luke 15:20-24 NKJV

"Well done," THEY kept saying! I said, "It seems like old times," and POPPA said, "No, like new times!" I could see a Glorious Kingdom behind THEM, and you're not going to believe it, but THEY took me to The Throne, an actual Throne Room experience, and I was there...

The Four Living Creatures, twenty-four Elders, the Sea of Glass...it was the Sea of Glass, and it was so amazing, absolutely indescribable; like John would say, it was like and like. There are no words to describe it, only slight references—slight in the way of not anywhere in comparison, not even in the ballpark. All I could do was stand on it.

THE THRONE ROOM OF HEAVEN

> *After these things I looked, and behold, a door standing open in heaven. And the first voice which I heard was like a trumpet speaking with me, saying, "Come up here, and I will show you things which must take place after this."*

Immediately I was in the Spirit; and behold, a throne set in heaven, and One sat on the throne. And He who sat there was like a jasper and a sardius stone in appearance; and there was a rainbow around the throne, in appearance like an emerald. Around the throne were twenty-four thrones, and on the thrones I saw twenty-four elders sitting, clothed in white robes; and they had crowns of gold on their heads. And from the throne proceeded lightnings, thunderings, and voices. Seven lamps of fire were burning before the throne, which are the seven Spirits of God.

Before the throne there was a Sea of Glass, like crystal. And in the midst of the throne, and around the throne, were four living creatures full of eyes in front and in back. 7 The first living creature was like a lion, the second living creature like a calf, the third living creature had a face like a man, and the fourth living creature was like a flying eagle. The four living creatures, each having six wings, were full of eyes around and within. And they do not rest day or night, saying:

"Holy, holy, holy,

Lord God Almighty,

Who was and is and is to come!"

Revelation 4:1–8 (NKJV)

The Sea of Glass is, once again, indescribable; it has fire, emerald colors, Heavenly rainbows of color, unimaginable things in it. It's HEaven... Then the emerald-colored rainbow, which is around The Throne, is, in itself, magnificent. It was all like the Heavenly colors THEY poured into my new heart; there are no words... I'm crying so hard editing this two years later... One day you're going to be living there if you've given your heart to *JESUS* and follow *HIM*.

If you haven't given your heart and life to *JESUS CHRIST* as your LORD and Savior or have fallen away from the Faith, please do it right now. You don't know when you're going to take your last breath, and you don't want it to be the second before going to hell for eternity. Hell is real, and it's not going to be a party at all; it's eternal damnation.

We can do it right now, together. Here no matter where you are, what you're doing. Say, "*JESUS*, I know *YOU* are GOD and *YOU* are fully man. *YOU* died for my sins as a perfect man. *YOU* never sinned and became the perfect sacrifice. I invite *YOU* into my heart. Please forgive me for all my sins. I want to honor and follow *YOU* every day for the rest of my life. Please take me to Heaven with *YOU* when I die. I ask all this in YOUR Name, *JESUS*. Amen." If you said this Prayer and meant it in your heart, *HE* accepts it and you. *HE* has forgiven you from all your sins no matter what they were and will honor your request like *HE* did the thief on the cross next to *HIM*.

Then one of the criminals who were hanged blasphemed Him, saying, "If You are the Christ, save Yourself and us." But the other, answering, rebuked him, saying, "Do you not even fear God, seeing you are under the same condemnation? And we indeed justly, for we receive the due reward of our deeds; but this Man has done nothing wrong." Then he said to Jesus, "Lord, remember me when You come into Your kingdom."

And Jesus said to him, "Assuredly, I say to you, today you will be with Me in Paradise."

Luke 23:39–43 (NKJV)

If you said this Prayer and meant it in your heart, you are forgiven. No matter what your sin was, it's forgiven and washed clean in The Blood of *JESUS CHRIST*. Now, live for *HIM* the rest of your life, and you will be with *HIM* in paradise when you die. Please tell someone who knows *JESUS* and loves you right away that you gave your heart to *JESUS CHRIST*.

This is the most incredible and gracious gift you have ever received in your entire life, but there's more...

"But as many as received Him, to them He gave the right to become children of God, to those who believe in His name" (John 1:12, NKJV).

You are now a child of POPPA's *love* instead of "HIS" wrath... Now that you are a loving child of GOD, you can become "HIS" favorite best friend... This is going to change your whole life. You don't have to be a *JESUS* freak like me, but if you dive in, you're going to want to. Stick your toe in; the water's warm, and you're going to want to dive into the deep end. Now, connect with a gospel-preaching church and run with *JESUS* and people who are like-minded. Please email me at testimonies@mikecollinsministry.com. I would love to hear your story and connect you with a church in your area if you can't find one. Welcome to the family of GOD; it's a great place to be. We're not perfect, but *JESUS* is...

"I will bless those who bless you, and whoever curses you I will curse" (Genesis 12:3a, NIV).

I looked, and there was the Altar with the martyrs. I asked LORD, "Please don't let me be painting this picture if this isn't true—please take it from me." "HE" said it was true, and "HE" didn't take it from me. I couldn't see anything perfectly clear; I was told it was muted. It all felt different than ever before, like when I went up last year and all the other times. With all we'd been through, I was always in my body, but now I was Spiritual. I was there on the Sea of Glass in full Spirit, but I felt like in my body. I believe it because now I was more Spirit in a physical body than I'd been a physical body with some Spirit...this is what I was speaking of earlier; it really hit me hard, and I wanted to wait to explain it. This was why Quinn Michael was so different; it was me, not her, me! I was different, seeing her differently. As me operating in my True Mike, my Spirit man, not the flesh...

Here I was on "the Sea of Glass," and I was looking at the Four Living Creatures. They are ginormous, with eyes all over them. I could see each of them, but not clearly. Utterances, indescribable utterances. I could see the twenty-four Elders with golden crowns. Absolutely amazing. They were eight to my right, eight behind me, and eight to my left; the Altar was in front of me, and there was The Throne of GOD up these stone stairs and these magnificent thrones. POPPA in the middle, *JESUS* to "HIS" right, and HOLY SPIRIT to "HIS" left. I could see *JESUS'* face perfectly clear. But not POPPA's face or body. Of course I couldn't see POPPA's face, or I would die.

"But He said, 'You cannot see My face; for no man shall see Me, and live'" (Exodus 33:20, NKJV).

I couldn't see HOLY SPIRIT either. I asked POPPA why *JESUS* was the only thing in focus, and "HE" said, "*JESUS* is all that matters!"

This is a drawing of *JESUS CHRIST*'s face, the Man with Fire in *HIS* Eyes, that I drew after seeing *HIM* face to face.

POEM BY VICKYD
(VICTORIA LYNN CHARLEY)[1]

Rejoice:

the darkness of dirt
was not always deemed discussing,
but good

I know a God
who makes mute light speak
and illuminates eliminates silence

and when the ground begged
to be able to vocally
proclaim the glory of God
God granted his dusty wish
drastically,

with dusky skin
meant to house his new breathe
a fresh wind now given greater purpose
to worship

and I can only imagine
what the worlds first
answered unspoken prayer looked like

I'm convinced
that our Faint whispers are Screams
to a God who has been intently listening

since the beginning of time
when our language consisted of soil
waiting for it's turn to reach the surface
and bask in his marvelous light

Oh how glorious it is
to have reached the surface

---

1   https://linktr.ee/EvanVicky

Where oxygen waits patiently
to be breathed into revival

perhaps the rise and fall of our chest
is the testimony of our body
breathe taken
as quick as it was given

he Fills lungs with such awe
that what goes in
doesn't leave the same

with every inhale
I immediately exhale
& C O's twice
when I see his name
God is good

Jesus!
Jesus...

He is the definition
Of an oxymoron
God Man
Fully God
Fully man
Fully fragile
Yet unbreakable
Yet was broken for me
With me

I will become a fool for him
I will become an oxymoron
I will command the air in my pockets
To tithe 110 percent of it's prophets
pulled from my reserves in heaven
Cuz Eventually on earth will be as it is

I will speak as a foolish Wiseman
And describe you
with the most elegant of words
Thought up from the
empty space of my understanding

And I'll stand over
Every tree taller than me
With paralyzed arms raised
And amputated hands
Grasping for you
I'll remove every contact
And break the glass shielding my eyes
So I can see you better
And share the vision

I'll toss o tanks in the ocean
And remove tubes
So I can breathe you in
with more ease
And breathe out testimonies
Until death does us part
And when I marry dust
And you rain on my parade
Even then
You'll see my fingers
Reaching for you
Cut constantly by everyday blades
Yet I steady my gaze
On one in the heavens
And next to me at the same time in root

Like a leader of leaders
Leading joy to the world
from the kids table

Heaven came down
 and if trees flip their hands
open to receive when
the heavens pour out

If the clouds uncontrollably
display a bright red blush
at the rising and laying of the sun &

If the moon can't help but smile
at just a glimpse of his glory

then
as a living breathing lump of soil
silly puttied into his likeness

I'll be damned
if I don't respond

They were blurry, foggy, or out of focus instead of muted. I didn't want to rush anything, so I asked POPPA, "What should I do?" "HE" said, "Take it all in, Mike." So that was what I did, and it was majestic, I guess...there were no words...I heard noises and thundering, and I saw lightnings...angels flying out from behind GOD, just utterly amazing, and I was there. I was still wearing Mike's sword, and THEY said it was okay...then I asked POPPA, "Are YOU taking me *Home*?" And "HE" said, "No, I want you to see OUR *Home*..." Can you believe that? POPPA's *Home*, and I was there.

Then Quinn Michael came up to me and was holding my left hand, it was so sweet. I felt Michelle for a moment, and She was gone. Barbara thought maybe that was POPPA letting Her see me in "HIS" environment. So, so kind! I just kept staring at THEM and looking at the Sea of Glass and everything. I could now understand that none of it was anything compared to THEM! It was all absolutely incredible, but nothing compared to THEM...and I was there...I couldn't dance. I couldn't move. I said hallelujah once, but not loud, and I couldn't do or say anything, I was in absolute awe! Then it all became dim and was over...absolutely unbelievable, incredible, awesome!

Then Barbara asked me to check in with my parts. Francis, Mary, and Bobby were so amazed; each of them was in The Throne Room of GOD. Francis was able to love and be loved by the girls. He was so HEaled. Then I saw the other guys, Gary, Harry, and Sal—they were different, but nothing like Francis...they were amazed and seeing things differently, but not there yet but doing better. She asked what I thought all this meant. I could only gather that they were so enamored by GOD and The Throne Room, and I needed to just keep moving farther and farther into THEM and not worry about anything...

04.14.22: BARBARA'S PRESESSION NOTES

She wanted me to share something from the extremely powerful session three weeks ago. So I shared, "I'm wrecked, ruined, undone!" and described a little of that session.

"So I said: 'Woe is me, for I am undone! ...For my eyes have seen the King, The Lord of hosts'" (Isaiah 6:5a, c, NKJV).

"Also I heard the voice of the Lord, saying: 'Whom shall I send, And who will go for Us?' Then I said, 'Here am I! Send me" (Isaiah 6:8, NKJV).

This is why I'm a missionary with GCHOP—to worship *JESUS CHRIST* twenty-four hours a day seven days a week like the Four Living Creatures and to bring the good news of the gospel of *JESUS CHRIST* to those who don't know *HIM*.

Then we jumped into the session, and I had something hit my gut and then work its way up and out of my mouth and ear like some of the manifestations in the past with my yawning and my ears popping. When it came out, it immediately hid in the woods. It seemed like a big werewolf or dragon and wouldn't show itself. I tried to get it to talk or show itself, and it wouldn't. I believe he said I would be afraid. I said, "It's okay." But he wasn't coming out, so I asked if I could come in, which I did, and he moved farther around the tree. Suddenly it manifested into a serpent around my legs and looked up into my face. I wasn't afraid, and it seemed to leave because of that. I saw a lion off in the distance that was wounded, circling around, and when it got a little past directly in front of me, I felt my two swords, and Mike A. showed up. We were both sitting there, and Barbara wanted to know why He came. He said He wanted to make sure they knew He had my back.

Barbara asked me to invite my parts. Sal and someone else showed up; I believe it was Gary... It turned out that these manifestations were more their insecurities, and Mike A. was there for them because they didn't trust me yet like the others did. I addressed Sal, and he said these were the dark thoughts they had about never seeing Michelle again, not getting funded, and maybe not ever seeing the girls, maybe even being martyred...I tried to empathize with him because I could relate to these concerns because they all could happen. He was afraid I might forget Michelle, especially if we heard bad news that She was never coming back...that was painful to hear, and I could feel it in my heart. I was glad that it wasn't just me feeling it and that I was encouraging myself out of it. I also wasn't scared by it because of all THEY had been doing in, through, and with us. He was looking at us in the promised land, couldn't see Michelle or the girls there, and wanted to make sure I wasn't going to remove Her from my heart and lump Her all into Egypt and just move on and forget Her altogether...

Barbara asked what would make him feel good; when I asked, he said to hear from Michelle, and things to begin to work out. Wisely she asked what he needed from me to make him feel 5 percent better. I didn't know if he answered, so I assured him; even if Michelle gave us horrible news that She was moving on, I assured him I wouldn't remove Her from our heart. I love Her and always will... I thanked him again for being so venerable and open with us.

I looked him in the eye and said there was a real chance that we could get bad news and never get Michelle back. That would be devastating, but we would be all right no matter what. I hugged him and said, "I will be there for you, and even more, *JESUS* will be…" I thought he was feeling a little better but scared…

08.25.22: Barbara's Presession Notes

They were closing down my campaign. I was only $82 per month short. I would think they would keep it going for a few more weeks for me to get funded, but I didn't know. I would meet with them tomorrow. I met with HR, and they said, "Of course you're going to be funded! We're just going to close down your campaign so you can be on staff." To be on staff vocational missionary at GCHOP (GateCity House of Prayer, formerly IHOP-ATL), which has been Praying and Worshipping JESUS CHRIST nonstop since 2006. You go out on a campaign to raise your budget. This way you don't have to do other work to be able to live and pay your bills. I am now a vocational part-time intercessory prayer missionary. Which means my part-time job is to be part of the twenty-four seven worship and prayer of *JESUS CHRIST* because *HE* is worthy and coming back soon. Michelle and I had been on over 200 face-to-face partner meetings eleven months out of eighteen from 2017–2018. We were very Blessed, favored, and successful, but I believe it cost us our Marriage, sadly, because this narcissist was more concerned about the task than my wonderful Michelle's heart and well-being.

On staff officially, officially and finally, but supposedly the entire time.

09.15.22: Barbara's Session Notes

This was the first 100 percent fully external manifestation, no internal parts at all. I felt a Spiritual (what I believe was good) being enveloping, encircling, and swirling around my lower torso and upper legs; it felt warm, comforting, and assuring. Then it went farther down to my lower legs and even to my feet but was completely external; it was odd. I didn't say anything to Barbara yet, and she asked, "Is it internal or external?" I didn't remember her ever asking me that, and I'd never had an external experience like this, so that was cool—like how Spirit-filled she is and connected. It was also the first time it wasn't at all painful and felt soothing. It looked like a beautiful woman; I asked, "May I please see you?" There was a lion's face, like the lion of Judea, then the woman again. Then it looked like a dragonfly, swirling around and above me instead of around my torso and legs. I love dragonflies. I asked, "Are you here to tell me something or ask me something?" And she wouldn't answer me. Then Barbara asked if there was any internal involvement. I checked, and there wasn't any. Everyone was fine and happy, so we went back to her, and she seemed a bit more real. I asked, "Please talk to me. I really want to hear what you want and have to say." I immediately started seeing an image from today's field trip at work with them digging the piers for the parking garage for a site.

They both seemed to be very much connected. I started seeing her floating, flying, and swirling away and up, and I asked her to please speak with me, and she called out, kind of like I imagine the angels did in times of old. She said, "Do your homework and do it well." I received it and asked her if there was anything else, and she said, "Do your homework and do it well" again while floating farther up like she was going to Heaven. I smiled, laughed, and said, "Thank you—is there anything else?" She just said it again, "Do your homework and do it well," not scolding me or mean, just comforting and loving. Then she disappeared into possibly Heaven and was gone.

Then suddenly it looked like Michelle appearing out of nowhere. It was so comforting to my soul to see Her. I told Her how glad I was to see Her; She looked at me lovingly, and She looked radiant and stunning. She said:

» "I'm proud of who you've become."

» "Do it well."

» "You're doing great."

Barbara thought that perhaps this was an external manifestation of my emotional longing for Michelle. When I was editing this, it was exactly 17:55 (5:55) that had always reminded me of POPPA, *JESUS*, HOLY SPIRIT, Michelle, and me times three. I was also taken aback afterward at the mention of the word *swirl*; the studio I was at was called Swirl...

09.29.22: Barbara's Presession Notes

I spoke with my old boss and a professional engineer friend of mine named Jeff; this guy's a forensic structural PE (professional engineer). I got my confirmation that I had good questions, and there were concerns regarding my questions. I had Spiritual warfare at 03:00, tough morning, and I Prayed and Prayed. I emailed one of the chiefs at around 08:00 and kept it very minimal and to the point. I believe I did my homework, did it well, and was obedient.

Bobby shared how much she was missing living with Michelle. Barbara said, "Ask her to get real." She said, "Well, I really miss being with Her." How's that for real? Then Mary and Francis spoke up in love, openness, and volubility about how tough it was at times, and Bobby just loved and greatly appreciated the dialogue. The three of them started talking intimately around a table, and Barbara said to invite *JESUS*, and there *HE* was...

JESUS started speaking directly to them: Bobby, Mary and Francis. I was standing right there and couldn't hear a thing. He convicted each of them sternly but in love for their part in the failed Marriage. *HE* then ministered to each of them so lovingly and kindly, but I still couldn't hear anything...then Barbara asked if anyone wanted to say something. Bobby immediately spoke boldly and asked with a smile, "When am I going to get Michelle back?" *HE* started ministering and speaking to them big time and once again. Once again, I couldn't hear anything. They each were touched and felt loved and blown away like *JESUS* always does!

Then *HE* left, ascended away, and said to me, "Take *MY* seat," and wow, was *HIS* presence there. Like sitting down after someone and feeling their heat in the seat. But way, way, way more. It was HIS presence, and wow, was it powerful. I just sat there for a moment and couldn't move or say anything...

Then Bobby looked me dead in the eye, like right through me, and said, "I love you!" I'd never heard it like that—so intimately, genuine, kind, and loving... Then Mary and Francis said it so kindly as well...then Bobby said, "I trust *JESUS*, and I trust you." The other two agreed wholeheartedly. Then Bobby added, "*HE* has such plans for you and us." We all just held hands and flowed in *HIS* love...

10.06.22: Barbara's Presession Notes

JESUS came, and everyone ran to see *HIM*...it was so amazing...*HE* showed them visions of *HIS* passion story...they were all so touched, and Bob became Robert!

I was absolutely exhausted from six days with no caffeine or ibuprofen... But Barbara kept wanting to press in! So we did...I had to work hard to answer her questions; she was so patient with me...then she asked me to have Robert get to know Bobby, and Mary jumped in. *JESUS* laid hands on all three of them, and they were so, so good!

Then the three other guys felt left out. I was really exhausted at this point, but Barbara said, "Go back." I went back, and it was Gary, Harry, and the artist (artist named Joel). I explained that "each of you all is just as important as the others."

> *For as the body is one and has many members, but all the members of that one body, being many, are one body, so also is Christ. For by one Spirit we were all baptized into one body— whether Jews or Greeks, whether slaves or free—and have all been made to drink into one Spirit. For in fact the body is not one member but many. If the foot should say, "Because I am not a hand, I am not of the body," is it therefore not of the body? And if the ear should say, "Because I am not an eye, I am not of the body," is it therefore not of the body? If the*

whole body were an eye, where would be the hearing? If the whole were hearing, where would be the smelling? But now God has set the members, each one of them, in the body just as He pleased. And if they were all one member, where would the body be?"

1 Corinthians 12:12–19 (NKJV)

I apologized for calling them the lesser, and I looked forward to growing in intimacy with each of them. They really appreciated that and agreed. I was glad Barbara made me hang in there and share with these guys.

10.27.22: My Notes

17:42: I'm in the Prayer Room, just sitting staring at *JESUS* with all my parts…*HE* is so beautiful… *HE's* on *HIS* Throne, the King of kings…then I ask POPPA if we can all go walking along the shoreline like "HE" and I used to always do. There we all are, POPPA, Bobby, and Mary on either side, then Francis next to Mary, Robert next to Bobby, then me, Gary and Harry next to me, and the Joel next to Francis. We're all walking, and POPPA picks us all up and puts us on "HIS" shoulders and carries us along the shoreline. "HE" is POPPA, and then "HE" starts heading into the water and keeps walking with all of us on "HIS" shoulders; it is so fun. HE's GOD. "HE" can do anything…we're all in the water together, and POPPA's walking under the water, so all of us are in the water. Then, of course, "HE" must take it to a higher level, and a whale comes up, and we're all riding the whale. We're whale sailing. We go for a while, and the whale starts going under; maybe my parts don't need air, but I sure do, but wait—we're with POPPA; therefore, it's HEaven, and I don't need air. We are whale sailing under the water, whale submarining! It's absolutely amazing. Unfortunately, a transition comes, and the room manager isn't there, so I jump up to do the transition. "HE" never ceases to amaze me. Thank "YOU," POPPA. I was very disappointed to have this vision time interrupted. "HE" is always so fun to be with. This is one of the biggest reasons, I believe, "HE" had me write this book. "HE" wants to have this much fun, if not more, with you.

"God is no respecter of persons" (Acts 10:34, KJV).

Therefore, if I can be "HIS" favorite best friend, so can you!

Back to the transition, at the House of Prayer, we have unceasing worship and Prayer in one-to-two-hour blocks twenty-four hours a day, seven days a week, and we have been doing it nonstop since 2006. When the worship leader changes, someone has to readjust the sound and maybe adjust some cameras for the livestream. This person is called the room manager, and sometimes I do that. While we're speaking of it, one of my other jobs on staff is Prayer leader. About six hours a week, I help lead the Prayer during our Monday evening Stern family set from 18:00 to 20:00. This is an amazing time to Pray and seek GOD's heart for Israel, and the other times we usually Pray for "HIS" love and the fear of The LORD. I also serve as one of the leaders in our 212 High School Youth Ministry. Our ministry is actually Gatekeepers International, and the name came from:

"Altogether, those chosen to be gatekeepers at the thresholds numbered 212" (1 Chronicles 9:22, NIV).

11.02.22: MY NOTES

17:05: I said to HOLY SPIRIT that I'd missed hanging out with HIM and asked if we could do something. Of course, HE was right there and wanted to show me the first and second Heavens. HE had me jump on HIS back, and we sailed around in the first Heaven (which is the sky where the birds fly). I saw Mount Everest and a few incredible points. HE then took me to the second Heaven (which is space or outer space). I told HIM I love the Cat's Eye Nebula, which, of course, HE knew well. I asked HIM what HIS favorite was, and we were just hanging in the middle or somewhere in space just watching everything. Then HE mentioned something about the birth of a star, and I was really intrigued. Right after HE said that, I looked out, and I could see a lion's face, and, sure enough, it was *JESUS*. I asked *HIM* to please join us, and HOLY SPIRIT ("BOB") agreed. It was the three of us, and it seemed like we were sitting on a swing...*JESUS* was on my right, and "BOB" on my left. We just sat there looking, and I said, "I love y'all" (that was one of the first times I'd ever said that), and a shooting star went by toward our right. Then another one directly over our heads. It was so cool. I would lie my head on *JESUS'* shoulder, then on BOB's, and then back...suddenly POPPA came and slid under me. I was sitting on "HIS" lap, and I was in Heaven. I would rest on POPPA's right shoulder and have *JESUS* there. Then I would move to POPPA's left shoulder, listen to "HIS" big bass drum heartbeat, and have "BOB" there. It was so much fun just hanging with the GOD of creation...we were all together, and I said y'all again. Just then my oldest brother, Larry, came to my heart, and I asked THEM if THEY would please heal him. I said, "Sorry to have an agenda, but please..." After that POPPA wanted to show me the sun, so there we were. It was so huge and beautiful, and, of course, since I was with THEM, I didn't melt. We just watched it; it was massive and so active. Explosion after explosion, the flairs would fly out, and one came right through us—wow! Then THEY put a song on my heart that Cate and I would sing when she was little about the sun being a great big hydrogen bomb or something. We started seeing more and more big ones, and it reminded me I had to get an old, old vehicle, like my 1950 GMC, so when the big one comes, I can still drive it...then I thought, *Yes, when the big solar flare comes, it will keep running.*

A month caffeine- and ibuprofen-free.

Everyone is really well! The camping has everyone in love and loving me well!

Dream about a little person crying about not being able to play baseball.

We started the session, and there was something in my gut, but it wouldn't come out. I asked, "Are you afraid?" I was saying, "I just want to meet you; I'll be eyes and ears, and I won't talk." I had a pain in my right arm, and it moved away toward my right side. Then I felt something say, "No, help me out!" I looked, and there was this old man around eighty-five years old. I helped him out of something—I don't know what, but I guess that doesn't matter. I got him out and asked if he wanted to sit down; he said "Yes, I'm exhausted..." So I helped him sit down toward my right.

I was listening for a while and then asked a few questions. He said, "I thought you were going to be eyes and ears." Not mean but in jest, I guess... "Oh, yes, I'm sorry." So I didn't say anything...he reminded me a bit of my Pop Pop (my dad's dad). Then he started reminding me of the times I had hurt or disappointed Mom and/or Dad.

1. I was around fourteen and supposed to put Pop Pop to bed. My friends (Arthur, Gary, and...) were outside with his car, and I left with them and Sean (my brother number seven—I'm number eight out of nine) instead of putting him to bed. I loved doing it, but I chose them in a car, and Mom had to put him to bed. This was embarrassing to both of them.

2. I got drunk and hit by a car at around fourteen and scared both Mom and Dad.

3. I got in a lot of trouble in school.

4. AA.

5. BB.

6. I ordered pizza for us and decided to share it with Joan's mom instead.

Then we jumped right to ninth-grade Mike (a lot of the times above around fourteen were his)... he just appeared there and was very upset. He reminded me of all his shame with cystic acne on my face, neck, and back from around seventh grade to a senior in HS, feeling ugly and shameful like the hunchback. So dumb because he wasn't doing good in school and was such a fool...he carried so much pain, shame, and jealousy. Sean was so good-looking and had great skin, getting all the girls... he had boils on his face and back. Acting out in school, getting in trouble, and drinking...I felt so, so very sad and sorry for what he had to go through. I just cried with him and told him I was sorry...then Barbara had me butterfly tap all the pain, and a lot of it went away. Thank *YOU, JESUS*. I saw him again, and some of it came back, so we did it again, and this time she didn't let me stop for a very long time, and that really did it...he apologized to me saying if he had done better in school, we could have become a pilot or done better in engineering, and he cried...I told him he couldn't feel that way; the enemy beat him up so bad—he did a great job! He had it so tough...I completely understood what was against him and what he had to walk through because of the Healing we got these last two and a half years. I told him I was so, so sorry I didn't get help for us sooner. I was sorry that all of my mes had to go through so much and we destroyed so many lives...

Then forty-year-old Mike started sharing what a horrible man he was—supposedly saved, but the way he acted...we tried so hard, but he had such a rotten heart; how could we have not invited *JESUS* and POPPA into our heart in high school when my friend John Pine evangelized me in 1980?

"*JESUS* answered and said to him, 'If anyone loves ME, he will keep MY word; and MY FATHER will love him, and We will come to him and make Our home with him'" (John 14:23, NKJV).

We didn't get this scripture until around June 9, 2021, at Restoring the Foundations Ministry. What a horrible mess of a man and such destruction...he continued how he screwed up. It cost us so very much money. I cried with him and told him the same thing, that it wasn't his fault...the enemy had his claws in us so deep and had us deceived for our entire life. I just wished that I would have fallen in love with *JESUS* as a kid and received the deliverance and HEaling that we got last year. Boy, would that have saved so very much pain for us and everyone around us, especially Michelle...he cried and cried and cried...

Then I figured out that the old man was old Mike (me at around eighty-five years old). He started telling all of us what a great job we did with all that we were against. He reminded ninth-grade Mike that he really loved...after a few years he really buckled down and worked very hard in engineering... to forty-year-old Mike, he said, "You did a great job raising the girls..." Then he told me he was so proud of how I'd surrendered to *JESUS*, actually gave my heart and life to *HIM*, and have gotten such HEaling and wholeness...I could see him looking younger and younger. We decided that the HEaling we were getting was making him healthier because he was me in around twenty-five years... then *JESUS* came in, held ninth-grade and eighty-five-year-old Mike's hands, and we all held hands and got such an incredible HEaling from *HIM*. Then all my parts came in for the HEaling as well...it was deep, deep HEaling down in the bowels on my soul. It felt so very peaceful...I was telling Barbara that this was a HEaling and wholeness of around seventy years and more...

I could see sixth-grade, molested Mike, and he wasn't happy or well. *JESUS* walked up to him, and he was resisting *JESUS*...not fighting 'cause you can't fight *JESUS*...but he was really resisting; it was so painful to watch. Then I realized when we were dealing with him and Wilber a long time ago, he got so mad and started screaming for Wilber to come out, so *JESUS* told him Wilber was in hell, and he was glad. He was still mad. That was when *JESUS* held him, and *Glory* came over both of them and pushed me away...it was one of the most powerful times in these sessions. The force of *Glory* pushed me away from *HIM* and Mike. I physically was pushed back in my seat and couldn't move...absolutely amazing. I described it like *JESUS* must have taken him to HEaven...here he was, and he was mad...I told him how sorry I was for all that he had to go through—clearly, the worst of all of us... And that it wasn't his fault—he did nothing wrong; he was the biggest victim of all of us at satan's hand...it started in the womb, and he took the worst shot of all of us. "Ninth-grade Mike had it bad, but you had it the worst, and I'm so very sad and sorry." We just cried and cried and cried; he felt loved and heard. We all had *JESUS* holding us, *loving* us, and healing all of us deeper and deeper...I told Barbara, "Thank you for your patience; we were able to get HEaling for both third- and sixth-grade Mike. That was now more than seventy-five years of Mikes that were healed and made whole...I saw us all at a table with *JESUS* while *HE* was HEaling, comforting, and making us whole...

It had been a long while since we'd done such deep soul surgery like this...

11.10.22: Barbara's Presession Notes

My weekend started!

Going away for four nights for Thanksgiving up in a North Georgia cabin in the mountains to start this book!

11.17.22: Barbara's Presession Notes

I had a dream sometime early yesterday morning. Sean (number seven) and I were at a table, and he was messing with me somehow, eating my food or something. I didn't fight back. I just strong-armed him like siblings do but firmly took my territory or something.

12.01.22: Barbara's Presession Notes

Cabin was awesome! Four hundred pages complied! Two thousand twenty Barbara notes edited; I got a lot of HEaling from all of it.

Two months with no caffeine or ibuprofen.

I had a very difficult day yesterday; laptop wouldn't do a mail merge correctly. I spent hours on it; while I tried to print it at HOP, the printer was sitting under a hole in the roof—it poured for days, and the paper trays had water in them, ugh, ugh, ugh...so I rearranged the copy room to move the printer and decided to leave after that. I got to the PO to find what looked like Amazon mailed me the wrong envelopes for my year-end updates that had to go out. At which point I said, "Typical of my life." I immediately felt such conviction...we decided to find the root of this frustration. I believe I was feeling hopeless and beat up. I really wanted to get these updates out, and none of it was going well. I'd ordered the correct envelopes weeks ago, and now I didn't have enough to do my year-end ask update... As a missionary I send updates to my partners at least every quarter, bringing them insight into my ministry for that period. So we went back to the time that Michelle called to tell me I was going to be served, which was the worst day of my life until being served, until, of course, the divorce...and a time that I felt absolutely hopeless and discouraged, so we did progressive counting. This time was an eight, from zero to ten, in pain. Barbara counted up to and then down from the number to the left, and the sentences contained ether good times or bad times.

We went to a peaceful spot.

Tree on the trail just below the curve up to top of Blood Mountain and the New York Trip.

Ten: POPPA, *JESUS*, and BOB (PJB) on trail. It's sad there with the girls.

Twenty: POPPA, *JESUS*, and BOB, dinner, crying—please don't D me (ten). Ali at her house.

Thirty: POPPA, *JESUS*, and BOB. Giant Fred Flintstone ribs. She's not there. Two-to-three-hour-in-Cate's-car talk.

Forty: Heavenly cheesecake, bringing a big piece for Michelle—She's not there. Cate's apartment.

Fifty: Great talk after dinner with Cate, enjoying the mountain view. I'm at Ali's house with her.

Sixty: Mike A. joins the talk, really enjoying the sun! Cate and I eating New York pizza.

Seventy: Chaise lounge at tree, chaise lounge in sun, with Ali.

Eighty: They all walk me up the mountain. Ali, Michael (Ali's fiancé, I know, another Michael, and he's an electrician—you just can't make this stuff up!), and Cate surprise me and meet us at the top of the mountain. All eight of us for my sixtieth birthday surprise party.

Fifty: All eight of us in chaise lounges in the sun. *JESUS*, Cate, BOB, Michael, Ali, POPPA, me, Mike A. Both the girls sitting, being loved on by GOD. An answer to my Prayer Leading Monday and calling out every day for them to come home.

Thirty: All eight of us playing frisbee in the sun.

Ten: All eight of us, four pairs, three-legged races, Cate and *JESUS*, Ali and POPPA, Michael and BOB, Mike A. and me. Reminded me of the last time I did three-legged races that I remember at Hempstead State Lake Park at the South Hempstead Fire Department's picnic in the '60s.

01.05.23: BARBARA'S SESSION NOTES

I show her the book; we chat quickly and jump into the session. I don't want to talk. I feel I need a session. I know I say this a lot, but it really is strange. No feelings or anything. I ask my core—that's where most happens—and nothing. I ask, "Is there anywhere else in my body?" Immediately my ears start popping big time—the only time I've ever had my ears popping more than a few times has been in deliverance. They are popping so much that it's more like crackling. I try to be patient but find it very funny, and I'm laughing a lot...I'm asking it to please give me space, and it's just popping for ten to fifteen minutes. I realize to ask it questions and say, "Pop once for no and twice for yes." I ask, "Are you in me?" Two pops. "Okay, yes." I ask a few more Qs, and it seems to be going along.

Suddenly out it comes on the run circuit near where the angels hang, and it is a beautiful blonde. I say, "I only use the word *beautiful* to describe *JESUS* and my three girls. Now four girls with Quinn Michael." I ask, "Do you mind if I describe you to Barbara as an attractive woman?" And she's fine with that. I ask if it's okay to update Barbara; she says yes, and that's what I do. We are then off walking the circuit, and she lovingly grabs my hand. We continue down to where the boys are, and they are so excited to see me. I don't know if they know her; they do and are excited to see her as well. The five of us continue walking the trail holding hands. I am enjoying holding her hand but think it best that each of us should be holding one of the boys' hands. I have Joshua on my right, Isaac to my left holding this woman's hand, and she's holding Caleb's hand. We walk down, as I affectionally call, C and J Lane—Caleb and Joshua Lane. This was before I met Isaac... Now we call it C, J, and I Lane. We get to the field, and we all lie down in the sunny grass next to the lake with Caleb—her, then Isaac and Joshua. We are just enjoying each other in the sun; it is so kind and sweet of POPPA. Then some big old white geese show up; she pulls out some bread, and we start feeding them. I say, "This really reminds me of feeding the ducks at Silver Lake in Baldwin, Long Island, New York, when I was a small child," and she remembers. I ask, "If you remember, does that mean you've been with me my whole life?" And she says yes. I say, "Oh good." I always try to get info of whether they are parts, mes, or messengers...we finish feeding the geese, and the boys start leaving like Spirits. I've never seen them leave like this. They usually just appear and disappear. I ask them, "Please wait. I would love a hug." They come back, and I hug, kiss, and tell each of them how much I love them. I cry and cry... She (I never even got a name) and I continue walking, but this time she grabs my arm and snuggles into my shoulder. I ask her, "Please don't leave me." I believe she immediately starts popping my ears to enforce my newfound security and not rejection. It starts getting dark Spiritually, and my crown and swords are on me now. There are demonic beings around and almost on me, and she's gone, but we go back to communicating with my ears popping. I'm alone on the bridge, but my ears are popping lovingly. I'm thinking to myself, *Am I to start walking the circuit myself?* I check in with Barbara, and that's what we decide. I'm walking up the first hump of a hill, and I can hear giants in the land. I think it's just thumbing of loud, huge feet, but I stay curious and keep walking. I'm about the crest of the hill and turn around, and there she is smiling and waving, and I hear the boys say, "We're proud of you, Dad, and love you..." I start crying again and continue. I see myself drawing my sword and say, "Let's not do that yet," and I put it back. We get to the clearing of the north powerlines, and I grab my sword and pull it out; it's not me, and I jam it into the ground right at the clearing. I figure this must be what we're supposed to do, but it is gorgeous and shining in the sun. I'm thinking, *Maybe we shouldn't leave it, and remember, we're in the Spirit here; it's okay—no one is going to be able to steal them...* So now both my swords are off me, and I continue walking; there's Mike A. in His usual spot, and I just say hi...now I'm at the big hump of a hill, and I continue walking to the top and down the other side. I think to myself, *If Michelle's around, She'll be on the other side of the two bends...* I continue, and no Michelle...my ears start popping big time as I walk up the last part of the hill, so I stop—nothing—and I continue. I get to the spot where we met, and nothing. I continue, go past where the boys usually are, and nothing again. I get to the spot of the one bench and think to stop and rest, but it's a new plastic bench and not my style. I feel her having me go down the hill to the right instead of up toward the left. I don't think I've ever done that, at least not more than one or two times out of hundreds. I sit down and remember this is where I texted Michelle after running my Triozathon. It was later a very bad experience, and I feel a giant coming toward me; my ears start popping and popping, and I start yawning uncontrollably. I remember that the yawning is a huge part of my deliverance as well as ear popping. I sit back and start manifesting a lot, yawning around ten times, and realize I'm being delivered from a lot of deep things from the Marriage and divorce...I'm sitting back, getting such peace...this is clearly POPPA! I rest in it for a few minutes and ask, "Is there anything more you want to tell me?" And I hear nothing...I wait, and there are still only peace and silence...

01.12.23: Barbara's Presession Notes

10:38: We now call her Popp'n; she came running up right after the bridge and grabbed my hand. I was so happy to see her. I said, "Do you like walking and running?" She said, "No, but I like being with you." We walked and ran to the top of the hill (hump one). (I got a strong feeling that maybe this was Michelle looking out Spiritually out for me, and that's why She was beautiful...listening and watching me. Not saying almost anything and just confirming I am really healed.) We walked to Mike A.; she didn't say anything (and I was getting the feeling it was Michelle). I introduced them; when we walked away, I asked if she knew Mike A., and I believe she clearly said no. We continued walking and running a bit and passed Michelle's spot, and She was not there. I asked, "Do you know Michelle?" And there was nothing. We got near the boys, and I could hear them, and so could she... when we saw them, they were very excited to see us, and we continued walking together. Caleb (the oldest) on my right, Isaac (now Issy, the youngest) on my left, her and Joshua (the middle boy) to her left. Caleb wanted to be on my shoulders. I was so glad to have him up there, and now I got to hold her hand with Issy on my right. We stopped on the new bench. I still had Caleb on my shoulders. After the pic we started up again, and Issy got on my shoulders, Caleb back on my right, and we walked. Issy let Josh get up, and when we got to the clearing, the boys wanted to run on their own. I remembered that the five of us were together in the open field we were heading for, lying in the grass in last Thursday's session. It was just her and me; we got to the clearing and caught up to the boy, and we all ran to the lakes. We walked to the car, and they all left...

We started chatting about how I felt that I believed I'd never been nurtured by a woman my entire life. There had never really been a nurturing mom, sisters, girlfriend, or wife who had truly loved and nurtured me. We were wondering who this lady Popp'n was. Barbara wanted to check in with my parts to hear how everyone was handling things. Suddenly Sal, Francis, Bobby, and Mary were at a table. Sal was upset; he kept hearing me talk to everyone explaining I gave my vow to GOD to love, honor, and serve Michelle till death do us part. Me saying I made this vow to a covenant keeping GOD for thousands of generations. How could I not keep it for one or two generations? He was very lonely, missing Michelle, and didn't really believe or feel okay with that. He said, "She left us; if She never comes back, how could we not find someone else? Why shouldn't we have someone else?" I cried and agreed on how much I missed Michelle. All the others joined me but also said firmly they agreed and understood the vow we gave to POPPA. We needed to and wanted to keep at least until Michelle came back, we died, or She did...they wanted to acknowledge Sal's feelings, but they knew he just didn't have that relationship with GOD to feel he wanted to. I appreciated everyone talking and sharing so peacefully. We asked him, "What would make you feel 5 percent better?" He said, "A hug, a real hug from Michelle." Barbara asked when the first time we can remember feeling this lonely was. Immediately we went to being with Michelle, how bad that was some of the time, arguing with girlfriends...then we shot all the way back to being six or seven at Grand Ave Grade School, crying because I couldn't get my ice skates on. Why couldn't Sean or Timmy help me put them on? I felt all alone and unloved. We asked Sal what this had to do with him. He said I (me) was too sweet as a very young child and kid, and he needed love and wanted to have someone to fill this lack of nurturing and love. He was mad and said I was such a prude my entire life, and he didn't like it; he hated it...

Barbara said for me to hug and love on little Michael trying to get his skates on right now as an adult. I did and started crying so deeply. He, me, felt so loved and held on so deeply...I asked him if he wanted me to get his skates on; he said, "No, please keep hugging me." I stayed there for a long time and felt such Healing. I (we) felt nurtured...then suddenly Mom took over for me; she came out of the blue... She held him (us) and held us like I didn't remember ever being held by her. She reminded us how much she had always loved us so.

Reminding us how she cried and cried the whole way home from kindergarten after dropping me off. How she had always loved me since I was born and my sweet, beautiful smile, plus how husky I was my whole life—not fat, husky. Then she put my skates on; he (we) asked her not to—to please just keep hugging him. But she said, "You're going to learn to skate." I didn't want to; I wanted to just be held. She knew best; she taught me to skate with the four blades, then a few years later with two blades, and then single-blade skates. I was figure skating; she was so proud of me and came to all my competitions. I was getting good...skating through my life, and then I was skating with Michelle, who excelled in anything She did. We were skating at Rockefeller Center in New York City, and I was keeping right up with Her and having a great time...I was seeing how that would have changed my whole life. I was never any good at any sports growing up. I was horrible at all sports and felt like a failure most of my life. Then I got cystic acne (boils) across my entire upper torso, neck, and face. That was the cherry on top of the biggest shame for me to carry the first twenty years of life. I watched how this love and nurturing from Mom change everything, giving me the confidence I needed to do well in all other sports, do well in school, not be so rebellious in school and life...it would have changed the trajectory of my entire life...I felt so loved and accepted... Thank *YOU*, *JESUS*.

01.19.23: BARBARA'S PRESESSION NOTES

08:33: I believe The LORD reminded me to "stop thinking about what was going on in front of you. Just remember what 'I' have told you to your face."

14:41: Tough, tough day. Trip again this week to Atlanta, but that wasn't bad. Yesterday an applicant kind of tore me to pieces, saying that it seemed to him that I didn't like my job and I didn't explain myself well. He wished I had some ownership, so I repented to him and said I was told by a lot of people that I did my job well, but I was sorry that I made him feel that I didn't like my job. He wanted to speak to me today and have me explain it all again.

I got home, and there was an email about another one of his jobs that he sent to someone else, and he started it with "I don't know what's with Mike Collins," and then he said I didn't do something that needed to be done. It was something that I was not supposed to do. I replied and copied all my bosses with what I did and the reason he didn't get what he wanted with a picture showing why.

Popp'n showed up, and she wouldn't come out of my ears, so I asked for help. Barbara's good at talking to some of the characters. She came out. She would only cuddle my left arm and wouldn't say anything. Barbara asked if she was afraid of someone, and yes, that was the case. It turned out to be, you guessed it, a huge Chinese dragon...I held her tightly and then had her go behind me while I spoke to it. I said, "You're going to have to come down to my size," which he did. He was still mad and scared Popp'n. We decided to have her step away so I could speak with him. He said he was pretty upset with the way the applicant was dealing with us yesterday. I agreed with him wholeheartedly and asked if he was a protector. He said yes; he was the one that kept me cool so I wouldn't go off on the dude. I thanked him and let him know how much I appreciated it and how hard it was not going off on the guy. I asked him his name, and he disappeared...

I called Popp'n back, and she asked if I wanted her to call him back. I said, "Yes, please." I saw a huge war horse, and then it morphed into a big storm. Then suddenly a knight or huge warrior appeared on the back of that giant black war stallion. This dude was tough. I asked him if he was on my side, and he said yes, so I said thank you. He had full armor on and a huge ball with spikes; it was connected to a pole by a chain. He said the enemy was attacking me big time. I said, "Yes, I know..." He said he was one of my protectors from them. I asked him if there was anything I could do to help. He said, "Clearly keep reading your Bible every day and finish the book." The enemy didn't want me to finish the book (this book). He was trying to distract me and prevent me from writing it. He had to leave but repeated loudly, "Keep reading your Bible every day and finish the book." I turned to Popp'n, and she said she was here to help with both...

02.01.23: Barbara's Presession Notes

Then we got into the session, and there were no internal manifestations. I was on the bridge of the run circuit; immediately my ears started popping, and there was Popp'n. It was so good to see her, even though I couldn't really see her. She grabbed my left arm, and we started walking hump one. I said, "How are you?" She said nothing. I said, "How am I?" And she said nothing... Immediately my Quinn Michael came and grabbed my right arm. I got a little concerned knowing she was a messenger...but we continued walking the circuit; we said hi to Mike A. and continued walking up hump two; when we crested it, I started thinking Michelle was not far, and I wondered if we'd see Her. We got to the big red, the uprooted tree, and, sure enough, there She was, and She ran up, gave me a hug and kiss, and grabbed Quinn Michael's hand. I immediately remembered Quinn Michael telling me months ago that she was going to be speaking with her stepmom... The four of us continued up the rest of the hill; when we got to the flat part, I saw this dude who was all hair like the yeti coming toward us, and he bumped Popp'n. I was thinking to myself, *Is he mad that I have these three ladies around me?* I checked to make sure she was okay, turned, and said, "I'm sorry we were taking most of the trail, but I believe you owe her an apology." He agreed, said he was sorry, and continued walking. I said, "Do I know you?" He said no. I said, "Can I get to know you?" He again said no and kept walking. I said, "Be blessed in the Name of *JESUS CHRIST*." And we continued walking. I told everyone, "If we come across anyone, Michelle and Quinn Michael will move in front and Popp'n and I will fill in behind them." Suddenly Quinn Michael grabbed Popp'n's arm and let me hold Michelle's arm...we continued across the powerlines, saw the angels, and walked down the hill. I was thinking if we were going to see the boys, and, of course, there they were. I grabbed Issy on my shoulders. Michelle had Caleb, and Quinn Michael had Joshua on her shoulders, and we continued walking C and J Lane...we got to the newer bench that we'd been hanging at; the boys wanted to go play and came off our shoulders; they went down the small ravine and toward the water... Suddenly this huge alligator appeared, so I jumped down with them, and it was okay. I sent them up to where Mom and I were. This dude, as I'm sure you now know, was huge! I told him how beautiful and big he was, and he started shrinking and disappeared. I believe it was because I wasn't scared at all. I updated Barbara, and she said, "Call him and the yeti guy back to talk" and reminded me that everyone up on the bench was in the book...and, therefore, probably represented the book. I reminded her that POPPA reminded me a few times to never leave Michelle in a possibly unsafe situation, so we decided to call yeti and the alligator to me, and here came yeti and the alligator...the alligator got uptight, so I asked yeti to hang; when I asked the gator what he needed, he asked that yeti to sit down. Then I remembered he was huge, so he sat down, and gator was cool. I reminded them both how big and beautiful they were, and gator came close to me around my right side; yeti was sitting to my left, and a huge crowd of warriors started coming from the front left. There were a bunch of them. I called out, "Don't get too close," and they stayed back. I could see that they were with yeti, and a few started approaching, and I signaled okay.

They reminded me they were the ones that came to me around a year or so ago when I was a judge with Mike A. They were unhappy; when they saw me last, I kind of disrespected them to rebuke and cut off the heads of the witches. I acknowledged them, and suddenly the witches came back, and I could feel confusion, so I immediately rebuked the curses and demanded they stop. They did but started hanging with the alligator, and I continued speaking with the man. Yeti said, "We're not happy about the book..." And the man agreed. Suddenly Popp'n was on my left. I put my arm around her, and she started talking with yeti and asked if they could go for a walk together. I reminded him if anything happened, there would be trouble...then Quinn Michael came, did the same thing, and walked away with the warriors. I didn't have to warn them because she was a Spirit... then Michelle came and sat to my left, and I put my arm around Her. Suddenly Joan came into the picture; I thanked her for her kind text for CHRISTmas, and she drove a huge steak through the head of the gator. It reminded me of Jael. The woman who did the same thing to an evil king.

And he said to her, "Stand at the door of the tent, and if any man comes and inquires of you, and says, 'Is there any man here?' you shall say, 'No.'" Then Jael, Heber's wife, took a tent peg and took a hammer in her hand, and went softly to him and drove the peg into his temple, and it went down into the ground; for he was fast asleep and weary. So he died.

Judges 4:20-21 (NKJV)

I didn't know what to do. I liked the gator but knew I would be in trouble with Barbara if I rebuked Joan. The witches disappeared...Joan said, "I killed the debt and broke all the curses I've ever spoken over you..." I cried and thanked her. I said, "Thank you, and we thank you," and then she smiled and left...the boys and Mike A. were so excited!

02.09.23: Barbara's Presession Notes

We went right into it, and there was Popp'n, and she was just really cuddling my arm at the bridge on the run circuit! She was freezing and wanted to walk fast, so we did. We just waved to Mike A. and kept going quite fast—no Michelle and no one else. We got to the new bench spot, and she was just really loving and cuddling on me. I turned, and there was Bobby cuddling on my arm and holding her as well. It was very soothing and nurturing for all of us. Something started manifesting across the way in the little ravine, and I believe Bobby said, "Let's go for a walk." I checked in with Barbara because I didn't want to miss anything with the manifesting, so she said, "Go with what they want," so we left. We continued on the trail, passed the bridge and up the first hump, and stopped at the little bench at the top. Now both Bobby and Popp'n climbed on my lap. Bobby is a brunette, and Popp'n is a blonde, so it reminded me of Ali and Cate when they were little playing on my lap...we decided after a bit to continue walking, stopped, had a hug fest with Mike A., and then walked more. When we got to the bench near the Heavenly host, I started actually getting itchy and tingly and wanted to stop and acknowledge it. The girls left, and I hung. I started seeing some black creeping around and asked if it would sit and speak with me. It didn't say anything but started having this electrical field going up and down its entire length. Suddenly a woman appeared in a hat, and all I could see was her hat and a bit of blonde hair. She said the dark guy who was creeping around was with her; she sat down and started complimenting my work at HOP. I thanked her and asked her if she had details for me. She said she liked my Prayer leading today for Israel but really made a big deal about the conference, especially Pastor Brian Williams of Hope City House of Prayer in Columbus, Ohio, and his teaching and exaltation of women at GateCity. She loved my Monday night Prayer leading, how I took ownership and repented for all my disrespect and not exalting women like I should have. How I may have kept them from being lifted up by *JESUS* in my ignorance, insecurity, and hurts. Barbara asked me to invite my parts; there were Francis, Sal, and Mary. The dark guy started sharing about his hurts from women and the story about my dad in the army. During WWII he was a staff sergeant doing KP (kitchen patrol), his job was to make sure all fires were out before dark so that the Germans couldn't see the smoke and bomb them. He was on the Rhine River in Germany on VE Day (Victory in Europe Day). While Stateside after the war, a higher-ranking female office said, "Collins, have your men service these men." My dad said, "My guys from overseas aren't going to serve your Stateside guys," at which time he was written up. He then appeared in from of a very high-ranking officer and told him the same thing he told the female officer—at which time he was told, "Okay, Collins, get out of here." I never thought of my dad as ever being condescending to women, but I guess with that and a lot of hurts I got from women, I became jaded and disrespectful in my insecurities. Then all the ladies circled around him and repented on behalf of all the women in our life who took advantage of and hurt us. It was so sweet to watch and feel the healing of it. Suddenly there was *JESUS*, and we all started a Davidic circle dance. It was amazing...*JESUS* is so, so good to me...I asked the woman her name, and she said, "Patty, and the dark guy is Joe." Barbara asked a bunch of Qs, and suddenly Bobby was being loved on majorly by Popp'n—then she said to have whoever wanted to step forward allow Bobby and Popp'n to love on them and I should just watch. Francis wanted first, so I watched him approach what looked like a huge light of love around Bobby and Popp'n, and he disappeared in it. Then Sal, Mary, Joe, and Patty...it was incredible... they all disappeared into a Heavenly cloud of light of love...I felt such peace and love in my entire being. Then Popp'n disappeared into Bobby, and there she was just looking at me so absolutely lovingly...then Barbara said something like, "Let's have you and Bobby work together this week," and I promised Bobby I would listen to her instruction, knowing that she would speak to me in love and nurture me like I'd never had my entire life was and excited to have it now... What Barbara said was that everyone was getting so comfortable with me and each other that they joined and made Bobby in charge to speak for all of them. I think that's so appropriate since Bobby is the most like Michelle, and it's so sweet that *JESUS* would have her as the spokesperson. It was also cool that *JESUS* had Popp'n go in last since she seems to be the manifestation of my feelings for Michelle.

02.10.23

18:00: I just finished my best picture of *JESUS* with fire in *HIS* eyes at GCHOP, and a little Hispanic boy showed me the picture he was coloring of *JESUS*; he loved mine.

02.11.23

21:00: Finished writing *Caveman to Priest*! Thank *YOU*, LORD *JESUS*.

02.17.23

Revival is hitting at a lot of colleges and countries around the world. I'd love to go to Asbury University, but I have to apply for the copyright at 18:43. I'm done! I hear POPPA say, "You're set to drive to Ashbury!"

02.18.23

10:30: Drove to Ashbury University Revival.

17:45: I ran into Coby Humphrey and Felipe and Hannah Saldana, friends from GCHOP.

20:00: In the Gymnasium overflow since I didn't get here until late. It was very anointed with a lot of worship. A young man started playing "How Great Thou Are" on a violin, and *Glory* came down.

02.19.23

Ashbury University Revival. Slept in van. "Beautiful," very tough morning in the '30s but worth it. I got into Hughes Auditorium at around 13:30 after standing in the cold since about 06:30, but it was so worth it...I was able to get my friend JD Russell and his daughter in. It was beautiful and peaceful. I was feeling a bladder infection since I got there. I didn't ask but received a HEaling from *JESUS*! I've been to revivals, especially up in the Toronto Fire and others, which were great, but they were mostly Fire and Wine from Heaven. This was just absolute peace...the *peace* of GOD. Thank *YOU, JESUS*, for allowing me to be at the last weekend of public worship at Ashbury University's revival before the city made them shut it down.

We tried something new. I put my hand on my heart, and I said, "We're okay." Someone said, "No, we're not. I'm mad at Joan and Michelle." She said the way Michelle treated us was wrong. When I asked if there was anything else bothering her, she said, "Yeah, Professor Zipper..." He was a professor at SUNY Farmingdale in Farmingdale, New York. Barbara said, "Let her take her frustrations out on Zipper." She had a baseball bat with a huge spike in it, and I said no twice and meant it. Believe me, as a young adult, I wanted to do more than that for giving me a D every semester for two years during my bachelor's degree. He had to give me a C in my last semester because I had the highest grade on my midterm exam in the class, and I believe that got him mad...that was the reason I only graduated with a C+. He is also the one who tried to prevent me from getting into the bachelor's program, but two professors with their doctor overrode him. Boy, did I want to hurt him, but I still couldn't let her pummel him; I just couldn't... But Barbara's in charge, so I had to let her loose... She approached him, got ready to swing, and dropped to her knees and started bawling and crying. *I can't...* Then she just disappeared, sort of like water running downhill away from us...Bobby was fine, so we did the hand on my heart and said, "I'm okay," and there was nothing but peace...

03.06.23

09:00: We've been really missing Michelle badly. I'm getting out of the shower, and I believe I hear "HIM" say, "She's missing you big time too."

03.07.23, 3:53

17:48: The LORD was stirring in the Prayer Room regarding all of Israel being saved. I believe "HE" marked me for Jerusalem. It was truly an Isaiah 6:8 "send me" moment. "Also I heard the voice of the Lord, saying: 'Whom shall I send, And who will go for Us?' Then I said, 'Here am I! Send me.'" (Isaiah 6:8 NKJV).

03.13.23, 04:54

14:53: I believe when I was walking up to the office building for my meeting with GateGity Pastor Hazen, The LORD said my buying my brand-new denim jacket was just the beginning of my spending money. After twenty-two years of lack, plenty is coming! "Now the Lord blessed the latter days of Job more than his beginning; for he had fourteen thousand sheep, six thousand camels, one thousand yoke of oxen, and one thousand female donkeys. He also had seven sons and three daughters" (Job 42:12–13a, NKJV).

"So I will restore to you the years that the swarming locust has eaten. You shall eat in plenty and be satisfied, And praise the name of the Lord your God, Who has dealt wondrously with you; And My people shall never be put to shame" (Joel 2:25a-26, NKJV).

03.19.23

10:30: At church, people started approaching the platform, so I backed off toward the door and was worshiping. I felt drawn to two of my ministry partners (Bobby and Nan) but felt hesitant about going up to them; they were both so deeply with *JESUS*. Then they called us to Pray for each other, and I turned around and laid hands on her, and there was such a powerful move of HOLY SPIRIT. I didn't remember it ever being so anointed; she was obviously moved. It was incredible. Then I felt The LORD calling me to Pray for a young man named Michael Boal, and once again it was very powerful. The next day he called me and thanked me for Praying for him. It is so cool being "HIS" favorite best friend. Animals come out of nowhere just to look at "HIM" and be in "HIS" audience when We're together. Thank "YOU," POPPA.

03.23.23

16:55: POPPA swims to Fire Island with me on "HIS" back. We sit with our feet in the sand on the water's end, and whales come up and show off for "HIM."

03.27.23

17:05: Hard, hard, heavy heart for moving to Israel. Like really, really.

03.28.23

16:23: "HE" opened the door to HEaven above the bassist on the platform at GCHOP. I said, "Tell me, and I'll come immediately, or else I'll just stare at 'YOU.'" Staring at "HIM" is what I did!

04.13.23

15:05: TBN wants to publish *Caveman to Priest*! Thank "YOU," POPPA!

04.16.23, 07:11

08:08: I believe it's the first time I genuinely said to POPPA, "If it's 'YOUR' Will for me to be single my entire life, then that's what I want," and I meant it and mean it.

10:43: I could see the statement above turn into a beautiful garden.
"Lush, fragrant, and thriving..."

04.19.23, 05:55

01:39: I woke from a sweet dream with Michelle to the dreadful thought of Her engaged...
It's 05:55. POPPA, *JESUS*, BOB, Michelle, and me.

04.21.23, 06:43

06:00: Before waking up, I saw Michelle. She was crying, and there was a man in front of Her. I stayed back to observe, and She came to me, apologized, and told me She loved me and wanted to work on our Marriage...

04.23.23

05:55: I had a dream I was Praying for this young black man at a table with, I believe, friends of mine. He suddenly started manifesting and Praying against me. I just started pressing in, in the *love* of GOD for him. It was very powerful. Thank YOU, POPPA.

08:19: Richard gave me a word, "Solidify my contacts in Israel."

12:08: Word from my friend Richard Dalton when I spoke of my very difficult day yesterday missing Michelle, "Michelle is the last thread."

19:12: Having a tough day missing Michelle. I listen to TobyMac's "21 Years," and I've lost Michelle and don't know if I'll get Her back. If I'm not Her husband down here, I won't mean so much up there in Heaven.

17:02: While we were worshipping during all-staff chapel, someone touched my back. I turned, and no one was there.

05.13.23

05:30: I spent time with POPPA, and "HE" let me know it was one of "HIS" favorite times with me. I won the battle, perhaps, when I blew the shofar for the first time. "HE" reminded me of when "HE" honored me at a banquet table with Mike A. and gave me my armor, royal crown, and robe. Thank YOU, POPPA.

05.18.23

11:02: After walking and tripping two times, one that would have been major two years ago:

For who is GOD except The LORD? Who but our GOD is a solid rock? GOD arms me with strength, and he makes my way perfect. HE makes me as surefooted as a deer, enabling me to stand on mountain heights. HE trains my hands for battle; he strengthens my arm to draw a bronze bow. You have given me your shield of victory. Your right hand supports me; your help has made me great. You have made a wide path for my feet to keep them from slipping.

Psalm 18:31–36 (NLT)

05.22.23

08:05: I believe POPPA said "HE" is with me and will not allow them, my enemy, which currently is my employer, to overtake me or take advantage of me. "Stay strong, Mike—stick with the plan and with 'ME.' You're doing great—keep up the great job!"

05.25.23

I had a dream, and my lead pastor, Dustin, was in it. It was clearly him. We were in a room with other people but weren't talking. Suddenly he walked up to me and handed me a fresh folded towel. Then it was over. He texted me back with his thoughts, "Your dream may make sense that you're entering into your rest period and don't need your workout towel anymore because you're entering rest. It's time for your beach towel."

05.28.23

08:10: I believe "HE" said, "Wait till you see the restoration story."

06.14.23

09:32: I'm having a conversation in the Spirit with one of the leaders. He asks me where I see myself in a year. I answer, "I believe I will be in Israel, married to Michelle, having our first baby, and writing my third book." Thank "YOU," POPPA

06.21.23

07:02: I was having a conversation with POPPA about Pastor Hazen's sharing yesterday afternoon at the 4:00 p.m. Prayer meeting. Hazen was speaking about my first book, about ultra visitations from GOD and angels. So I was talking to POPPA about the visitations and how incredibly wonderful they were, and, of course, as my book says, after three years of visitations on steroids, I would cry to "HIM" and say, "POPPA, I miss those visits when 'YOU' would come in, in Glory and blow things up," and "HE" said, "You have 'MY' presence now, Mike. 'MY' presence is so much better than visitation." Then, "HE" said what was really incredible just now was that it was like when I was dating Michelle and I was so excited to see Her and spend time with Her. That was what those visitations were, but now I was married and always had THEM there in true intimacy, relationship, and love...

07.08.23, 03:33

06:53: "HE" told me that today starts my new season with the return of all that the locusts have eaten. New Kia Soul! Thank "YOU," POPPA. It'd been a very hard and long twenty-three years ..."HE" said, "'I' know, Mike. You've done great. Well done, 'MY' favored son! Come into the kingdom!"

08.03.23, 02:46

10:00: Today was the first Trader Joe's (TJ) run in two months. I've been picking up 800–1,000 pounds of everything TJ sells as part of my ministry. I load thirty to forty banana boxes of yummies every Wednesday and bring them back to the GateCity mission's base for the last five years. The ministry is coming to an end, and that's why it's been two months. I'm driving back and heading up to North Carolina this afternoon. I call my friend Gary Clem and ask if he would like a palm tree. He says of course; he loves plants and flowers like me. I get off the phone and think to myself, *That would look great on my bathroom next to the money plants*. I say, "Oh well." I get home, and there are two. POPPA, "YOU" are so good to me. Thank "YOU."

18:24: I'm in Clayton County, Georgia. I can see the hospital that I parked in the parking lot in September 20, 2021, when I drove as far as I could after Michelle divorced me. I'm just kind of thinking, and I'm just letting my feelings feel, and all of a sudden, I listen to the radio, and it's saying, "GOD's not done yet." Thank "YOU," POPPA. "YOU" are so kind to me. I'm on my way to Franklin, North Carolina, to visit my dear friends Gary and Trish Clem, and this is my second trip in less than a month. "YOU" are so good to me.

08.08.23

10:00: I believe I heard POPPA say Donald Trump is going to endorse *JESUS CHRIST Is behind NESARA/GESARA* (JBN), my second book. Hallelujah!

NESARA: National Economic Security and Recovery Act.

My next book will be called *JESUS CHRIST Is behind NESARA/GESARA*.

Many people are confused about the subject matter of this book. They think it's about current events, news, science, conspiracy theories, and/or politics. I don't see it that way. This book is about the move of GOD we're experiencing now in "the end times" but before "the great tribulation."

We have been in "the end times" since the day JESUS CHRIST ascended back to HEaven. I believe "the great tribulation" is near but at least a few years away. The intent of this book is to describe what has been going on behind the scenes of America and the world for hundreds of years from a biblical lens.

I believe we, the people called by GOD's Name, have humbled ourselves, Prayed, sought "HIS" face, and turned from our wicked ways of federal abortion and "HE" is HEaling our land after fifty years of us legally, federally, killing "HIS" children. Roe vs. Wade was fifty years ago. Fifty years is Jubilee in the Old Testament, freedom from bondage, slavery, and debt. This is what NESARA is all about. POPPA GOD is sending a refreshing for "HIS" church. We are not in the great tribulation yet, and I believe "HIS" church is fainting already. "HE" is freeing "HIS" people of the debt that has been illegally imposed on us for centuries, the poisoning of us, the killing, sex trading, and organ and adrenochrome harvesting of "HIS" *SON*'s bride. I think all the revival that has been going on this past year (Ashbury & Lee Universities; Athens, Georgia; Uganda; Israel...) is the proof of it.

POPPA GOD is bringing revival and a refreshing to "HIS" people so that we can stand and walk into tribulation as opposed to crawling under all this oppression... That is what this next book is about. It's a move of *JESUS* to revive and refresh *HIS* church and bride. I also call it a political/science nonfiction book. Stay tuned on cavementopriest.com and/or mikecollinsministry.com.

"If My people who are called by My name will humble themselves, and pray and seek My face, and turn from their wicked ways, then I will hear from heaven, and will forgive their sin and heal their land" (2 Chronicles 7:14, NKJV).

15:03 (3:03): Katie, one of the ladies at the HOP, walked by with her little baby, and I heard, "Yes, you will make a good dad soon."

08.12.23, 02:40

I wake up and believe POPPA has said to print a copy of my manuscript for *JESUS CHRIST Is behind NESARA/GESARA*, my second book, which isn't finished yet, and go see Chris Reed, president of MorningStar Ministry, about thirty minutes away and give it to him. He had a dream about it not long ago.

13:11 (1:11): I get to the church Chris Reed is speaking at and walk in, and he is selling his book right there. I introduce myself and give him the manuscript for *JBN*, and he seems locked on! I believe he is genuinely interested. He seems to know what NESARA is. Thank "YOU," POPPA.

15:00: Chris Reed starts reading my mail about NESARA, regarding tunnels and a ministry HEaling people involved with tunnels, and even lays hands on me (which I'm told doesn't happen often)! Then Ken Fish starts prophesying over me being around eight years old, and that's when the enemy really starts attacking me; it is so spot on...it's over now! But like the king of Persia was sixty-two, sixty-two is going to be huge! He prophesied *Caveman to Priest* and Chris prophesied *JESUS CHRIST Is behind NESARA/GESARA*! Come on!

08.13.23

10:33: I hear I'm dual resident and soon tri-resident.

08.14.23

10:00: I took the van to Pep Boys in Buford, Georgia; there was a very small screw in the rear driver's tire that they patched and didn't charge. Thank *YOU, JESUS.*

08.15.23

17:05: "Those who sow in tears Shall reap in joy. He who continually goes forth weeping, Bearing seed for sowing, Shall doubtless come again with rejoicing, Bringing his sheaves with him."

Psalm 126:5–6 (NKJV)

08.21.23

19:00: My first worship with the Word set with the Sterns. This is when we Pray through sections of the Bible. I would read a passage and they sing that part of the Scripture. It's very powerful. It was just Jim and Jess. I loved it. Thank "YOU," POPPA.

08.22.23, 03:13

09:50: I'm on my run circuit and in a bad mood. I call out to Popp'n, and immediately she's there; it is so good to talk with her. I ask her what is going on, and then, I ask, "Do you miss Michelle?" She really surprises me; she says, "It was really bad. I don't wanna go back there, so no, I really don't." Then she says that she's looking forward to us being Married again, but only if that will never happen again.

I had a dream about 04:00 this morning. The number four with POPPA, Cate, Quinn Michael, and me. Quinn Michael was hanging with Catherine Michael; that was very sweet. I remember asking POPPA to come have some time with me, and "HE" invited the two girls. Thank "YOU," POPPA.

17:30: I was worshipping with flags, and I believe I heard "HIM" say "worship leader," maybe even 212.

03:23: I trust "YOU," LORD! POPPA, I believe I've been hearing from "YOU" and doing "YOUR" will. Please help me, *JESUS*. POPPA, I need "YOU" to come through in the Mighty Name of *JESUS CHRIST*. Amen.

Chapter 8

MICHELLE VISITS ME OUT OF THE BLUE?

19:30: Finished helping a friend work on his veranda in North Carolina!

08.27.23

14:43: I'm driving home from the Smokies on 23 in Clayton. I see this blonde woman, probably middle age, holding this pretty, little, blonde baby girl, and I believe The LORD says that's gonna be me one day driving home to Michelle with our baby girl (or boys) on Her side. Thank "YOU," POPPA. I love "YOU."

15:00: My friend Richard calls me and tells me a woman stopped by looking for me, but she wouldn't say who it was. She said, "I'll stop back—don't say anything." He walked back to his room, and *JESUS* told him it was Michelle. He felt The LORD said to call me.

I get home from the Smokies at about 16:15. I'm trying not to be too excited, but I'm really just so blessed to know that Michelle is coming to see me. Right around 17:00 the doorbell rings, and I go out, and the most stunningly beautiful, wonderful, and incredible woman to have ever touched this earth is there in this beautiful outfit. She looks like HEaven. She's disappointed because She knows I know. I'm disappointed because I know; we stand there at the front step for probably thirty minutes, and I'm just looking into Her lovely face. She tells me The LORD told Her to come face Her enemy, me, and tell me that She forgives me. I immediately cry and thank Her for Her forgiveness, and I start repenting for all the pain I caused Her and how I hurt Her so badly... We decide to meet over in the old IHOP (International House of Prayer Atlanta) parking lot. We meet there, and She starts telling me so very much. And She tells me She's been to the old IHOP; She's been to GateCity; She's been to the post office. She's been around here for at least a week, and I didn't even know it. We go into the old IHOP. And we sit in my car for at least an hour. She loves my new soul car, Kia Soul, as well as the one in me, and we just talk and talk and talk. Then She asks if I want to go to Brewster's for ice cream. So we drive separate cars over to Brewster's. And this is my old Michelle—actually, it's a new Michelle. But it is so soothing to my heart to watch Her as She deeply thinks and carefully thinks before She speaks. We get to Brewster's, and we are in line. She's trying to decide and is so adorable—actually more than adorable. She gets a raspberry chocolate cone, and it looks good, but the raspberry is dripping all over the place, so I'm getting her a bunch of napkins. We sit down, and POPPA gives Her the most delicious ice cream. It's dripping a little bit but just full of raspberry, and I'm helping Her but trying not to do too much but helping Her, and She's appreciating. So I let Her know that I don't eat in the car, so we eat on the bench, and then She decides to sit in Her truck, and She's got a beautiful truck (She calls it a car). And I am outside, kind of, looking in and trying not to get too close, and then She comes out, and we talk, but She really needs to sit. And we talk until 01:45. Before 01:45, probably the last half hour, we just hugged and hugged and hugged! She let me hug Her, and She hugged me probably six times, and She held me so. We just really kind of became one; She held me and allowed me to hold Her. It was all so redemptive to hear Her sigh.

Before the hugs we just spoke for hours, and She explained and shared how I hurt Her from two days after the wedding up in Saratoga, New York. I believe I understood more deeply how I hurt Her and how painful it was for three or four years, and She hung in there. We both cried and cried and cried. During one of the hugs, She said that I had red glitter on my face. But now with all of these visits around here, the apartment, the hospital, IHOP, GateCity, She'd been using red glitter to sanctify, restore those memories, and all. She started prophesying that this glitter on my face was redeeming me, us. And that was what She said about the hugs; it was the hugs that were putting the broken pieces back together of both our hearts. I believe She made some type of reference of not only individually healing them but healing them together. I kept on asking Her if She needed to go because it was so late and She was staying forty-five minutes away, and then finally by 01:45, I said I needed to go. She promised me She would text me. She waved goodbye to me so sweetly. And I woke up and opened my phone to do my Prayer time, and there was a text from 02:20. So I wrote Her a text to say how sorry I was I missed the text. But I didn't beat myself up. I didn't get anxious or nervous, and I just explained myself. I told Her thank You for the most wonderful night in years.

My Lovely Michelle and me at the old IHOP-ATL building

"By YOU I have been upheld from birth; YOU are HE who took me out of my mother's womb. My praise shall be continually of YOU."

Psalm 71:6 (NKJV)

"He who tills his land will be satisfied with bread, But he who follows frivolity is devoid of understanding."

Proverbs 12:11 (NKJV)

08.29.23

17:13: Billy Humphrey, director of GateCity, is Praying at the mic for 1,000 intercessors full time, and I immediately see Michelle here with me, running that dance ministry that Billy wanted Her to do a few years ago here and in four others twenty-four seven in Atlanta.

"Wise words bring many benefits, and hard work brings rewards."

Proverbs 12:14 (NLT)

16:53: Michelle called me; we spoke for an hour; it was so kind. I ended up at 212 late, and we texted back and forth during service. We decided to both catch sleep and not speak.

At 212 Youth Ministry

We didn't have a worship leader tonight for 212, so we did a video, and I was crying my eyes out the entire time.

"Everything you've lost, *love's* Returning."

21:56: Michelle called me, and we talked for around three and a half hours. It started great but quickly went south when we started speaking about how I betrayed Her to almost all the leadership. I babbled and talked in circles for around twenty minutes, which hurt Her badly. Also, I didn't address Her lovely heart. It was so painful, but we both hung in there, even though we were exhausted and made it through! Thank *YOU, JESUS.*

I started by saying how proud I was of Her for coming to my door. How courageous She was to have done that. She explained also that *JESUS* showed Her when She was ringing my bell that it was exactly three years ago, 08.27, that I texted Her the triathlon pic, and She removed my ring and never put it on again. That was the day She was divorced from me, sadly. Here it was exactly three years later that She was at my door. Thank "YOU," POPPA.

08.31.23

11:45: I had an amazing short conversation with one of the leaders at GCHOP. He asked how I was doing, and I said that was a very complex Q. I expect to retire in days, weeks, or months from engineering, my book should be out in a few months, and Mike Collins Ministry Inc. A 501.c.3 soon too!

13:36: I believe POPPA just told me that I was not on trial with Michelle. "HE" said to relax and enjoy becoming Her best friend. Thank "YOU," POPPA!

"My mouth shall tell of YOUR righteousness And YOUR salvation all the day, For I do not know their limits."

Psalm 71:15 (NKJV)

"The generous soul will be made rich, And he who waters will also be watered himself."

Proverbs 11:25 (NKJV)

15:30: I'm working on the agenda for Michelle for our time tomorrow, and I just start really weeping deeply, and I don't know why. I'm calling out to *JESUS*, and I hear, "Mike, it's okay. You're going through a lot of emotional stuff. Michelle's in your life. I'm closing a season of engineering, which you did a great job with, and opening a season with Michelle, ministry, books...it's okay to cry, but remember it's *ME*; it's okay; 'I' have you."

09.02.23

08:42: I believe I heard POPPA say, "Yes, a lot like last time. You're going to lose your job, but you're going to do it right this time, Mike. 'I' *love* you. 'I' am with you, and it's 'ME.'" Thank "YOU," POPPA. When we Married in 2015, I lost my job three days before the Wedding on Long Island, New York.

11:22: Second time together with Michelle at McCray's rooftop in downtown Lawrenceville. POPPA, please rest my emotions, calm my mind, hold my tongue, and open my ears and heart to listen to Michelle's heart and emotions in the Mighty Name of *JESUS CHRIST*. Amen. Please give me wisdom to not say anything that isn't of "YOU" and to make sure I say everything that is of "YOU." Please keep me humble and inquisitive.

12:00: It was so Healing to have the most incredible and stunning woman in the world walk into McCray's today. So, so much She shared from Her heart...

My Lovely Michelle and me at McCray's roof top for lunch.

Lunch was lovely and sunny; we just talked and talked. Afterward we walked down to the local coffee shop and chatted; that was when I gave Her a copy of this manuscript. She started sharing a lot of what The LORD had been doing in South Carolina and Georgia over the last few months and about Her new book. We walked over and sat in my car in the parking garage, and She just continued sharing Her heart and lots of pictures of butterflies, Her on the swing, the red boots. She shared for hours...

Then we were walking on CJI Lane, and I asked, "Do You want me to hold Your arm?" She doesn't even answer, and I stumble. She said, "Should I hold your arm?" And I wish I said yes please. I gave Her a beautiful little black backpack purse. I wasn't certain if that was really what I was to do, but "HE" made it pretty clear. So I gave Her the purse, and She really loved it. She said something like, "I wish it had room for this cell phone." I was just listening and listening to Her heart. In the past that would have gotten me insecure, like "oh, well, I made a mistake," like She doesn't like it. But now I know what to look for when I'm buying a purse for Her. I didn't make a mistake, and She doesn't not like it. Thank *YOU, JESUS*. I love what *YOU*'ve done to my heart and my entire being, breaking *insecurity*.

09.03.23

13:00: I found a beautiful acorn near big red on the run circuit!

"They will be called oaks of righteousness a planting of the Lord for the display of his splendor" (Isaiah 61:3c, NIV).

09.04.23, 02:42

12:00: Michelle called me. She was so thankful for me having so many beautiful things for Her. It went really well but then turned, unfortunately, and I hurt Her badly again, like thousands of times, if not ten thousands of times. It was very painful for me to hurt Her with not knowing details, remembering later, which makes it look like I'm lying like I have so very many times. I said a few times that I knew I'd upset her. I asked if She would please lower Her tone and that I felt like I was being berated, and She apologized and changed the way She was speaking with me. Thank "YOU," POPPA.

17:37: *JESUS* came while I was getting ready for the Prayer set. *HE* put *HIS* head on my shoulder; it was so kind. This had never happened before. I asked *HIM* why I'm such a knucklehead. I'm the chief of knuckleheads. *HE* said, "You're not a knucklehead." I asked *HIM* if *HE* could give me a heart to truly hear Michelle's heart and listen patiently and lovingly while She shared Her emotions on anything, but especially how I'd hurt Her. I didn't want to react but respond in love. That was when the Sterns came in.

18:20: I asked *JESUS* to dance with me, oh Lover of my soul, and we started holding hands, and we were like sky diving in a circle, and suddenly, *HE* took off like a rocket, and I followed *HIM*. It was like I had a jet pack with no pack, of course, because I was with *HIM*, and I'm following *HIM* up and down and all around…it was so cool and beautiful. Thank *YOU, JESUS*. Then I Prayer lead.

> *"For you shall go out with joy, And be led out with peace; The mountains and the hills Shall break forth into singing before you, And all the trees of the field shall clap their hands."*
>
> Isaiah 55:12 (NKJV)

09.05.23, 07:14

07:38: It was very painful how much I hurt Michelle once again in our conversation yesterday. But I believe it revealed to me that I can't work for DeKalb County because of the stressful nature of what they want me to do and the environment they want me to work in. Thank "YOU," POPPA, but it was and is so painful when I hurt Michelle with the way my brain works or actually the way it doesn't work, sadly.

11:49: I believe HOLY SPIRIT told me to leave Michelle be. "Let Her miss you and let ME bring to remembrance all that is good and different about you." Thank YOU, BOB! I love and miss YOU so much.

16:56: Billy said, "Every step in joy!"

"When my steps were bathed with cream, And the rock poured out rivers of oil for me! When I went out to the gate by the city, When I took my seat in the open square."

Job 29:6–7 (NKJV)

Then I felt to share with Rolando and Olivia that we have a new worship leader and we are stepping into a season of joy as a church and 212. We were Praying; it's not hard when you are working in joy!

09.06.23

"My lips shall greatly rejoice when I sing to YOU, And my soul, which YOU have redeemed. My tongue also shall talk of YOUR righteousness all the day long; For they are confounded, For they are brought to shame Who seek my hurt."

Psalm 71:23–24 (NKJV)

09.07.23

12:29: I keep hearing a man's voice behind me during the Israel set, and there is no one there.

15:15 to 20:15: Michelle asked me if I would met Her at the run circuit. She responded to all my hurts and how I hurt Her. She responded so lovingly—then Smoothie King and to my place! Thank YOU, LORD! I was able to repent, and She repented for so much; it was beautiful.

09.08.23

12:45: I called Michelle to let Her know about the meeting with my employer. She allowed me to share, and it went well. She didn't understand everything, but we were both good with that. Then She told me The LORD was putting Her on a ten-day fast, which included no seeing me, no communication, and just juice/smoothies. I was proud of Her but would miss Her terribly. This reminded me about when She left the third and final time we separated—She texted me that She was doing a fast and Praying about moving to Kansas City. Sadly, I didn't even address the moving to Kansas City part; She moved thinking I didn't care She moved. Boy, was the enemy vicious, and I was such a jerk. Please forgive me, POPPA, for hurting Her so much. Please heal us both! In the Mighty Name of *JESUS*. Amen.

I was a jerk, but as I was able to explain to Her, that was the weekend She visited Kansas City and Her car was having trouble. I repaired it; She asked me to lock the keys in it at the apartment. When I left, my van broke down, and I found out that my brother Kerry's son was found dead only about four hours away. I had no vehicle, and I couldn't go to the funeral. While I was picking up my van from the mechanic, She texted me that. I addressed the fast, but not Her Praying about moving some 1,000 miles away...it was so stupid of me to not read the text completely and carefully; perhaps if She stayed here, it would have worked out better...this action of mine sent Her away feeling that She wasn't worth loving...and that I didn't care. I still cry so hard over this...I can't believe I sent the most incredible, wonderful, beautiful, anointed, gifted woman in the world away, thinking She wasn't worth loving...I have to live with that for the rest of my life...

17:27: We talked for hours. She shared Her heart that when I said if The LORD wanted me to sell the van, I would and I was fine either way, that reminded Her that She believed I didn't love Her or the Marriage. The van is mine, and I can sell it, but it reminded Her of feeling like I didn't care. I was able to talk to Her heart. It was so beautiful. Thank "YOU," POPPA.

09.09.23

07:40: I believe I am to join Michelle on the ten-day fast. Out of solidarity and crying out for friendship with Michelle and our Marriage, so I am to do a ten-day fast with her.

19:00: Michelle said that She felt *JESUS* had made Her healed and whole while driving the van and all the redemptive work. That was so incredibly warming to my soul. I'd love to have Her back as my Wife if that's "YOUR" will and we're both healed and whole in "YOU."

Most incredible time with Michelle. She drove the van all day today and asked me to come sit with Her. She shared so very much, gave me a beautiful sweet card, and good and plenty candy; we sang the Tim Reimherr song "More Than Ashes." It was so beautiful and HEaling to my soul. Then we went to Waffle House.

09.10.23

07:31: I had a dream that I was meeting with General Flynn. He was busy with someone before me but came out and said, "A lot of people are writing about NESARA, but I'm excited to read your book, *JESUS CHRIST Is behind NESARA/GESARA*, Mike."

"FATHER, I desire that they also whom YOU gave ME may be with ME where I am, that they may behold MY Glory which YOU have given ME; for YOU loved ME before the foundation of the world."

John 17:24 (NKJV)

09:11: What I believe "HE" told me today was that I was not remembering things as well as I used to; now I'm not working so hard in the flesh to remember and allowing HOLY SPIRIT to bring things to remembrance. It's okay if I don't remember everything.

09.11.23

17:05 (5:05, SOS): Billy's Praying out of Daniel 9. Release the spirit of understanding of the end-times. Why not me, POPPA, and why not now! Release revelation of the end-times now in the Mighty Name of *JESUS CHRIST*. Pretty amazing that I'm on a ten-day fast with Michelle!

09.12.23

17:57: Send me, LORD.
I had a dream that I met Michelle's mom and dad. They were shocked and so very excited.

09.13.23

10:39: While in the shower, I heard Michelle say, "Yes. I believe The LORD wants us to reMarry." I was crying. I said, "I believe that's 'YOUR' plan, but I believe we are to court, and I'm to love Her well. Then we are to become engaged, enjoy the engagement, and then be remarried." Thank "YOU," POPPA!

10:53: The enemy may have won the battle, but he didn't win the war. I believe POPPA has great plans for Michelle and me to remarry.

16:01: Having a tough, tough day. I really have such trouble fasting. *YOU*'re worth it, *JESUS*, but I do so very poorly!

07:13: My HEaling cost me everything—my life, Marriage, girls—this is tough for me to say but was worth it to have such an incredible personal relationship with POPPA, *JESUS*, and HOLY SPIRIT. It's sad, but as Billy Humphrey and Jamie Boy Pridgen said three years ago, it's all a light affection; losing everything is not easy, especially my Michelle and girls, but I gladly lost my life, but losing the Marriage was so very gut-wrenchingly painful. It's so, so very sad how I hurt Michelle, and I'm so very sorry for the pain I caused Her, but I don't think I would have this relationship if it wasn't as painful and costly. I would cry so hard that I couldn't breathe. As I've said, I would tell POPPA, "If 'YOU' don't put air in these lungs, I'm coming to see 'YOU.'" Then when I had a Throne Room experience for an hour, starring into the "Eyes of Fire" of *JESUS CHRIST*, I now cry so hard when I think, Pray, or sing about *HIM* that I can't breathe and say, "POPPA, if 'YOU' don't put air in these lungs, I'm going to come see 'YOU.'" This has been my life for three and a half years. I worship hard, loud, and right up front... For the first two years, I would be crying in anguish for not having my Michelle, but then, after seeing *JESUS*' face, I now worship and cry in joy and can't breathe either way. People who don't know me don't know the difference. I believe POPPA told me it was like people who don't know me and stay far off could not discern the difference between me Worshipping in anguish for two years and now in joy.

Restoration of the Temple Begins

Now in the second month of the second year of their coming to the house of GOD at Jerusalem, Zerubbabel the son of Shealtiel, Jeshua the son of Jozadak, and the rest of their brethren the priests and the Levites, and all those who had come out of the captivity to Jerusalem, began work and appointed the Levites from twenty years old and above to oversee the work of the house of The LORD. Then Jeshua with his sons and brothers, Kadmiel with his sons, and the sons of Judah, arose as one to oversee those working on the house of GOD: the sons of Henadad with their sons and their brethren the Levites. When the builders laid the foundation of the temple of The LORD, the priests stood in their apparel with trumpets, and the Levites, the sons of Asaph, with cymbals, to praise The LORD, according to the ordinance of David king of Israel. And they sang responsively, praising and giving thanks to The LORD:

"For HE is good, For HIS mercy endures forever toward Israel."

Then all the people shouted with a great shout, when they praised The LORD, because the foundation of the house of The LORD was laid. But many of the priests and Levites and heads of the fathers' houses, old men who had seen the first temple, wept with a loud voice when the foundation of this temple was laid before their eyes. Yet many shouted aloud for joy, so that the people could not discern the noise of the shout of joy from the noise of the weeping of the people, for the people shouted with a loud shout, and the sound was heard afar off.

Ezra 3:8–13 (NKJV)

I was so foolish and ignorant; I was like a beast before YOU. Nevertheless I am continually with YOU; YOU hold me by my right hand. YOU will guide me with YOUR counsel, And afterward receive me to Glory. Whom have I in Heaven but YOU? And there is none upon earth that I desire besides YOU. MY flesh and my heart fail; But GOD is the strength of my heart and my portion forever.

Psalm 73:22–26 (NKJV)

09.15.23 07:10

22:30: I believe "HE" is telling me "HE" has got a gaggle of feelings for me in New York.

09.17.23, 08:00

10:00: While showering, I believe I heard POPPA say, "Do you trust 'ME,' Mike?" I said, "Yes, I trust 'YOU' with my entire life, Michelle, the girls, finances, and being..." "HE" said, "Good. 'I' *love you*, Mike."

19:12: I spoke with Cate for around three hours (165 minutes). At first it was about her life and my life. I repented for any pain I caused her, for not being caring or not loving her well, for not being there for her senior year of high school and all of college. She appreciated that, forgave me, and said she always felt loved by me. We talked about playing Barbies until high school and cooking and baking together. The second two hours were about *JESUS CHRIST Is behind NESARA/GESARA*, and she listened well, asked great questions, and received. She did take one (two) vax and a booster, three total, but will take my pine needle extract. Thank "YOU," POPPA.

Michelle, 12:00–22:45: At the Jones' most amazing redemption. Then at Stone Mountain, tough spot for a bit. Back at Jones' help load car and...tough, but we worked through it. I shared my unfiltered heart of never feeling loved, and that really hurt Michelle, and She got really upset. I stayed till late to work it out, and we really did. Thank "YOU," POPPA.

09.19.23, 05:15

11:57: I believe POPPA just told me that Michelle got really hurt and upset; we worked it out, and I needed to learn to be even better when I upset Her. This was still very painful for Her, but She was doing great! "Keep doing your best with Her as you are, Mike."

14:31: This came from my gratitude list. Yesterday with Michelle at the Jones' ministering to Her and the HEaling and redemption. Then Stone Mountain with lunch and climbing the mountain with Her was just so incredible. Then to going back to the Jones', helping Her pack for the car, and being able to continue ministering to Her and loving on Her. Thank "YOU," POPPA.

16:33: We started Praying against the wiles of the enemy, and I was crying so hard for me, Michelle and me, the girls, the entire work situation. Then it absolutely lifted, and I felt a full tank of gas, full bank account, peace and *love* tomorrow and the entire eighteen-hour drive to New York, and our Marriage and friendship. Then Billy had us really pressing and laying hands on each other; it was powerful. Then he started Praying against curses against us, and it got even stronger. Thank "YOU," POPPA.

09.20.23, 05:42: Two years from divorce, but I'm seeing Her and celebrating my sixtieth birthday.

07:24: "HE" just showed me a picture of Michelle walking out of the restroom on top of Stone Mountain. We were being rushed by a huge angry female security guard, but I was able to take in Her beauty. "HE" just showed me again and said, "That is a new, healed woman." Thank "YOU," POPPA.
We went to Olive Garden and had a beautiful birthday dinner for me. Then we went back to Bogart, and She tried almost all the clothes I gave and what She had just recently gotten. It was an even kinder gift from POPPA than I could have ever wished or Prayed for. I stayed with Her until 03:45!

09.21.23, 09:01

20:02: I was leaving after spending about three hours with Michelle at Bogart, and we just spent so much time together. It was so beautiful; we blew the shofar when I was leaving. She was probably twenty feet away. I said, "I love You, Michelle," and She said, "I love you too, Mike." Thank "YOU," POPPA. This was twenty-six days with Michelle around, and seven of those days, we were completely together. I would've guessed more than that.

09.22.23, 04:36

04:45: I had such a tough time falling asleep last night. I went to bed at 21:45 but saw 22:30. We had such a beautiful time together then texting about it and sharing pics.

04:56: The enemy is really beating me, and *JESUS* just told me, "Remember the last thing you heard from Her was 'I love you too, Mike.'"

05:45: I heard "HIM" say, "'I' wonder how that new makeup bag is."

06:11: I believe "HE" just told me, "Michelle's not remembering any good times with you because She's still very hurt and sad." She will!

I'm heading out later than I wanted, but I couldn't fall asleep remembering twenty-six days total, seven together, my birthday celebration on the second year, the last day, and the last thing I heard from Her was "I love you too, Mike."

06:44: There's going to be full restoration between Michelle and Dad and the entire family.

09.23.23, 07:53

16:10: I'm at the spot at Dean's Creek in Upstate New York where I was drowning, and Mom came running in to save me. I was probably between five and seven. I got a lot of peace being there. Thank "YOU," POPPA.

19:34: I'm tired! I hear myself say, "I miss You so much, Michelle," and I believe I hear "HIM" say, "She misses you too, Mike."

04:04: I believe POPPA gave me even more insight. I've been wanting to be secluded, and "HE" gave me seclusion here in New York with Ali and Michael not here. They don't get in till sometime today, so it's really nice. I've enjoyed this time alone and going up in the mountains up in Greene County. I didn't see anybody that I knew, and I really didn't wanna see anybody that I knew. I was not hiding from anybody, but I believe The LORD said I still need to be guarded because I'm still not healed. *HE* just gave me a reference in John when Mary saw the resurrected *CHRIST*. *HE* said, "Jesus said to her, 'Do not cling to Me, for I have not yet ascended to My Father'" (John 20:17, NKJV). Not that I'm ascending to POPPA too soon... Thank *YOU*, LORD *JESUS*. *YOU* are awesome.

16:00: Ali and I met Cate at a nice seafood restaurant in Salisbury, Connecticut, and had a wonderful time for my sixtieth birthday with both my girls! Thank "YOU," POPPA!

Me, Ali and Cate for my 60th BDay dinner in NY.

Some of the places I went to:

Dave Schneck's apartment—I believe it was building eleven. I blew the shofar outside, laid my hands on the door of 11D, and released Michelle and me from all traumatic bondages in the Mighty Name of *JESUS CHRIST*.

Montgomery Place, where we took our wedding pics. I didn't want to see Her before the wedding but was so glad we did it Her way. I took pics in the garden, around the mansion, and the little pond. I blew the shofar over the mansion, pond, and garden. Then I took a pic of me with the shofar at the trellis, which is where my favorite picture was taken.

09.26.23, 07:52

15:18: Michelle texted, "Can we talk?" I called Her, and we talked for fifty minutes. I told Her I missed and loved Her and all about Green and Dutchess County trips. She wanted me to blow the shofar with Her over the Lawrenceville gazebo. But I called Her too late. We had such a nice talk. I told Her about my almost drowning as a kid, and She wanted to know details and was quite concerned for me.

09:27.23, 08:05

07:30: After stopping by Bagel World in Wappingers, New York, around twenty minutes out of my way. When I drove past my former Lead Pastor Marlow's road, I wondered how he was doing. I was driving over the Newburgh/Beacon Bridge (in New York), and there was Marlow driving his pickup. I waved and signaled to pull over. We said hi, he mentioned not hearing from me, and I reminded him that the phone was bidirectional; he laughed and said he'd do better. We chatted for a moment, I told him I loved him, and we left. It was nice that he was the last person I saw in New York.

09.28.23, 04:32

22:30: I drove 1,000 miles in sixteen hours from Ali's to Atlanta and am feeling good! Thank "YOU," POPPA! I listened to all my voice memos the trip up and down.

12:15: I've tasted HEaven being Married to Michelle, and I'm not looking anywhere else ever again.

12:39–13:41: I believe I spoke to my Michelle in the Spirit and shared how vicious the enemy was by stealing intimacy my entire life and how much I missed out by not having it with Her. She agreed and said I couldn't have had it with Her because I didn't even have it with POPPA. So very sad!

10.02.23, 09:29

16:55: "The secret of The LORD is with those who fear HIM, And HE will show them HIS covenant."

Psalm 25:14 (NKJV)

17:18: I was so reminded of not having intimacy with the most incredible woman in the world and the most wonderful GOD, who *loves* me and wants such intimacy with me.

10.04.23

01:45: I have the thought of when my landlord was doing a job for a hotrod shop I was managing, Stardust Hotrod, we needed a trailer truck removed and he misquoted us; he brought the wrong truck for the job. When I was moving out of the house I was renting, he decided to keep some of my security to make up for it. I told him that wasn't right, and he didn't care. Well, a few short years later, I became the CEO (code enforcement officer) for the town. You should have seen the terror on his face when I walked onto the multimillion house job he was general contracting. He wasn't a believer and thought I was going to get even with him, which I could have very easily done, especially with my being such an arrogant, prideful narcissist... Thank "YOU," POPPA, that I didn't...

02:02: I'm asking POPPA what "HE" is doing, and at 01:58, I'm that little boy with my right arm around the Great King's left leg while "HE" is ruling from "HIS" mighty Throne. Some man looks down snidely and says, "Why's he here?" POPPA immediately says, "He will be a king one day soon. Mind your manners..." That's my POPPA. Thank "YOU," POPPA. "YOU" are so good to me!

15:38: On my way to the Prayer Room, I saw a couple walking and holding hands, and I believe I heard POPPA say, "Michelle is getting such HEaling, Mike. Wait for it, Mike. Trust 'ME.' Do you trust 'ME,' Mike?" "Yes, POPPA, I trust 'YOU,' will wait for 'YOU,' and know 'YOU' will do it!"

17:09: I heard POPPA whisper, "Michelle's beginning to know that you really love Her, Mike. Keep waiting. 'I' know it's hard. Hang in there and know 'I' am working. Trust 'ME,' Mike."

10.05.23 06:23

08:50: I believe "HE" said with my accepting 100 percent responsibility for all the problems with the Marriage and repenting immediately, without hesitation, it was dropping Michelle's guard and allowing HOLY SPIRIT to remind Her of Her involvement. If I didn't or don't, it gave Her flesh a chance to rear up. "You're doing great, Mike. Keep it up. Keep doing what you're doing, and let 'ME' work on Her lovely heart." Thank "YOU," POPPA.

10.06.23, 05:00

Our two-hour talk. TY, *JESUS*!

10.07.23, 03:33

I want to be Your best friend.
I want You excited to share what GOD is doing in Your life that day and me not interrupting You.
I want You to feel safe to share Your heart with me and excited to do it anytime You want.
I want You to share Your dreams and desires with me freely.

03:45: I believe "HE" just told me "HE" was going to remind Michelle of some really sweet times with me while She was in Loveland, Ohio. JEHOVAH Sneaky! That's "YOUR" name. Oh, how "YOU" *love* me and my beautiful Michelle. Thank "YOU," POPPA.

10.09.23, 03:14

14:00: Thoughtful and frugal with my finances (Richard).

"Where no oxen are, the trough is clean; But much increase comes by the strength of an ox."

Proverbs 14:4 (NKJV)

10.10.23, 05:51

17:13: *"Seek good and not evil, That you may live; so The LORD GOD of hosts will be with you, As you have spoken. Hate evil, love good; Establish justice in the gate. It may be that The LORD GOD of hosts Will be gracious to the remnant of Joseph."*

Amos 5:14–15 (NKJV)

Feeling:

Then Job arose, tore his robe, and shaved his head; and he fell to the ground and worshiped. And he said: "Naked I came from my mother's womb, And naked shall I return there. The LORD gave, and The LORD has taken away; Blessed be the name of The LORD." In all this Job did not sin nor charge GOD with wrong.

Job 1:20–22 (NKJV)

17:30: POPPA cast out all evil from Israel. If it's not "YOU," cast it out in the Mighty Name of *JESUS CHRIST.*

18:05: While talking with a friend, another friend, Beto, gave me a hug and said to keep practicing for the audition. I guess that means I didn't pass the audition, which is okay.

10.12.23, 07:18

10:36: I'm in the Prayer Room, and I believe The LORD put on my heart Michelle and I being healed and raising our own new family.

"I call to remembrance my song in the night; I meditate within my heart, And my spirit makes diligent search."

Psalm 77:6 (NKJV)

08:43: I believe POPPA reminded me when I speak with people about *JESUS CHRIST Is behind NESARA/GESARA* and all *HE* is doing, it's like *HIM* talking with Nicodemus. If you don't believe earthly things, how can I tell you about Heavenly things? "I have told you earthly things and you do not believe, how will you believe if I tell you heavenly things?" (John 3:12, NKJV).

"Will The LORD cast off forever? And will HE be favorable no more? Has HIS mercy ceased forever? Has HIS promise failed forevermore? Has GOD forgotten to be gracious? Has HE in anger shut up HIS tender mercies? Selah."

Psalm 77:7–9 (NKJV)

"Most assuredly, I say to you, he who believes in ME, the works that I do he will do also; and greater works than these he will do, because I go to MY FATHER. And whatever you ask in MY name, that I will do, that the FATHER may be glorified in the Son."

John 14:12–13 (NKJV)

"The wisdom of the prudent is to understand his way, But the folly of fools is deceit."

Proverbs 14:8 (NKJV)

There shall come forth a Rod from the stem of Jesse, And a Branch shall grow out of his roots. The Spirit of The LORD shall rest upon HIM, The Spirit of wisdom and understanding, The Spirit of counsel and might, The Spirit of knowledge and of the fear of The LORD. HIS delight is in the fear of The LORD, And HE shall not judge by the sight of HIS eyes, Nor decide by the hearing of HIS ears; But with righteousness HE shall judge the poor, And decide with equity for the meek of the earth; HE shall strike the earth with the rod of HIS mouth, And with the breath of HIS lips HE shall slay the wicked. Righteousness shall be the belt of HIS loins, And faithfulness the belt of HIS waist. "The wolf also shall dwell with the lamb, The leopard shall lie down with the young goat, The calf and the young lion and the fatling together; And a little child shall lead them."

Isaiah 11:1–6 (NKJV)

14:13: "The Spirit of The LORD GOD is upon me, because The LORD has anointed me to bring good news to the poor; he has sent me to bind up the brokenhearted, to proclaim liberty to the captives, and the opening of the prison to those who are bound."

Isaiah 61:1 (ESV)

"And I said, 'This is my anguish; But I will remember the years of the right hand of the Most High.'"

Psalm 77:10 (NKJV)

"If you ask anything in MY name, I will do it."

John 14:14 (NKJV)

"Fools mock at sin, But among the upright there is favor."

Proverbs 14:9 (NKJV)

16:58: I don't know if it was me, but I thought I heard in the Spirit Michelle say She wishes I was with Her going to Mom's eighty-fifth birthday party.

10.16.23, 08:42

11:23: *Ralked* (ran/walked, but more ran than walked) one point five out of one point eight miles CHPN. Mike A. joined me on the run circuit. He was so funny. He didn't run hump two; He did whatever and met me on top. We walked. He didn't have much to say except love on me. We even held hands; it was powerful.

When we got to the boys, I got a huge hug from them, and He stayed with them. While I was saying goodbye and I love you, Michelle, in the Spirit, came to walk with me. My heart melted; my Michelle came to walk with me. She grabbed my left arm and loved on me well. One of the old Asian women in the natural walked by. I was in a T-shirt, and it was only fifty, so she said, "You're a Superman." Michelle said, "You're my Superman." My heart completely melted! Then Popp'n came and grabbed my right arm. I said to Michelle, "That's where she usually is, but that's all right. My left arm is always and will always be

Yours," and she (Popp'n) agreed. When we got to the clearing, I took Michelle to the table I wanted to take Her when we were repenting a few weeks ago, but it didn't happen. It was supposed to happen today in the Spirit. I repented to Her more about six things I did and tried to name them and give the name of how it must have hurt Her. She said She appreciated it, that She'd already forgiven me, and that I didn't have to repent for them. I said, "Thank you, but I believe I'm going to be repenting for the rest of my life, and I want to. It's what's going to keep me humble, and I want that as much as POPPA wants to give it to me."

13:43: Michelle called. Thank "YOU," POPPA. She was just so tired and sore. LORD, please give Her rest, peace, protection, wisdom, and comfort. Thank "YOU," POPPA, for Mom's eighty-fifth birthday dinner cruise to have gone so well. Thank "YOU" for having Michelle hug Dad and for them all to dance and have so much fun, as Michelle said, like they hadn't in years. Also, thank "YOU" for Dad dancing with Michelle. Redemption and restoration over Dad, Michelle, and the entire family in the Mighty Name of *JESUS CHRIST*. Amen.

10.17.23, 08:11

15:51: A feeling word. Grateful. YOU are so very good to me and love me so.

"There is a way that seems right to a man, But its end is the way of death."

Proverbs 14:12 (NKJV)

10.19.23, 07:32

05:29: I had a dream last night; suddenly I saw Michelle, and She looked Heavenly, absolutely darling, gorgeous, and lovely. She started prophesying about our son or sons. It was very, very powerful. As I said, She, Michelle, was radiant.

12:40: So glad I chose ("HE" chose).

Therefore I positioned men behind the lower parts of the wall, at the openings; and I set the people according to their families, with their swords, their spears, and their bows. And I looked, and arose and said to the nobles, to the leaders, and to the rest of the people, "Do not be afraid of them. Remember the Lord, great and awesome, and fight for your brethren, your sons, your daughters, your wives, and your houses." And it happened, when our enemies heard that it was known to us, and that God had brought their plot to nothing, that all of us returned to the wall, everyone to his work. So it was, from that time on, that half of my servants worked at construction, while the other half held the spears, the shields, the bows, and wore armor; and the leaders were behind all the house of Judah. Those who built on the wall, and those who carried burdens, loaded themselves so that with one hand they worked at construction, and with the other held a weapon. Every one of the builders had his sword girded at his side as he built. And the one who sounded the trumpet was beside me.

Nehemiah 4:13-18 (NKJV)

First for my Prayer set. My friend, the local Messianic Rabbi David Otero from Tzur Yisrael, and his wife were here, and they were in full agreement. Thank "YOU," POPPA, for giving me a Spirit to listen to "YOUR" ways.

19:48: Michelle called me for seventy minutes. The perfect number times ten. She had just finished dinner with Mom and Dad! Dad said he missed her. She told them about me, us, and it was so comforting to my heart and soul. She continued about not knowing about driving to Columbus or where She was going to stay and appreciated my advice on that. She was also thinking about driving to Kansas, Dallas, and then Atlanta. I suggested that might be too much for Her to do and weather could get bad. She was not sleeping well and was very tired. It was so nice to have Her share Her lovely heart and catch up. I just love Her so much, POPPA. Thank "YOU"!

10.21.23, 07:06

"Now to HIM who is able to do exceedingly abundantly above all that we ask or think, according to the power that works in us, to HIM be Glory in the church by CHRIST JESUS to all generations, forever and ever. Amen."

Ephesians 3:20–21 (NKJV)

08:41: I believe The LORD told me to give Joan a chance to be kind to me.

10.25.23, 12:01

I want to repent for being a liar for our entire Marriage. "HE" has been giving me deep revelation and understanding to this problem I've had my entire life and into our Marriage. As an engineer in New York, I would always exaggerate and embellish things like resume experience, work, salary...I would always know that I would exaggerate by a factor of four and think that was okay. A lot of this was before I was a CHRISTian, but my actions really didn't change when I became a Believer, as You know and brought to my attention many times.

I want to repent for allowing the enemy to cause such disruption and confusion in my mind and soul. I have a man here at the house who speaks in such a confusing manner. It's really difficult to talk with him, like it must have been with me. I am so sorry for frustrating You and provoking You to anger with my absolute confusing and combating conversation almost all day every day of our Marriage. "For where envying and strife is, there is confusion and every evil work" (James 3:16, KJV).

I had one of the missionaries who used to live here visit me around a year ago. He let me know that he could only speak with me or take me for around twenty minutes because I was so shallow. He visited me for hours...he was amazed at my transformation.

10.26.23, 02:22

13:03: I'm in between Prayer cycles and use the bathroom. One tiny hair is a bit long, and it makes me think of Michelle. She would cut my hair and/or fix it, and every single hair would be perfect. She would break out Her Big, Sexy hair spray and make sure it looked great. Boy, do I miss Her and that!

10.27.23, 07:36

21:08: I felt while we were Praying for the baptism of HOLY SPIRIT, the Girls were hit in the Mighty Name of *JESUS CHRIST*.

10.28.23, 08:58

09:24: I keep hearing something in my noise machine, *isop*.

10.29.23, 07:28

09:40: I'm in the shower. I believe I hear POPPA say, "'I' am stopping the bleeding. It doesn't mean you and Michelle aren't going to feel the crunch, but it's going to stop." Thank "YOU," POPPA.

12:45: While sharing with my friend Franky about everything that is going on, he said I've become gentle. Thank "YOU," POPPA.

16:00: I feel heavy-hearted, reserved, opened, quiet, and open.

11.02.23, 09:03

19:26: Michelle calls me from my driveway and spends five hours with me! It is so kind and sweet of "YOU," POPPA. I am able to feed Her my roasted potatoes, which She just absolutely loves. I lend Her a portable heater and get Her AirPods working. While She is sitting in my new leather seat, it's very low, so I give Her my hand; She is amazed at how soft my hands are and caresses them for what seems like five minutes. I am able to romantically hug Her around three times, and one time I just start repenting again and again, and She receives it. She looks at some of my books next to my bed and asks why I have them. "Are you looking for a wife?" I say, "You are the only woman for me until I die." I don't think She believes me, and I say, "You'll see." I tell Her, "Michelle, I love only You." I am able to say that twelve times, and She doesn't rebuke me. I am able to tell Her I miss Her about the same, and I am able to caress Her lovely face at least six times. The last time when She was in Her car, She said something like, "Maybe we shouldn't do that," but it was very lovely and kind. Also, I kissed Her lovely face at least three times. I lent Her a heater, which really made Her beam, and gave Her one of my flannel pillowcases. It wasn't clean, so I handwashed it and dried it for Her. It was so kind of "YOU," POPPA!

11.03.23, 04:17

15:33, 3:33: POPPA, Michelle, and I, *JESUS*, Michelle, and I, HOLY SPIRIT, Michelle, and I. Having a tough day today. I thought I was tired from staying up till basically 23:00 with Michelle, but I'm thinking now, while sitting in my car at CHP (the run circuit), it's more like today's my last day as a fire protection engineer for DeKalb, but maybe forever as an engineer. Not being paid in two months and maybe ending a thirty-five-plus-year career as an engineer and a fifty-year career overall. As Paul said, "It's all dong anyway but still hard." Thanks for letting me share. "I count all things but loss for the excellency of the knowledge of Christ Jesus my Lord: for whom I have suffered the loss of all things, and do count them but dung, that I may win Christ" (Philippians 3:8, KJV).

11.05.23, 04:14 (05:14 DLS, Thank You, Jesus)

"Wisdom rests in the heart of him who has understanding, But what is in the heart of fools is made known."

Proverbs 14:33 (NKJV)

11.06.23, 07:02

07:25: I believe POPPA told me, "Since you're helping everyone, Mike, I'm going to help you." Thank "YOU," POPPA.

14:02: Michelle called me and asked if I would help Her at Marshalls since She didn't feel good. I went to see Her at Marshalls to help Her decide on clothes; this was one of my most favored things to do with Her. I would hold Her clothes, water, or anything else She needed for hours. I missed doing that more than almost anything...then went to where She was staying to help Her pack until 17:30. Wow, YOU are so kind to me.

18:30: While doing lyrics I was crying for HIM to please not leave me.

18:40: Having a tough time. I walk out of Prayer Room, and a young man asks how I am, and I say good. But then he asks, "Really?" And gets more honest, and he starts prophesying POPPA's *love* and encouraging me—how I've encouraged him and how I'm a light. It is clearly GOD. He is crying, and so am I. I tell him I have really received his word. He calls me Frank.

19:17, 17:17: Why wouldn't "HE" show up? "HE" always has!

11.07.23, 01:58

02:12: I Pray boldness and truth and protection over Mike Bickle and his family.

07:39: Jim Stern Prayed; we need to hold on to some things and let other things go. I need to hold on even tighter to "HIM" and let Michelle go.

10:26: Michelle woke up with a headache and asked if I was still willing to help at Bogart. I said yes, and She asked if I would help Her at Aldi's, which I immediately agreed to.

11:15: We meet at Aldi's and have a lovely time shopping for Her. It was so, so sweet. She was cold, so I offered my demon jacket. She said, "No, it smells," and immediately She said, "No, it doesn't smell; your cologne is strong." Thank *YOU, JESUS*. When we couldn't find everything, I volunteered to go to Walmart. I put the stuff in my car; She went to Bogart. Then we proceeded to shop by pictures and text. It was so cute!

13:26: I get to Bogart; Michelle's not feeling well, so I bring the groceries in, help put them away, and put a few chicken breasts in the oven for Her, and then we unloaded Her car. She greatly appreciated all I did because I wouldn't let Her do anything. I feel so bad. She didn't feel well at all. She is just so absolutely gorgeous and wonderful...

Chicken was done; She ate...it was so, so sweet. Only *JESUS* could do that. I was there until 15:45 and had to run to Prayer Room, or I would maybe still be there. Thank "YOU," POPPA.

17:05, 5:05: SOS. Hazen was sharing what revelation he was getting with this fast. I believed there was no way I would be able to make it through this shaking "HE" was allowing me to walk through if I wasn't fasting.

17:09: I get an email from TBN. "It is going to be an honor to publish your book when you're ready." Speaking of my second book *JESUS CHRIST Is Behind NESARA/GESARA* as well as *Caveman to Priest*.

17:11: I can't take "YOUR" kindness!

17:25: It's been a while since I've had my usual Tuesday 16:00 trivial, and boy was it a good one! Thank *YOU, JESUS*!

11.08.23, 06:34

06:46: I believe POPPA told me "HE" is proud of me. I've survived another very dark night of the soul. Thank "YOU," POPPA.

> *"Yet HE had commanded the clouds above, And opened the doors of Heaven, Had rained down manna on them to eat, And given them of the bread of Heaven."*
>
> Psalm 78:23–24 (NKJV)

"You did not choose ME, but I chose you and appointed you that you should go and bear fruit, and that your fruit should remain, that whatever you ask the FATHER in MY name HE may give you."

John 15:16 (NKJV)

"A soft answer turns away wrath, But a harsh word stirs up anger."

Proverbs 15:1 (NKJV)

17:13: "Awake, O north wind, And come, O south! Blow upon my garden, That its spices may flow out. Let my beloved come to his garden And eat its pleasant fruits."

Song of Solomon 4:16 (NKJV)

I believe "HE" is letting me know that if it wasn't for the twenty-one-day fast, I might not have made it through this extreme, dark night of the soul. "HE" purposely kept Michelle away so that all I could do was press into "HIM" and a few brothers. It was such a tough season.

11.09.23, 03:51

09:43: I'm listening to the livestream from this morning, and the dude is Praying, "'HE' will strengthen your brain." I receive that in the Name of *JESUS*. Amen.

"Men ate angels' food; HE sent them food to the full. HE caused an east wind to blow in the heavens; And by HIS power HE brought in the south wind."

Psalm 78:25–26 (NKJV)

"The tongue of the wise uses knowledge rightly, But the mouth of fools pours forth foolishness."

Proverbs 15:2 (NKJV)

11:27: After getting encouraged by Richard, driving to the Prayer Room, the song "What Doesn't Kill You Makes You Stronger."

11:37: The crushing and shaking have just been ratcheted up a few more notches, like it wasn't tough enough before.

16:30: I went to Pray over Pastor Casey. Afterward he reached over and said I was his favorite person to have Pray over him. Thank "YOU," POPPA.

17:42:

Though the fig tree may not blossom, Nor fruit be on the vines; Though the labor of the olive may fail, And the fields yield no food; Though the flock may be cut off from the fold, And there be no herd in the stalls—Yet I will rejoice in The LORD, I will joy in the GOD of my salvation. The LORD GOD is my strength; HE will make my feet like deer's feet, And HE will make me walk on my high hills. To the Chief Musician. With my stringed instruments.

Habakkuk 3:17–19 (NKJV)

11.20.23

10:00: I'm getting the last of DeKalb County stuff together, and I'm considering keeping the Samsung charging cable. I hear HIM say, "You have the riches of the kingdom. Why would you want from the world? Give the world back what's the world's and take and enjoy from the kingdom!"

11.21.23, 02:38

15:25: I believe POPPA said "HE" was going to lift the roof off the joint at the 16:00 Prayer meeting.

So David, the elders of Israel, and the captains over thousands went to bring up the ark of the covenant of The LORD from the house of Obed-Edom with joy. And so it was, when GOD helped the Levites who bore the ark of the covenant of The LORD, that they offered seven bulls and seven rams. David was clothed with a robe of fine linen, as were all the Levites who bore the ark, the singers, and Chenaniah the music master with the singers. David also wore a linen ephod. Thus all Israel brought up the ark of the covenant of The LORD with shouting and with the sound of the horn, with trumpets and with cymbals, making music with stringed instruments and harps. And it happened, as the ark of the covenant of The LORD came to the City of David, that Michal, Saul's daughter, looked through a window and saw King David whirling and playing music; and she despised him in her heart.

1 Chronicles 15:25–29 (NKJV)

15:44: I believe "HE" may have been saying that "HE" ripped the roof off so that there could be an open HEaven for my full HEaling today from all the brain disorder in the mighty and powerful Name of *JESUS CHRIST*. Amen.

16:26: It is well with my soul. I lost everything like the writer of the song, and it is well with my soul.

16:30: Hazen started Praying for mental illness, and I believe POPPA said to have Jim Stern and then Pastor Dustin Pennington Pray for me; they did, and I'm believing in 100 percent HEaling and deliverance in the Mighty Name of *JESUS CHRIST*. Amen. I feel completely clear-headed. In the Name of *JESUS CHRIST*.

17:00: Sarah Pearl, a young lady from HOP, got up and said there was a breaker anointing on the room. Dean, Craig, Maria, and Phylicia Prayed for me. I started shaking Craig's hand, and it felt like I was in a HEavenly hospital having the brain surgery I so needed. Dean started hitting it hard. I believe it broke the depression and the onset of dementia in the Mighty Name of *JESUS CHRIST*. Amen.

17:50, 5:50: Dean Prayed.

The Spirit of The LORD GOD is upon me, because The LORD has anointed me to bring good news to the poor; he has sent me to bind up the brokenhearted, to proclaim liberty to the captives, and the opening of the prison to those who are bound; to proclaim the year of The LORD's favor, and the day of vengeance of our GOD; to comfort all who mourn; to grant to those who mourn in Zion—to give them a beautiful headdress instead of ashes, the oil of gladness instead of mourning, the garment of praise instead of a faint spirit; that they may be called oaks of righteousness, the planting of The LORD, that he may be glorified.

Isaiah 61:1–3 (ESV)

11.24.23, 04:46

12:59: I believe "HE" just told me "HE" is gearing me up for big things.

14:30: After listening to the Derik Prince video that Carol Rosenbusch gave me plus the next one, I Prayed to be released from thoughts of Michelle. While I was drinking in *JESUS* and exhaling the demon, my ears started popping about the fourth breath and for about four more times, bad. It was so good!

21:45: Finished the CHRISTmas tree—odd but nice. Texted the girls—they liked it.

11.27.23, 06:39

08:02: I spent time with The LORD after my Prayer time and must have fallen back to sleep. It was such a sweet time and reminded me of times in the past. The last moments of sleep, I was with Michelle. Oh, was that glorious. She called me, and I played running away like She used to, like a little bunny. Then I turned and said, "No way, I'm not going to miss this time with You." I enjoyed being with Her. She was sitting on a big, beautiful white chair. I crawled up to Her and sat on Her lap. Then I woke up. Thank "YOU," POPPA!

11.28.23, 06:17

06:00: While still sleeping I heard myself say, "Many international economies are falling and failing."

"Folly is joy to him who is destitute of discernment, But a man of understanding walks uprightly."

Proverbs 15:21 (NKJV)

13:45: I realize that I haven't seen Michelle's gorgeous face in three weeks. I say, "It's okay. I need to give Her time to herself and to miss me." Thank "YOU," POPPA.

11.29.23, 06:10

Psalm 118:5–6.

"Plans fail for lack of counsel, but with many advisers they succeed."

Proverbs 15:22 (NIV)

12.01.23, 05:50

I want ministry to be my full-time vocation and career!

12.02.23, 06:17

12.04.23, 06:48

09:07: I believe The LORD let me know it was not just Michelle testing me to see if I was going to honor Her boundaries. HE wanted to make sure of it as well. Thank *YOU, JESUS*.

I had a dream with Terrance, my brother number nine. I don't remember much; we were hanging out as adults, maybe even now. We were in a camper, bus-like, and climbing out the window instead of using a door. I don't know if there was a door.

16:00: I'm beginning to get good at monotasking.

19:05: I Prayed at the mic, "POPPA, thank 'YOU' for beginning the restoration process in my home and household in the Name of *JESUS CHRIST*."

12.05.23, 07:43

I had a dream with Michelle in a lovely red ballroom gown. It looked stunning on Her; She kissed and hugged me very romantically!

12.06.23, 05:42

12.07.23, 07:42

12:34: Walked CHPN with Popp'n holding my left arm at the bridge, and then she grabbed my hand near big red. Michelle wasn't there, so Popp'n said she liked how I held Michelle's hand the other day and wanted to try. I was asking her about everyone, and Bobby grabbed my right hand. We chatted, and then Mary grabbed her right hand, and Francis grabbed Popp'n's left hand. It was so sweet. Then I asked if I could hold their hands, so we swapped and made the right after the batting cages. After making sure they were good, we went back. I asked Popp'n who she was. I said, "I don't want to know unless you want me to know," just like Michelle. She didn't want to say. As we were walking CJI Lane, I thought of the Wizard of Oz with the five of us walking together. I don't know who's who.

Bobby: Dorothy

Popp'n: The Lion

Me: Scarecrow, maybe Mary

Francis: Toto

Mary: Tin Man, maybe me

18:55: I'm doing something at home, and the enemy is messing with me. I say, "I'm doing my best," and I hear Michelle say, "And you're doing a great job!" Boy, did I need that. I haven't heard a thing from Her in four and a half weeks. I love You, Michelle, and miss You terribly.

12.11.23

00:48: I watched a video about how curses can't land on the righteous, but the enemy gets us to curse ourselves.

"Like a fluttering sparrow or a darting swallow, an undeserved curse will not land on its intended victim" (Proverbs 26:2, NLV).

So I confessed that I'd cursed myself, repented, asked for forgiveness, received it, closed any open doors, and asked HOLY SPIRIT to sweep me clean and fill my house like that of Solomon's temple. I woke again at 01:38 to a very painful dream of Dustin calling me to let me know he heard from Pastor Jeff Lyle my beloved Michelle had passed away. I cried and cried and said, "I have to see Her." I got to the morgue and cried, Prayed, lay on Her wailing out loud, and She came back to life through the power of the Blood of *JESUS*. I had to give Her my jacket to cover Her up; after they gave Her a robe. *JESUS* brought my baby, my love, back! If it hadn't been so real, I wouldn't have added Dustin to my favorite list to be able to ring through on my phone's *do not disturb*. Then at 03:38, in a dream, Michelle and I were sitting at a desk somewhere in public, and She kissed me romantically; it was so passionate, kind, gentle, and lovely. I didn't want to kiss Her until our wedding, but this was so sweet.

07:40: I'd rather have my Michelle back than NESARA, POPPA.

12:22: "HE" reminded me that what DeKalb was doing was unjust, but I'd rather have justice in HEaven than here on earth.

16:28: Dream interpretation—Michelle dead. I killed Her. *JESUS* used me to bring Her back to life, and we're going to reMarry. Thank "YOU," POPPA.

12.12.23, 03:18

While awake, I believe POPPA told me that the dream of Michelle was "HIM" speaking to me. More from after the interpretation, of course. My jacket was Michelle's Spiritual covering…"HE" was confirming in me that I was Her Spiritual covering. "Keep pressing in for Her, Mike. She needs it and you. Trust 'ME,' Mike. Do you trust 'ME'?"

Then, as Job would continually sacrifice for his children, I repented for myself, Michelle, Ali, and Cate for any transgressions in our lives.

> *And his sons would go and feast in their houses, each on his appointed day, and would send and invite their three sisters to eat and drink with them. So it was, when the days of feasting had run their course, that Job would send and sanctify them, and he would rise early in the morning and offer burnt offerings according to the number of them all. For Job said, "It may be that my sons have sinned and cursed God in their hearts." Thus Job did regularly.*

Job 1:4–6 (NKJV)

12.13.23 05:24

Michelle made a cameo in my dreams sometime early this morning before I woke up. It kind of seemed like we were in a university class. Maybe tables, maybe at an auditorium. I don't think we were together, and Dustin was speaking. He was speaking to Michelle, acknowledging how much fun She was or what a great job She did doing something. She and I weren't together, and I was just so excited for Her that he was acknowledging Her.

12.15.23, 03:59

10:19: My young friend Jonathan Bucksot sent me this, and I cried and cried!

"Was listening to this song just now. And I thought of you dancing to this song. And you told me you like this song. It brings me joy to see you dance before the LORD."

13:14: I'm driving on Taylor Road and pass the lake. I think, "Aw, that's where Michelle and I had a date on the lawn." I believe POPPA said, "Yes, Michelle is thinking of the good times as well." Thank "YOU," POPPA.

12.19.23, 08:16

11:18: Catie sent me fingerless gloves that She made for me as well as the card She made. All I could do was cry!

12.20.23, 03:17

09:07: I'm looking out the kitchen window to see a male cardinal and three bluebirds. I don't think we ever had bluebirds in New York. Thank "YOU," POPPA.

12.23.23, 08:11

07:00: I'm doing dishes, and I decide to wash the Starbucks cup that Michelle left in the van. I heard Her say, "Why would you keep something like that?" I said, "You just don't know how much I love you," and She said, "I'm beginning to." Thank "YOU," POPPA.

11:29: Popp'n met me on the circuit near the bridge; she now liked holding my hand after she saw Michelle do it. I told her I preferred her holding my arm but wanted her to do what she wanted. We walked and ran together until we got to the boys—boy, did I cry and love on them. She decided she wanted to stay with them, and I also wanted her to. It was all so, so nice; she really didn't pop—almost at all. I thought things were different. She didn't speak much, except about the van, and I wasn't sure if she had much to do with it, except maybe that night in the national park in Blairsville, Georgia, when we camped in it. But I think we have a different relationship now, and I'm looking forward to cultivating it.

Me leading Worship for JESUS CHRIST's Birthday celebration!!!!

12.24.23, 07:28

17:01: I got to church around 16:15 because there was a problem in the student auditorium. They told me I'd be fine keeping the fire burning in room twenty-three, meaning continuing the Worship. They set a pad on the keyboard, and I just played chords. Could you imagine? I was not approved yet, but I get to lead worship to *JESUS* for *HIS* birthday celebration! Come on!

12.25.23, 06:24

Then the seventy returned with joy, saying, "LORD, even the demons are subject to us in YOUR name." And HE said to them, "I saw satan fall like lightning from Heaven. Behold, I give you the authority to trample on serpents and scorpions, and over all the power of the enemy, and nothing shall by any means hurt you. nevertheless do not rejoice in this, that the spirits are subject to you, but rather rejoice because your names are written in Heaven."

Luke 10:17–20 (NKJV)

10:48: I believe I heard Michelle say in the Spirit, "I love you, Mike. Please be patient. I'm a little scared." Thanks, POPPA!

"Give ear, O Shepherd of Israel, YOU who lead Joseph like a flock; YOU who dwell between the cherubim, shine forth!"

Psalm 80:1 (NKJV)

12.26.23

10:05: Just a little sad not to hear anything from Michelle for CHRISTmas.

I did hear from both of the girls after I texted them at around 18:00. Catie loved the color of Her wallet.

That's my little girl, Cate Mike.

"And the Glory which YOU gave ME I have given them, that they may be one just as We are one."

John 17:22 (NKJV)

"Pride goes before destruction, And a haughty spirit before a fall."

Proverbs 16:18 (NKJV)

12.29.23, 01:59

02:22: I believe POPPA just told me that 222 doesn't just mean HIM, *JESUS*, and HOLY SPIRIT and me three times. It also means Michelle and me three times.

12.30.23, 08:56

05:14: I had a dream that I woke up and Michelle had made me Belgian waffles for breakfast in bed. She was stunning.

13:50: While showering POPPA showed me a vision of Michelle coming to church with me. Dustin and Billy apologize for not believing Her. It was so incredibly kind to have Her there, but even more for them to apologize. Thank "YOU," POPPA!

12.31.23, 07:32

Praise The LORD! Blessed is the man who fears The LORD, Who delights greatly in HIS commandments. HIS descendants will be mighty on earth; The generation of the upright will be blessed. Wealth and riches will be in his house, And his righteousness endures forever. A good man deals graciously and lends; HE will guide his affairs with discretion.

Psalm 112:1–3, 5 (NKJV)

Michelle was visiting me for the entire second half of my dreams. We had a son and daughter; I believe we named Her Michelle Lynn McKirahan Collins and called Her Lynn. We all spent life together all night. It was just so, so sweet. I just loved being with Her and them!

23:23: I was blessed to be able to Pray over around twenty young men less than thirty years old who came forward. I asked around four young boys, but they said no, and then I asked a fifth and he said yes. Thank "YOU," POPPA.

Ten people gave their life to *JESUS*!

01.01.24, 10:18

"An ungodly man digs up evil, And it is on his lips like a burning fire. A perverse man sows strife, And a whisperer separates the best of friends."

Proverbs 16:27–28 (NKJV)

01.02.23, 06:54

11:53: I'm on my run circuit. I've seen three beautiful hawks, and I asked POPPA, "What does that mean?" I believe "HE" said, "Birds of prey for the man of Prayer." Thank "YOU," POPPA.

01.03.24

May HIS Blessings unfold to more blessings and unfold to more blessings and more blessings… and I saw a beautiful canvas or tapestry unfolding in front of me by HOLY SPIRIT HIMself, and it was opening in more of a triangular figure; it was getting wider and wider as HE unfolded or rolled it out.

Then I see the walkway to our house, and the pavers are gold. It looked like the house on Wildcat... We got rid of all the vinyl and put brick throughout and then smeared it. It was gorgeous; the small triangles were copper.

"Now I am no longer in the world, but these are in the world, and I come to YOU. Holy FATHER, keep through YOUR name those whom YOU have given ME, that they may be one as We are."

John 17:11 (NKJV)

"I do not Pray for these alone, but also for those who will believe in ME through their word; that they all may be one, as YOU, FATHER, are in ME, and I in YOU; that they also may be one in Us, that the world may believe that YOU sent ME."

John 17:20–21 (NKJV)

"Return, we beseech YOU, O GOD of hosts; Look down from Heaven and see, And visit this vine And the vineyard which YOUR right hand has planted, And the branch that YOU made strong for Yourself."

Psalm 80:14–15 (NKJV)

01.04.24, 03:24

10:44: I'm getting ready to eat my apples with peanut butter, and I forgot my honey. I say to myself, *I've got to get my honey*, and I hear, "Mike, you're going to get your honey soon!" Thank "YOU," POPPA.

11:42: I'm walking up to the PO, and I see this lady holding the hand of a little girl, and I believe I hear, "That's going to be your Michelle walking with your Michelle Lynn." "Lynn" someday soon.

"HE who is slow to anger is better than the mighty, And he who rules his spirit than he who takes a city."

Proverbs 16:32 (NKJV)

I'm still going through a lot of pain and questions, but I believe "HE" is using all the pressures to make beautiful things.

01.07.24, 07:50

11:48: I'm at GateCity in worship and suddenly feel such peace—all my anxieties, which are a lot, just fall off!

01.08.24, 08:52

15:15:

Therefore if there is any consolation in CHRIST, if any comfort of love, if any fellowship of the Spirit, if any affection and mercy, fulfill my joy by being like-minded, having the same love, being of one accord, of one mind. Let nothing be done through selfish ambition or conceit, but in lowliness of mind let each esteem others better than himself. Let each of you look out not only for his own interests, but also for the interests of others. Let this mind be in you which was also in CHRIST JESUS, who, being in the form of GOD, did not consider it robbery to be equal with GOD, but made HIMself of no reputation, taking the form of a bondservant, and coming in the likeness of men. And being found in appearance as a man,

HE humbled HIMself and became obedient to the point of death, even the death of the cross.

Philippians 2:1–8 (NKJV)

01.09.24, 08:34

13:11 (1:11): I'm hurt, upset, disappointed, angry, confused, and a bit mad.

14:30: I'm wearing my green button-down shirt that has the black, red, yellow, and orange stripes. I look at the picture of *JESUS* on my phone and say, "This shirt would look great on *YOU*." *HE* agreed, and I asked if *HE* wanted to wear it.

"For I will rise up against them," says The LORD of hosts, "And cut off from Babylon the name and remnant, And offspring and posterity," says The LORD. "I will also make it a

possession for the porcupine, And marshes of muddy water; I will sweep it with the broom of destruction," says The LORD of hosts.

Isaiah 14:22–23 (NKJV)

Three different times I begged The LORD to take it away. Each time he said, "MY Grace is all you need. MY power works best in weakness." so now I am glad to boast about my weaknesses, so that the power of CHRIST can work through me. That's why I take pleasure in my weaknesses, and in the insults, hardships, persecutions, and troubles that I suffer for CHRIST. For when I am weak, then I am strong.

2 Corinthians 12:8–10 (NLT)

17:25: They called a rapid-fire Prayer, which means a bunch of folks go up to the microphone and Pray a ten-to-fifteen-second Prayer. I had no thought of going up, and suddenly I heard, "Perfect love," so I went up.

"There is no fear in love, but perfect love casts out fear."

1 John 4:18a (ESV)

01.10.23, 08:29

16:33: If I keep crying like this, I'm gonna blow a gasket!

Peace I leave with you, MY peace I give to you; not as the world gives do I give to you. Let not your heart be troubled, neither let it be afraid. You have heard ME say to you, "I am going away and coming back to you." If you loved ME, you would rejoice because I said, "I am going to the FATHER," for MY FATHER is greater than I.

John 14:27–28 (NKJV)

01.11.24, 06:49

08:24: I'm looking out my bathroom window and see a beautiful pair of cardinals. There's a third one, a female, and the male has no interest. I believe POPPA said this is Michelle and me, and I have no interest in any other. Thank "YOU," POPPA.

10:28: I believe POPPA reminded me that I always told Michelle that I was going to get a black Suburban and was going to carry all the equipment needed, lights and sound for Her conferences across the country, and what does POPPA give me yesterday to borrow? A huge black Suburban.

He said, "I will certainly return to you according to the time of life, and behold, Sarah your wife shall have a son." (Sarah was listening in the tent door which was behind him.) Now Abraham and Sarah were old, well advanced in age; and Sarah had passed the age of childbearing. Therefore Sarah laughed within herself, saying, "After I have grown old, shall I have pleasure, my lord being old also?"

And the Lord said to Abraham, "Why did Sarah laugh, saying, 'Shall I surely bear a child, since I am old?' Is anything too hard for the Lord? At the appointed time I will return to you, according to the time of life, and Sarah shall have a son."

Genesis 18:10–15 (NKJV)

01.13.24, 08:38

01.16.24, 06:28

15:15: I get to the Prayer Room, left side since it's Tuesday, and I look over to the other wall and see one of the leaders: Theresa. She's reading her laptop with her head against the wall, and the light is shining making her look like an angel. I believe The LORD wants me to say something, and I walk over to her. She's having a tough time; she's reading about angels and shows me an article; it says something like I understand about angels and feel them around me but want to know more about them...she really appreciated it. Thank "YOU," POPPA.

"Let a man meet a bear robbed of her cubs, Rather than a fool in his folly."

Proverbs 17:12 (NKJV)

16:53: Hazen was Praying.

The believers heard this. Then they raised their voices together in Prayer to GOD. "LORD and King," they said, "you made the heavens, the earth and the sea. You made everything in them. All the believers were agreed in heart and mind. They didn't claim that anything they had was their own. Instead, they shared everything they owned."

Acts 4:24, 32 (NIRV)

In Closing

On 08.27.23 The Love of my life rang my doorbell and spent three weeks with me including days before my sixtieth birthday. I had made plans to visit my daughters up in New York, or we probably would have spent the actual day together. I hadn't seen Her glorious, loving face for three and a half years. The LORD told Her to face Her enemy and tell him (me) that She forgave him. I immediately cried and cried and cried, then repented, repented, and repented. We spent eight hours together until I had to get to bed, unfortunately. We probably would have gone on all night. It was the sweetest thing POPPA could have done for me in my entire life.

ABOUT THE AUTHOR

Mike Collins was born on Long Island, New York, and lived in Rhinebeck, New York, before moving to Atlanta. He's been a follower of The LORD *JESUS CHRIST* for over twenty-one years and an intercessory Prayer missionary with GateCity House of Prayer (GCHOP), formerly the International House of Prayer Atlanta (IHOP-ATL), for eight years. He's blessed to have two beautiful daughters, Alexandra (Ali) and Catherine (Cate).